Andrew Jackson and the Constitution

Andrew Jackson and the Constitution

The Rise and Fall of Generational Regimes

Gerard N. Magliocca

University Press of Kansas

© 2007 by the University Press of Kansas

Published by the University Press of Kansas (Lawrence,
Kansas 66045), which was organized by the Kansas Board of
Regents and is operated and funded by Emporia State Uni-
versity, Fort Hays State University, Kansas State University,
Pittsburg State University, the University of Kansas, and
Wichita State University

Library of Congress Cataloging-in-Publication Data

Magliocca, Gerard N.
    Andrew Jackson and the Constitution : the rise and fall of
generational regimes / Gerard N. Magliocca.
        p.   cm.
    Includes bibliographical references and index.
    ISBN 978-0-7006-1509-4 (cloth : alk. paper)
    ISBN 978-0-7006-1786-9 (pbk : alk. paper)
    1. Constitutional history—United States. 2. Jackson,
Andrew, 1767–1845. 3. United States—Politics and
government—1829–1837. I. Title.
    KF4541.M27 2007
    342.7302'9—dc22   2006037920

British Library Cataloguing-in-Publication Data is available.

Printed in the United States of America

10 9 8 7 6 5 4 3 2 1

The paper used in this publication meets the minimum
requirements of the American National Standard for Perma-
nence of Paper for Printed Library Materials Z39.48-1992.

For Mom and Dad, the best teachers anyone could ever have

Contents

Illustrations

Preface to the
Paperback Edition

Reading a book that you wrote several years ago is like looking at a photo album. Some things bring a smile to your face; others make you wonder what you were thinking about back then. Unlike old pictures, a book can be changed, but it is better to avoid that temptation and let the work stand as is. Nevertheless, I would like to make a few fresh observations about what you are about to read.

This book operates on two levels. First and foremost, it is a constitutional history of Jacksonian Democracy. The focus is on the two great controversies of the 1830s, which involved the Second Bank of the United States and the removal of the Cherokee Tribe from Georgia. Obviously, they were not the only significant constitutional issues during this period, and my treatment of the others, most notably the Nullification Crisis of 1832–1833, is more cursory. Likewise, the discussion of what happened after the 1830s is largely limited to the fallout from the Bank and the Cherokee Removal debates, especially for the abolitionists and for the Supreme Court's decision in *Dred Scott*. Thus, this is not a comprehensive account of the law in the antebellum era, but it is a thorough examination of the most important subjects at that time.

The book also sets forth a theory about how the Constitution changes. In that respect, this is a work in progress. My central claim is that there is a regular pattern to how our higher law evolves. This "generational cycle" takes approximately thirty years to unfold and is closely tied to the periodic realignment of the party system. Each of these generational regimes evolves in a similar way, which opens the door for comparisons between otherwise unrelated events that share a common point in time within their respective generations. Jacksonian Democracy is one of these distinctive constitutional periods, and in this book I examine the relationship between that regime's early and late stages to show the cycle in action and to explore the powerful insights that come from using a temporal model.

An obvious problem with my approach is that one example is not enough to prove that there is an overarching structure to constitutional development. So why didn't I delve into other periods and provide more proof that there is a universal generational cycle? The answer is that I think books should be short. A few slim volumes, each organized around a specific topic, are far better than one tome. Short books get read; long ones get praised and gather dust. What you see here is the first part of my project. The second part is a book about the Populist generation of the 1890s led by William Jennings Bryan, which was unsuccessful and triggered a massive backlash that endured as the constitutional settlement until the middle of the twentieth century. The third one will cover the New Deal and expand on the discussion that I started in this book about the role that luck plays in shaping legal principles during moments of generational transition. There might be more, but I am not sure.

Finally, I should say something about how the Obama administration fits within the constitutional cycle. My view is that the 2008 election marked the start of a new generational regime, but at this point it is impossible to say whether this should be called the "Yes We Can" or the "Tea Party" generation. Historians are not fortune-tellers. The 2008 result certainly looked like a political realignment similar to what occurred when Andrew Jackson took the White House in 1828, as Obama was the first Democratic presidential candidate to win a popular vote majority in over thirty years. Like Jackson, President Obama used that mandate to push a transformative statute through Congress over intense opposition. Unlike Jackson, though, Obama suffered a sharp setback in his first midterm election. That may just be a bump in the road, but it is also possible that the backlash against President Obama will be the defining event for our generation. Moreover, the Supreme Court is still waiting in the wings, and an opinion striking down health care reform as unconstitutional could make the difference.

One thing is certain—the generational cycle grinds on. Abraham Lincoln told the nation during the Civil War that "we cannot escape history." That's why we need to keep studying it.

Acknowledgments

Though this book bears only one name, all authors know that their work could not shine without the assistance of many dedicated people. I want to start by thanking Debra Denslaw and Kiyoshi Otsu, who provided key library support; Kenny Crews, who offered his advice on copyright issues; and Joshua Claybourn, my research assistant for the past two years. Next, I would like to express my heartfelt gratitude to Donald Cole, David Fontana, Jay Koh, R. Kent Newmyer, Amanda Tyler, and George Wright for reading my drafts and offering their insights. In this spirit, I also salute the members of the Legal History Colloquium at New York University Law School, whose pointed criticisms forced me to rethink my arguments at a crucial juncture. And I want to acknowledge the law reviews that gave me permission to reprint parts of my prior work. These source materials are "The Cherokee Removal and the Fourteenth Amendment," *Duke Law Journal* 53 (2003): 875–965; "Preemptive Opinions: The Secret History of *Worcester v. Georgia* and *Dred Scott*," *University of Pittsburgh Law Review* 63 (2002): 487–587; "A New Approach to Congressional Power: Revisiting the Legal Tender Cases," *Georgetown Law Journal* 95 (2006): 119–170; and "Veto! The Jacksonian Revolution in Constitutional Law," *Nebraska Law Review* 78 (1999): 205–65.

Paying my largest debts last, I thank my colleagues at Indiana University–Indianapolis, whose good cheer and generous financial support have sustained me throughout this project. Michael Briggs and the staff at the University Press of Kansas also provided indispensable guidance and encouragement. Finally, this book would never have been written without Bruce Ackerman, whose friendly badgering convinced me that I had something here.

Introduction: On the Constitutional Rhythm

> We are engaged in just such a contest as every generation must pass through. In times of quiet, abuses spring up. . . . The people suffer until suffering ceases to be virtue; they are patient until patience is exhausted, and then they arouse themselves, take the reins of government and put the government back upon its old foundation.
>
> *William Jennings Bryan,*
> The First Battle: A Story of the Campaign of 1896

In 1763, the Treaty of Paris ratified England's triumph over France in the Seven Years' (or French and Indian) War. With this victory, the Crown's empire reached its greatest extent up to that time, particularly in North America. Faced with enormous debts incurred during the war, Parliament decided to take advantage of this overwhelming power by imposing new customs duties on the colonists. This policy was criticized by a small group of agitators, based largely in Massachusetts, who said that these taxes infringed their right of self-government. We know what happened next. The struggle between the Crown and the colonists escalated over the next ten years, resulting in the "long train of abuses and usurpations" that culminated in the Declaration of Independence.[1] In 1783, another Treaty of Paris ratified our victory (this time with help from France) and the revolutionary generation wrote a new Constitution designed in part to prevent the wrongs imposed by imperial power from ever being repeated here.

This story is familiar because it recounts the birth of our nation, but these events are just one part of a recurring pattern in our history. Every generation of Americans, not just the Framers, acts to correct the abuses tolerated by constitutional law and must overcome opposition from a political establishment committed to a different set of ideals.[2] In one age, these reformers were abolitionists such as William Lloyd Garrison and John Bingham fighting to end slavery. In another, they were Populists such as William Jennings Bryan and Thomas Watson trying to blunt the harsh edge of capitalism by redistributing income and expanding public ownership of the economy.[3] More recently, they were Republicans such as Ronald Reagan and Newt Gingrich arguing that the welfare state should be curtailed because it imposed a crushing burden on personal freedom. These movements were not equally ambitious or successful, but each left an indelible mark on the fundamental principles that govern us.

Although the call for renewal is a common one, the process of reform also has a distinctive rhythm best captured by the title of the British television drama *Upstairs, Downstairs*, which followed the lives of the aristocrats and servants in a single Edwardian household. At any given time, a ruling consensus is busy implementing its legal principles (Upstairs), while a host of fringe groups are developing a critique (Downstairs) and waiting for the day when they might seize power. As each Upstairs movement reaches the peak of success, its excesses create a backlash that lets one of the Downstairs groups emerge from the wilderness. In time, these challengers gather into a mainstream force and enter a battle between what Senator Thomas Hart Benton called the "old light shining steadily in a calm atmosphere" and "a new light, suddenly breaking out, and flashing fitfully in the bursts of a raging tempest."[4] When this clash between traditionalists and reformers is resolved, a new establishment assumes power and the cycle begins anew from a fresh legal baseline.

This cycle in constitutional law is fueled by the fact that each generation goes through a unique set of collective experiences that sets its views apart from its predecessors. Only one group can grow up during the Depression, fight in the Civil War, or live through the terrorist attacks of September 11. Of course, not everyone draws the same conclusion from a given experience. Americans were bitterly divided during the Revolution, the Civil War, and Vietnam, but there is little doubt that the people who lived through these trying times were responding to them. Some love what the 1960s represent; others hate it. Some Civil War veterans saw it as a noble cause; others saw it as a foolish adventure.[5] Either way, this kind of event or atmosphere becomes the chief frame of reference for political actions taken by that generation. Eventually, a majority opinion forms around these experiences, and that creates a relatively stable set of political preferences. This claim finds support in the literature on "generational cohorts," which explains that people who come of age at the same time tend to view political and social issues in the same way throughout their lives.[6] In the real world, this tendency is reflected by the "party system," which describes a pattern in which one party dominates during the time when one generation makes up a voting plurality (for example, Reconstruction Republicans or New Deal Democrats).[7] While personal views on politics frequently change, in the aggregate they shift decisively only on those rare occasions when one generation gives way to another.[8]

This analysis indicates that although there are many factors that influence the evolution of constitutional attitudes, one element that deserves more attention is time.[9] The passage of time explains why legal reform tends to move in a cyclical fashion, because everyone in a specific generation (that is, folks with firsthand knowledge of a given transformative event) eventually dies. They are then replaced by a group of people driven by other equally profound experiences from which they draw different conclusions about fundamental issues. By looking at constitutional law temporally, rather than doctrinally, scholars and judges can obtain insights into a host of problems precisely because there is a consistent and predictable repetition in how Americans confront the major questions posed by our legal system.

The main point that flows from this temporal analysis is that the friction from the regular clashes between "constitutional generations" is the primary force shaping the first principles of the Republic.[10] This view challenges a powerful metaphor in our legal discourse, which is that the Constitution was the product of careful and thoughtful deliberation. The images that come to mind are the Framers in Philadelphia, meeting behind closed doors and discussing the intricacies of statecraft at a leisurely pace, or the Supreme Court justices, meeting behind closed doors after weighing the arguments of counsel according to time-honored customs. These calm and reflective acts do play a role in our legal system, but they are not the most important factor. Instead, most of our constitutional practices get their start from one generation's desire to defeat another in the rough-and-tumble of politics. Thus, a more apt metaphor for how constitutional law develops is "creative destruction," a term coined to describe how free markets generate wealth by unleashing the disruptive energy of competition.[11] The legal rights and institutions that we cherish are the wealth that free citizens have created through uninhibited political competition.

To see the dynamic cycle of constitutional reform at work, this book looks at one turn of the wheel during the Jacksonian era. Jacksonian Democracy presents a compelling case study for four reasons. First, the politics of the day were filled with intriguing figures discussing issues that illustrate the themes of this project better than any other era. Second, there is now enough distance from the events of the mid-nineteenth century to evaluate them dispassionately. Third, these years receive less attention than they deserve because they lack a connection with a major war. Nonetheless, they marked the first broad public debates on issues that we still struggle with, such as the role of the presidency, the protection of minority rights, and the separation of church and state. Finally, the Jacksonian experience gives a more representative picture of our democracy because it saw significant advances in freedom and horrific injustices at the same time. Books on popular constitutionalism tend to emphasize only the heroic stories (for example, the abolition of slavery or the civil rights era).[12] Majority action, though, can also have a dark side. By focusing on a period that captures both aspects, I hope to provide a more persuasive analysis of the interaction of law and politics.

Chapter 1 traces the rise of Jacksonian Democracy, which started as a radical attack on Chief Justice John Marshall's statement of Federalist dogma in *M'Culloch v. Maryland*.[13] Chapter 2 shows how Jackson responded in his first term by advancing an agenda of white supremacy and states' rights in the Indian Removal Act, which essentially authorized Georgia to deport the Cherokee Tribe, and in the veto of the Maysville Turnpike, which contested federal authority to support projects that were beyond the powers expressly granted to Congress. Chapter 3 explores Chief Justice Marshall's effort to rally the traditional establishment by expanding Cherokee rights and federal authority in *Worcester v. Georgia*.[14] Chapter 4 focuses on Jackson's answer—the veto of the Bank of the United States—that framed the president's successful reelection campaign. Chapter 5 recounts the old guard's last stand during the Deposit Crisis, which was quickly followed by Jackson's successful effort to pack the Court and drive the Cherokees into exile on the "Trail of Tears." Chapter 6 wraps up this part of the story by describing the unsuccessful Whig effort to overturn this new order.

After following the arc of Jacksonian Democracy from its origins to the seat of power, the book comes full circle by chronicling the challenge posed to that order by a new generation. Chapter 7 observes that the rise of abolitionism was in part a response to abuses that the Jacksonians inflicted on the Cherokees and that these wrongs and the counterexample of *Worcester* exerted a pull on antislavery thought during the antebellum years. Chapter 8 reviews the growth of these radicals into the Republican Party and analyzes the reaction of Chief Justice Roger B. Taney. Like Marshall before him, Taney sought to rally support for the establishment, but this time by contracting African American rights and federal power in *Dred Scott v. Sandford.*[15] Chapter 9 looks at the last gasp of the Jacksonian generation under President Andrew Johnson and at the Republican answer—the Fourteenth Amendment—that became a central legal text for all time. Finally, the conclusion explores what a fuller appreciation of the constitutional cycle can teach us about the great legal questions of our time.

In sum, this book is about how our Constitution changes, not how it should be read. Part of the birthright of every American, as Thomas Paine once said, is "to begin the world over again."[16] The only thing that remains constant from age to age is the pattern by which this desire for reform unfolds. Understanding that process of collective rebirth can unlock the mysteries of our constitutional past, present, and future.

1

The Rise of Jacksonian Democracy

> If a corporation may be employed, indiscriminately
> with other means, to carry into execution the powers
> of the government, no particular reason can be as-
> signed for excluding the use of a bank. . . . The time
> has passed away, when it can be necessary to enter
> into any discussion, in order to prove the importance
> of this instrument, as a means to effect the legitimate
> objects of the government.
>
> M'Culloch v. Maryland

Since constitutional law is always in motion, there is no natural starting point for this analysis. The question that every ragtag group of dissenters asks itself, though, is how a winning political movement gets started. Thus, this chapter examines the birth of a constitutional generation and shows that there is a relationship between the rebels and the established principles that they are seeking to overturn. This "feedback effect" suggests that each generation carries the seeds of its own destruction, as its very success eventually triggers a backlash.

No constitutional consensus looked more invincible than the one represented by John Marshall in 1819. It was the "Era of Good Feelings," when party competition was nonexistent and President James Monroe was coasting to an unopposed reelection. In that year, the chief justice wrote for the Court in three cases that cemented the establishment's vision of a strong national government that protected property rights. *Dartmouth College v. Woodward* accepted the position of Daniel Webster, the undisputed leader of the bar, and held that the Contracts Clause barred a state legislature from amending a charter granted to a corporation.[1] That emphatic statement was accompanied by *Sturges v. Crowinshield*, in which Marshall held that the Contracts Clause invalidated state efforts to provide retrospective debt relief to farmers and small businesses.[2] Last but not least, the Court held in *M'Culloch v. Maryland* that the National Bank rested on a valid exercise of Congress's implied power and could not be taxed by the states.[3] Moreover, as the quoted passage suggests, the chief justice all but declared the Bank's validity settled law beyond the realm of discussion by reasonable people.

Although *M'Culloch* is one of the greatest cases in constitutional history, Marshall was largely restating the consensus of the political branches on the question of whether Congress could create a bank. Hamilton and Jefferson fought tooth and nail over this point when they served in George Washington's cabinet, but by the mid-1810s almost everyone agreed that the Bank was constitutional. The most vivid example of this shift came in the attitude of James Madison. In 1791, Representative Madison spoke against the Bank and explained that the Constitutional Convention (of which he was a member) had specifically rejected a motion to grant a power to create corporations.[4] Twenty-five years later, however, President Madison held that any constitutional objection was "precluded in my judgment by repeated recognitions under varied circumstances of the validity of such an institution in acts of the legislative, executive, and judicial branches of the Government, accompanied by indications, in different modes, of a concurrence of the general will of the nation."[5] This quote came in the president's veto of the Bank, but Madison's objections were on policy grounds alone and he signed a subsequent bank bill.[6]

Three years later, Marshall upheld the constitutionality of the Bank with a stirring defense of popular sovereignty. Responding to the argument that the Constitution was only a compact between the states, he wrote: "The government of the Union . . . is, emphatically and truly, a government of the people. In form and substance, it emanates from them. Its powers are granted by them, and are to be exercised directly by them, and for their benefit."[7] The chief justice added that "a government, intrusted with such ample powers, on the due execution of which the happiness and prosperity of the nation so vitally depends, must also be intrusted with ample means for their execution."[8] After explaining why a bank, like any other corporation, was a useful means for executing Congress's powers, he rejected the proposition that the Necessary and Proper Clause limited federal action to means that were indispensable.[9] Marshall said this would impute to the Framers "an unwise attempt to provide, by immutable

Chief Justice John Marshall, the pillar of the legal establishment. Painted by Robert Matthew Sully. Library of Congress.

rules, for exigencies which, if foreseen at all, must have been seen dimly, and which can be best provided for as they occur."[10] The chief justice concluded that the Constitution was "intended to endure for ages to come, and consequently, to be adapted to the various crises of human affairs."[11] Little did he know that *M'Culloch* would provoke a crisis that would lead to the demise of his constitutional generation.[12] In constitutional law, the peak is always close to the fall.

Like every generation at its height, the confidence expressed by the chief justice was based on a political winning streak that seemed without end. Although the Federalist Party was routed by Thomas Jefferson in the 1800 election and never recovered, Marshall's skillful leadership and other external factors thwarted his cousin's efforts to change the Court's trajectory.[13] The Court's opinions were criticized by a few states' rights radicals like John Taylor of Caroline, but they enjoyed almost no support in the 1810s.[14] Indeed, it is difficult to imagine a bleaker landscape for potential challengers. Every constitutional movement begins, though, as some quixotic association. The gulf between the substantive views of Samuel Adams in 1770, Thaddeus Stevens in 1832, and Ronald Reagan in 1964 should not obscure their common status as figures that were considered outside the mainstream, even dismissed as crackpots, before they attained power.

Under the surface, there were cracks in the ruling order. One was attributable to Father Time. Marshall and Monroe were foot soldiers in Washington's army (Marshall at Valley Forge, Monroe at Trenton) and represented a generation that was showing signs of mortality.[15] More important, overwhelming success tends to breed complacency and corruption. Complacency is a problem if elites are confronted by a crisis and fail to respond with enough urgency because they are convinced they will retain their majority no matter what. One-party government is also notoriously susceptible to bribery, and therefore it should come as no surprise that the "Era of Good Feelings" was the most corrupt period in the early Republic.[16]

Indeed, corruption became the watchword for a new generation of reformers as a sharp economic panic hit home, ironically enough, in 1819.[17] The 1810s were a boom time that sparked a frenzy of land speculation on the frontier that was fueled by the credit of the Bank of the United States, led by William Jones.[18] When the bubble inevitably burst, the Bank began calling in its loans, and state banks throughout the West and South failed. That catastrophe was especially painful because in this era people who could not meet their obligations were often thrown into debtors' prison. Even though financial crashes are driven partly by investor greed, the victims prefer to blame somebody else.[19] In 1819, they turned on the Bank. The Bank's visible role as the debt collector for the Panic led many people to question why a private firm should have so much power. This sense of outrage only intensified after an investigation disclosed that Jones was skimming money from Bank operations.[20] Many states responded by enacting measures to block the Bank from collecting its debts. In Kentucky, the conflict over debt relief grew so fierce that rival factions actually created separate supreme courts that issued conflicting rulings on the issue.[21] Amos Kendall, who later became a close advisor to Jackson and helped draft his 1832 message vetoing the Bank, exemplified the reaction of the frontier.[22] Before the panic, Kendall wrote articles supporting the Bank; now he denounced it as a "monster" arrayed against "the honest yeomanry of the country."[23]

The Panic of 1819 is just the type of shock that can jolt citizens loose from their allegiance to a particular constitutional regime. Economic distress is frequently a catalyst for electoral realignments, most notably following the Great Depression, because hardship invites scrutiny of traditional institutions and dogma. The scam at the Bank triggered a cascade of revelations about bribes to congressmen, graft in the Indian Bureau, fraud in the War Department, and favoritism in the Treasury's work on behalf of local banks.[24] Doubts were sown about the wisdom of vesting so much authority in the national government. Perhaps the states' rights critics of Marshall were not so crazy after all.

In this combustible environment *M'Culloch* acted like a lighted match, proving that even our greatest chief justice could have a tin ear.[25] Marshall's broad assertion of federal power and praise for vesting discretion in Congress was not welcome news in the midst of a panic that was blamed on the Bank and on grasping national officials. Notwithstanding the holding in *M'Culloch* that Maryland could not tax the Bank, states such as Georgia, Kentucky, and Ohio openly defied the Court by passing punitive levies on the Bank's branches.[26] Indeed, Ohio went so far as to declare the entire Bank illegal, citing the Virginia and Kentucky Resolutions and their endorsement of state sovereignty as support.[27] When the Ohio law was challenged, counsel for the State urged the Court to overrule *M'Culloch*, arguing that the Bank was a private entity that could not be chartered by Congress or exempted from state taxation. Marshall rejected this plea in 1824, opining that "the Bank is not considered as a private corporation . . . but as a public corporation, created for public and national purposes."[28]

Nevertheless, the political atmosphere was dramatically different by the time the chief justice reaffirmed *M'Culloch*. Marshall and his allies were now on the defensive, confronted by a new movement dedicated to a major revision of constitutional principles. For these upstarts, *M'Culloch* symbolized everything that was wrong with the law. In 1824, their candidate—Andrew Jackson—would carry the popular vote in the presidential election.

THE JACKSONIAN RESPONSE AND THE FRONTIER

Each constitutional generation is distinguished by its unique time and set of collective experiences, but Jacksonian Democracy also marked the rise of a new geographic region—the West and the Deep South. Ever since the Founding, political power had been monopolized by Eastern states, particularly Virginia and Massachusetts. Jackson, by contrast, was from Tennessee and came to fame fighting redcoats and Native American Tribes.[29] The sensibilities of the frontier were evident in the reaction against the Bank and in the other major issue on the new generation's agenda—eliminating the sovereignty of the Tribes. Indeed, the coming years were dominated by this contest over whether America's future rested with the commercial world exemplified by the Bank or with the simple agrarian life that evoked the Minutemen of the Revolution.

NARROWING THE FEDERAL TROUGH

The main tenet of the emerging critique was that the federal government threatened individual freedom because it was too powerful and controlled by unaccountable elites. Jackson himself told John C. Calhoun that he feared "a central power will arise here; who under patronage of a corrupt, and venal administration, will deprive the people of their liberties."[30] One of his remedies for this threat was what Jacksonian Democracy is best known for—more democracy. To reduce the probability that public officials would abuse their power, reformers sought to expand the right to vote and limit the tenure of civil servants with a rotation system.[31] Likewise, activists sought to demystify a common-law process that they considered undemocratic by codifying existing precedents and limiting (or so they thought) the discretion of judges to make law.[32] At the state level, they endorsed the election of judges, which became the norm for those courts and remains so today.[33] Accordingly, the new Democratic Party worked to weaken all bastions of "aristocracy," especially the National Bank, by introducing more popular control.

Notwithstanding these structural initiatives, Jacksonians also held that the federal establishment would always be captured by the wealthy and used to create special privileges. This line of thought contradicted the views of Madison in his famous essay in Federalist #10, where he argued that local government was more prone to corruption and the abuse of power. In his view, if you "extend the sphere, and you take in a greater variety of parties and interests[,] you make it less probable that a majority of the whole will have a common motive to invade the rights of other citizens."[34] By contrast, Democrats argued that "while a large nation gave special interests room to intervene between the people and their government, the state was a unit small enough for effective popular control."[35]

Since the national government was vulnerable to corruption, Democrats asserted that the best preventive measure was to reduce federal authority and spending. As one of their campaign pamphlets succinctly said, "The only use of government is *to keep off evil.* We do not want its assistance in seeking after good."[36] Cutting back funds to internal improvements (for example, roads and bridges) would give wealthy interests fewer chances to divert money into their own pockets. The most significant point from a constitutional perspective was that removing power from federal officials would give the states more power, which was viewed as conducive to honest government. *M'Culloch* stood in the way of this aspiration, and therefore the Jacksonian movement was committed to overruling that opinion and limiting the scope of Congress's implied power over economic questions. Thomas Hart Benton, who once shot it out with Jackson in a duel but later became his main supporter in the Senate, said that "it was not merely the bank which the democracy opposed, but the latitudinarian construction which would authorize it, and would enable Congress to substitute its own will in other cases for the words of the constitution, and do what it pleased under the plea of 'necessary.'"[37]

The Jacksonian view of federalism illustrates how the narrow perspective of experience often dictates legal philosophy. One might think that Madison's rosy vision of national power states a universal truth, but in reality Federalist #10 largely reflects the adverse reaction of the Framers to the tyranny and malfeasance in the states right after independence.[38] Others may feel that the Jacksonian position is right, but it should now be clear that this assessment was driven more by a different historical context than by novel insights into human nature. The upshot is that there is not always a "correct" answer to the dilemma raised by structural questions such as how state and national power should be divided or how church and state should be separated. Instead, each constitutional generation responds to the concrete problems that it encounters and attempts to make the necessary adjustments according to its own unique perspective.[39]

Native Americans and the Shadow of Democracy

For all of its egalitarian aspirations, there is little doubt that Jacksonian Democracy was also the most prejudiced movement that ever won the support of the American people. These two elements were linked. As the first generation to advocate equality for white men regardless of wealth, Jacksonians needed to explain why African Americans or Native Americans should not share in this new birth of freedom. Their basic answer was that these groups were culturally or racially inferior and did not deserve inclusion.[40] Unfortunately, this bigotry against Native Americans gets less attention from commentators than it deserves, probably because the plight of African Americans dominates our historical narrative. That oversight is regrettable, for it was the fight over the freedom of the Cherokee Nation that led to the first great national debate over the meaning of equality.

A Tradition of Tolerance

The constitutional tradition that Jackson inherited gave broad recognition to the rights of Native American Tribes on humanitarian and pragmatic grounds. No constitutional expertise is needed to know that the enforcement of these rights left a lot to be desired, but there was a difference between the way Tribes were treated before the 1830s and after.[41] By way of background, the legal status of Native Americans was not addressed by the Framers. Article One, Section Eight, of the Constitution states only that Congress has the authority to "regulate Commerce with foreign Nations, and among the several states, and with the Indian

Secretary of War Henry Knox, who developed the civilization policy. Painted by Gilbert Stuart. Library of Congress.

Tribes."[42] This text does not indicate if Congress has exclusive control over tribal commerce or whether that authority is shared with the states. Nor does it say if the Tribes had any rights that Congress or the states were bound to respect.

One of the many challenges facing George Washington's administration was how to handle Native American affairs. That task was taken up by Secretary of War Henry Knox, who responded with a "civilization" strategy that was designed to introduce tribes to Western culture in the hope that this would keep the peace.[43] Knox's view, which remained official policy until Jackson arrived, was that tribal communities had sovereign rights. He was adamant that these Native Americans could not be forced to sell their land and should be allowed to govern themselves, though the scope of their autonomy was left ambiguous.[44] Consistent with this view, Knox persuaded Congress to pass the Trade and Intercourse Act in 1790, which (1) barred whites from buying tribal land without federal approval; (2) imposed penalties on whites who entered tribal land without a permit; and (3) required that tribal trade be conducted under a federal licensing scheme.[45] As befit relations with sovereign entities, the United States also negotiated treaties with tribes rather than passing laws to govern them. In part, this policy was adopted because the Tribes were strong in the 1790s and federal officials could not, as a practical matter, interfere with their internal affairs. On the other hand, Knox argued that any other approach "would be a gross violation of the fundamental laws of nature and of that distributive justice which is the glory of a nation."[46]

Even though he was the Secretary of War, Knox argued that the best way to achieve peace with the Tribes was through cultural exchange. The key to the civilization plan was that "missionaries, of excellent moral character, should be appointed to reside in the [Indian] nation. . . . They should be their friends and fathers."[47] This might not convert Native Americans to Western ways, but Knox thought it "would most probably be attended with the salutary effect of attaching them to the interest of the United States."[48] He saw these missionaries as more than spiritual guides; they were federal agents who would encourage assimilation. To support this ambitious project, the War Department gave missionary groups financial aid in the form of surplus goods and technical assistance.[49] Congress also appropriated funds for Native American education and handed the money over to religious groups in the tribal areas.[50] In exchange for all of this largesse, these missionaries were required to give progress reports to federal officials. At the time, virtually nobody objected to this commingling of church and state.

Thus, the civilization program sounded the same notes that Marshall was playing on the Court. Broad power vested in federal officials pursuing benevolent policies was the path to progress. This did not sit well with the ascending movement any more than the Bank did, especially in the midst of an economic panic where the land occupied by the Tribes must have looked like ripe fruit ready for the picking.

A Cauldron of Resentment

Andrew Jackson's career as an Indian fighter epitomized the aggressive posture that the frontier took toward Native Americans. People in the West and Deep South saw the existence of autonomous groups in their midst as a security threat.[51] In addition, they resented the fact that federal authorities had control over tribal relations and left the locals with no say over what they saw as their territory. This policy had a disparate impact, to use the modern parlance, because by this time there were no organized tribes in the Eastern states that were supporting tribal autonomy. Reformers were also skeptical, to put it mildly, about the idea that the Tribes could be civilized since it was said that "you can't tame a savage."[52]

Jackson's position on the constitutional issues raised by the Tribes' presence was harsh and clear—Native Americans had no rights and were aliens that could be ruled by Congress and the states as they saw fit. He argued that the government should start "legislating for, rather than treating with, the Indians."[53] From the Democrats' perspective, this was an issue of equality, odd as that may sound. By stripping away the sovereignty of Native American groups, all people in the states with tribes would theoretically be on the same footing before the law. This change also would put states with tribes in an identical position to states without tribes. Finally, wiping out the notion of a protected tribal homeland would open huge parcels of land for the poor and create greater economic equality among whites. The only wrinkle, of course, was that many tribes refused to relinquish their land and could call upon treaties and federal law in support of their rights.

Democrats held that the best way for the states and Congress to exercise their authority with respect to a tribe that continued to assert its independence was by ordering its removal to the wilderness. Put another way, the Tribes would have a choice. They could maintain their sovereignty (for the time being) if they left their homelands and moved to a much less hospitable place outside of any existing state. Or they could surrender their rights and submit to state law, with no guarantee that the state would treat them as equal citizens. All that stood between the Tribes and this doom was the will of the political establishment to defend the traditional constitutional understanding.

In conclusion, there are two points worth making about the incipient agenda of Jacksonian Democracy. First, the substance of this legal insurgency was nothing more than a response to an immediate set of problems. A panic brought criticism down on the Bank, *M'Culloch* was issued in the teeth of this storm, and this created a rallying cry against federal power. The challenge to tribal policy drew from the same distrust of national action, along with the anger of western and southern whites that they were poor while their Native American neighbors sat on incredible wealth. Only with the rigor of time and criticism would these knee-jerk reactions develop into a semicoherent system. Second, even though Jacksonian Democrats pursued significant change, there were also important lines of continuity with the past. It would be wrong to say, for example, that reformers always backed states' rights over federal authority, cast aspersions on all of John Marshall's leading cases, or held different views from their predecessors on fundamental issues like slavery or judicial review. With a bow to these similarities, the rest of this analysis focuses on the Bank and Indian Removal issues, where there was a sharp break with precedent.

THE CORRUPT BARGAIN AND GENERATIONAL DISRUPTION

Suspicions that aristocratic interests controlled the government were confirmed in the eyes of many observers by the defining event in Jackson's climb to power—his defeat in the 1824 election through the "Corrupt Bargain" between John Quincy Adams and Henry Clay. Despite winning the popular vote by more than

Senator Henry Clay, the leader of the conservative resistance. Artist unknown. Library of Congress.

40,000 votes out of 350,000 cast, Jackson was unable to secure a majority in the Electoral College because there were four candidates who won at least one state.[54] Pursuant to the Twelfth Amendment, this sort of electoral deadlock is broken by the House of Representatives, which chooses from among the top three candidates. Clay, who was a strong supporter of Marshall's views, finished fourth but decided not to sit idly by. To stop Jackson, he offered his support to Adams, the runner-up, and this was decisive. Shortly thereafter, Adams chose Clay as his secretary of state.

The Jackson men cried foul and condemned Clay as "the Judas of the West" who betrayed the American people for "thirty pieces of silver."[55] What made the episode particularly unseemly was that in those days the secretary of state, rather than the vice president, was seen as the political heir apparent.[56] Though Adams and Clay denied any wrongdoing, a reasonable person at the time could conclude that Clay was bribed into delivering the presidency. The important thing is that most Jacksonians and many others did believe that the election was stolen by Washington insiders seeking to protect their privileges. The Panic of 1819 shook their faith in the establishment; the Corrupt Bargain of 1824 shattered it.

Pivotal as this event was in its time, the Corrupt Bargain also provides an early glimpse of the themes that accompany the ascendance of every constitutional movement. Let us begin with the collapse of the existing party structure, which is usually a harbinger of a major shift in first principles.[57] Sometimes legal revolutionaries simply form their own party, as was true with Republicans in the 1850s or Populists in the 1890s. At other times, insurgents seize control of one of the existing major parties and transform its ideology. In the Jeffersonian era, the transformation took a different form since there was only one party and the presidential succession had passed in royal fashion to the most prominent Virginians (Jefferson, Madison, and Monroe). This genteel tradition came to an abrupt end in 1824. Old institutions and customs could not handle the disruptive energy unleashed by the new generation, and four candidates—representing no parties—ran in the election. That result is particularly astounding when one recalls that just four years earlier Monroe was reelected without opposition. A political group has never fallen so far so fast.

Naturally, this implosion was unwelcome news for the ruling elite, and the Corrupt Bargain indicates just how far constitutional conservatives will go to retain power. A disinterested statesman might conclude that the best solution was for Clay to support the candidate who got the most votes or abstain from taking a position adverse to the popular will. The problem is that Clay was not disinterested; he was fervently against everything Jackson stood for. When a constitutional establishment is staring defeat in the face, even the most high-minded of its members fall prey to the desire to use all means at their disposal to win. There was nothing illegal about Clay's action, in spite of the suggestions of bribery. In later years, however, he would take more aggressive steps to stop Jackson that stretched the law to its limits.[58] When a constitutional challenge arises that is ideologically distinct and has a reasonable chance of winning, the established order does not just curl up into the fetal position. Instead, it fights back and fights back hard. Idealism drives reformers in a transitional time, but terror is what motivates traditionalists.[59]

Lastly, the Corrupt Bargain also shows how resistance to reform can backfire. Politics is a dynamic process in which each side reacts to the other side's moves and every action tends to lead to a stronger reaction. This tit-for-tat cycle usually continues until one party is overwhelmed or capitulates and strikes a deal.[60] The arrangement between Adams and Clay just enraged Jackson's supporters and made them more determined to win the next election. As one of them said about the Bargain, "Thus it is that treachery and duplicity fall in their own snare, and the acts of the villain return the poisonous chalice to his own lips."[61] Jackson vowed that "the constitution will be so amended as to preserve to the people their rightful" role, and he spent the next four years organizing the country to achieve that end.[62] This would be the first of many rounds of escalation between Jackson and his conservative foes as both sides sought to redefine the meaning of the Constitution.

When Adams and Jackson met again in the election of 1828, no last-minute maneuver could prevent the rising movement from taking its rightful place in the national government. The new political landscape, which was somewhat obscured by the four-way race in 1824, reflected the growing influence of the frontier. Adams won the old Federalist strongholds of New England, but Jackson swept the West and South in piling up a 150,000 vote majority.[63] The president-elect said that this was a "triumph of the great principle of self-government over the intrigues of aristocracy."[64] For the first time, a westerner would occupy the White House, and the magnitude of this change was "revealed in the lamentations of the ousted elements, which resembled those of the Federalists at the election of Jefferson in 1801 and somewhat also those of the South at the election of Lincoln in 1860."[65] The constitutional cycle was starting to turn.

2

Presidential
Reconstruction

> The blessings of freedom cannot be employed without
> a frequent recurrence to fundamental principles. . . .
> Thirty years ago, at the opening of the present cen-
> tury, our Government was drawn back to its original
> principles; the vessel of State, like one at sea, had got-
> ten upon a wrong tack, and the new pilot who was
> then placed at the helm brought it again into the right
> course. . . . In the progress of a long voyage, it has
> again declined from its proper course; and I congratu-
> late the whole crew that we have found another pilot.
>
> *Representative Phillip B. Barbour*

The triumph of Andrew Jackson brought his gen-
eration from political obscurity to the seat of power. Now the hard part was
about to begin. In our constitutional system, a general election victory gives a
coalition the opportunity to put together a new consensus. There is no guarantee of success. A new party is largely an empty vessel into which anybody who is
upset with the status quo can place his or her hopes. This presents a problem
because there is no way that everybody with a grievance can agree on a platform,
and thus many will lose faith as policy choices are made. Fractures within the
new coalition are inevitable, and this is the great hope for conservatives trying
to resist the growing clamor for change.

The other cold reality for reformers is that the ruling establishment always
retains a power base after its first loss. Due to the separation of powers and the
fact that the branches are selected at different times, it is virtually impossible for

a new movement to seize power all at once.[1] That split gives each side a platform from which to appeal to voters and ensures that the debate between their competing visions will be protracted. In 1829, Jackson controlled the presidency and little else. After all, Marshall was still chief justice and held sway over a Court committed to *M'Culloch* and its other landmarks from 1819. In Congress, the situation was muddled at best. People calling themselves Democrats were a majority, but the president could not rely on them because there was no agreement on what being a Democrat meant.[2] Indeed, for the next six years Jackson would square off against a Congress that was closely divided or openly hostile to his constitutional goals.

Managing these twin difficulties of internal cohesion and external resistance is the challenge for every ascending movement, and the strategy for resolving them is dictated by institutional forces. Put simply, policy choices in these transitional periods are shaped by the happenstance of which side controls which branch. In Jackson's case, he could not change the law by putting sympathizers on the Court or by ratifying a constitutional amendment because his supporters did not control the Senate.[3] Working with the cards that he was dealt, the president instead settled on a two-track strategy. One involved the Indian Removal Act, a radical piece of legislation that sought to end the special status of the Tribes and shift power over them to the states. The other involved using the veto to dismantle economic programs that rested on a broad reading of federal authority. With these acts, the new leadership threw down the gauntlet. The Upstairs and Downstairs generations were about to meet.

THE INDIAN REMOVAL ACT OF 1830

To understand how a new generation lays the foundation for its break with precedent, let us begin by examining how the Jacksonians approached the issue of Native American sovereignty. The contrast between Secretary Knox's liberal approach toward the Tribes and the punitive view of the rising movement was never clearer than in Georgia's relationship with the Cherokee Nation. Considered the most sophisticated tribe, the Cherokees maintained a sizable homeland (about 6.2 million acres) that carved a big hole in Georgia's sovereignty.[4] In 1802, the State of Georgia entered into a compact with the federal government and agreed to relinquish its land claims in the western territories in exchange for a promise to extinguish the Cherokees' presence.[5] Federal officials, though, did little to carry out this promise.

The Missionaries and the Cherokee Codes

Increasingly irritated by this stalemate, Georgia focused its frustration on the missionaries and other whites who were getting federal aid from Knox's civilization program and encouraging the Tribe to maintain its independence. The largest of these groups was the American Board of Commissioners for Foreign Missions, which was founded by Massachusetts Congregationalists in 1810.[6] Though proselytizing was its main focus, the board's missionaries did more than provide religious instruction. In fact, most of their focus was on secular education and vocational training. To publicize its work, the board put out a journal that had one of the largest circulations of any periodical at the time.[7] Although the board worked with many tribes, its showcase project was the Cherokee mission. By the mid-1820s, that tribe had a written language, published a paper, and was writing a formal constitution. News of their progress spread far and wide and seemed to herald a growing acceptance of their equal status. The Tribe's leadership was also optimistic, telling John Quincy Adams that their efforts would soon end white prejudice against them.[8] A Cherokee on a national lecture tour captured this spirit when he said that "a period is fast approaching when . . . [we] will be admitted into all the privileges of the American family."[9] Not everyone, though, was thrilled with the missionaries' work. Representative Lumpkin of Georgia described them as "the fanatics . . . from these philanthropic ranks, flocking in upon the poor Cherokees, like the caterpillars and locusts of Egypt."[10] In 1824, the same year that Jackson was robbed of the presidency and the Bank's legality was challenged by Ohio, Georgia forced Congress to open an inquiry into whether the missionaries should continue to receive federal funds. The Committee on Indian Affairs, though, issued a report praising the program and declined to change course.[11]

Matters came to a head in the late 1820s. As part of the new Cherokee Constitution of 1827, the Tribe declared its independence and claimed absolute sovereignty within its borders.[12] This move, combined with the discovery of gold on tribal land, convinced Georgia to take drastic action. The state enacted a series of laws, which I will call the "Cherokee Codes," aimed at forcing the Tribe to leave so that the state could annex its land. In case there was any doubt about Georgia's intent, one of the new statutes was entitled "An act to add the territory . . . now in the occupancy of the Cherokee Indians, to the counties of [Georgia], and to extend the laws of this state over the same, and to annul all laws and ordinances made by the Cherokee nation."[13] Another law made assisting a meeting of the Cherokee government a crime punishable by four years in jail.[14] The governor of Georgia was also authorized to raise a militia to protect the gold on tribal land and arrest suspects.[15] That militia would also assist in a survey of the Cherokee lands, which was the prelude to a lottery that would give the area to whites.[16]

If the end of tribal independence and the confiscation of its property were not bad enough, the Cherokee Codes also sought to inflict as many burdens as possible on the state's newest subjects so that they would want to leave. One law provided that "no Indian or descendant of any Indian . . . shall be deemed a competent witness in any court of this state to which a white person may be a party."[17] Other acts voided all contracts between Cherokees and whites and barred whites from employing Native Americans.[18] More broadly, the application of Georgia law to the Tribe meant that its members were now considered "people of color" and thus could not vote if they chose to remain. Lastly, the legislation provided that anyone who attempted to prevent a Cherokee from emigrating or stop a tribal chief from negotiating an agreement to leave was subject to a lengthy prison term.[19]

In a final effort to facilitate the Tribe's departure, the Cherokee Codes sought to drive sympathetic whites out. The crucial provision provided that all white males who wanted to live in the tribal area had to first swear an oath acknowledging Georgia's sovereignty and then obtain a license from the governor.[20] At the time this provision was enacted, there were fifty-six whites living with the Cherokees, of whom eighteen were pastors—the rest were farmers, teachers, and mechanics who supported Cherokee freedom and were giving them secular instruction.[21] Georgia's hope was that they would refuse to take the required oath and thereby give the state an excuse to kick them out. This loyalty oath would ignite a firestorm.

Changing the Constitution with Legislation

Georgia's undeclared war against the Cherokees gave the president the opportunity to launch his movement's first significant initiative.[22] Jackson responded to the crisis by breaking with Knox's long-standing policy and refusing to interfere with the state's exercise of its internal police power. In his 1829 Annual Message (the State of the Union), he explained that the Constitution forbade the erection of a state within a state as the Cherokees were attempting.[23] He noted that Native Americans in northern states were governed by state law, and thus "there is no constitutional, conventional, or legal provision which allows [the southern states] less power over the Indians within their borders, than is possessed by Maine or New York."[24] Jackson thus "informed the Indians inhabiting parts of Georgia and Alabama, that their attempt to establish an independent government would not be countenanced by the Executive of the United States; and advised them to emigrate beyond the Mississippi, or submit to the laws of those States."[25] The president was convinced that whites and Native Americans could not live together and that separation (or geographic segregation) was the best solution.[26]

Shortly thereafter, Jackson's supporters introduced a removal bill in Congress. The bill set aside land west of the Mississippi for a new Cherokee homeland and authorized the federal government to assist the Tribe's move if it refused to submit to Georgia law.[27] This proposal turned standing constitutional principles on their head. Up until then, federal authorities had held that the Tribes were sovereign and that states had no right to regulate them. The Removal Act, by contrast, held that state law could act upon the Cherokees and denied their choice to remain free in their homeland. The act did stop short of ordering the Tribe to leave, as Jackson informed Congress that the "emigration should be voluntary, for it would be as cruel as unjust to compel the aborigines to abandon the graves of their fathers, and seek a home in a distant land."[28] Even that nominal respect for tribal autonomy, though, would ebb as the confrontation escalated.[29]

The Removal Act has a counterpart in almost every generation and sheds light on the fact that much of constitutional law is just a set of customs that exist outside of the courts. To take a simple example, Article Two says that the president "shall from time to time give to Congress information on the State of the Union."[30] In the nineteenth century, this was a written proclamation. Today, of course, the State of the Union is a major speech before Congress. The modern custom did not come about through a textual amendment or a case, but the practical meaning of the State of the Union Clause was altered nonetheless. Article Two also says that a treaty needs the support of two-thirds of the Senate for ratification.[31] Until the twentieth century, almost all international agreements were ratified under this standard. But over the last sixty years most of them have been ratified by a majority of each house of Congress as an "executive agreement." Lowering the bar for entering into binding foreign obligations has had profound implications for our role in the world. No amendment or court decision brought about this change either. Instead, the practice just evolved through the joint action of the president and Congress, largely in response to the view that the Senate's defeat of the Treaty of Versailles (by a minority) contributed to the Second World War.[32]

Like the legislation of Franklin Roosevelt's first Hundred Days or Jefferson's repeal of the Judiciary Act of 1801, Jackson's first act did not directly challenge the Constitution as construed by judges.[33] Knox's civilization program, including his view on the power of the federal government and tribal sovereignty, was never reviewed by a court prior to the 1830s. In spite of this omission, that interpretation was authoritative and reflected a web of understandings that Jackson was determined to change. No campaign for legal reform can succeed without a plan for legislative action, since Congress is a leading source of constitutional custom. This sort of opening gambit also galvanizes the factions within a reform movement and sustains the momentum garnered from the initial election victory.

Religious Opposition to the Removal Act
Those who believe that most antebellum Americans were uninterested in civil rights might be surprised by the hostility that greeted the Removal Act. As Martin Van Buren, Jackson's close advisor, said, "A more persevering opposition to a public measure has scarcely ever been."[34] At the forefront of this opposition were the missionaries of the American Board. The board's secretary, Jeremiah Evarts, penned a pamphlet condemning removal that was the most widely read political work in the United States since Thomas Paine's *Common Sense*.[35] Evarts was also instrumental in organizing large antiremoval protests that led to the first national petition drive against a specific piece of legislation. These petitions came pouring in from university campuses, women's groups, and town meetings with such intensity that "the tables of the members (of Congress) [were] covered with pamphlets devoted to the discussions of the Indian question."[36]

The board's work against the Removal Act was part of a broader fight against Jackson's plan by faith-based groups. Religious periodicals and pulpit sermons across the country attacked removal and lionized the Cherokees. The most biting comments were reserved for Georgia and its discriminatory Cherokee Codes. One editorial said the state's annexation of tribal land "awaken[s] our indignation and lead[s] us almost to wish that the Cherokees had the power to vindicate their rights."[37] The *Missionary Herald* commented that "now is the time when every Christian, every philanthropist and every patriot in the United States ought to be exerting themselves to save a persecuted and defenceless people from ruin."[38] If the Removal Act passed, another said, the Cherokees would become "living monuments of the white man's wrongs."[39]

The president and his supporters were vexed by this fierce public opposition. Democrats in Congress blamed the missionaries and denounced their activities as "the wicked influence of designing men veiled in the garb of philanthropy and Christian benevolence."[40] Jackson himself thought that the missionaries' battle against removal was motivated by a fear of losing their federal subsidies. To hit them where they lived, the president told the War secretary to impound all funds appropriated to the American Board and the other missionary organizations.

The secretary made it clear that this was in retaliation for their political speech, stating that "the Government by its funds should not extend encouragement and assistance to those who . . . employ their efforts to prevent removals."[41]

Here we see the outlines of a debate that would preoccupy this generation and every other—what was the appropriate relationship between church and state? Notwithstanding the rhetoric of some judges that the Founders wanted a strict separation between them, in truth there was little concern expressed in the early Republic about the symbolic endorsement of religion by the government or about public funding of religion among the Tribes.[42] The Jacksonian regime was the first to take a more skeptical view of this funding, not in order to protect freedom of conscience but because the clerics receiving the money were critical of their agenda.[43] In other words, their insistence on separation was all about silencing religious expression rather than promoting it.[44] On the other side, missionaries had good reason to complain about state involvement with religion since their right to preach to the Cherokees was threatened by the Georgia oath law. The state statute was also motivated by a desire to suppress their critical speech, but this infringement of free exercise would become a rallying point for conservatives in the wider constitutional struggle.

Opposition in Congress
Debate on the Removal Act lasted for three months, and the leader of the opposition was Senator Theodore Frelinghuysen, who was known as the "Christian statesman" for his fervent support of Native American rights.[45] His opening speech made a passionate case against asking Cherokees to suffer for the benefit of others: "The confiding Indian [has] listened to our professions of friendship: we called him brother, and he believed us. . . . We have crowded the tribes upon a few miserable acres on our Southern frontiers; it is all that is left to them of their once boundless forests; and still, like the horse-leech, our insatiated cupidity cries, give! give!"[46] Other critics were horrified that the president intended to dump tens of thousands of men, women, and children into an area known as the "Great American Desert" because it was viewed as unfit for human habitation.[47] Likewise, the act's foes mocked Jackson's claim that the Tribe would be unmolested after it moved to its new home. They saw that this removal would be just the first of many migrations that Native Americans would have to make.

Next, Frelinghuysen eloquently defended his generation's view that the choice posed by the act was improper because the Cherokee Codes were invalid. Echoing Knox's position, he told the Senate that the Framers "wisely determined to place our relations with the tribes under the absolute superintendence of the General Government."[48] While individual Native Americans in the North were

Senator Theodore Frelinghuysen, who challenged the Indian Removal Act. Artist unknown. Library of Congress.

governed by state law, that custom was distinguished on the grounds that they were few in number and no longer retained their tribal identity.[49] The senator also noted that the United States was a party to treaties with the Cherokees that represented "fresh and strong proofs of the sacred estimation always accorded to Indian rights."[50] He cited the text of the Treaty of Holston, signed in 1791, which said that "the United States solemnly guarant[ees] to the Cherokee nation all their lands not hereby ceded."[51]

Senator Peleg Sprague of Maine made the more fundamental point that the existence of treaties between the United States and the Tribe proved that the Cherokee Nation had sovereign rights. Treaties are signed with nations, not with aliens or subjects, and hence the Framers' decision to use treaties rather than laws in regulating the Tribes was significant. Consistent with the legal method of the age, Sprague said this unbroken legislative custom settled the constitutional issue. To support this view, the senator cited Madison's decision to endorse the validity of the Bank under similar circumstances: "Mr. Madison, who has, with so much justice, been denominated the great constitutional lawyer of this country, declared . . . that the constitutionality of the Bank of the United States, had been so settled by the sanction of the different departments of the Government, that it was no longer to be agitated; and yet only one bank had then been chartered. If his argument had, in that instance, any force it is here irresistible."[52] This would not be the only time that Madison's analysis of the Bank would be invoked to defend the traditional Constitution from the new generation's attack.

Finally, the act's foes were upset by the Georgia law excluding Native American testimony in cases involving whites. Frelinghuysen laid out this objection with vivid imagery: "A gang of lawless white men may break into the Cherokee country, plunder their habitations, murder the mother with the children, and all in the sight of the wretched husband and father, and no law of Georgia will reach the atrocity."[53] The senator had a name for this kind of conduct: he said it "shut [the Cherokees] out of the protection of Georgia's laws . . . [and] stripped these people of the protection of their government."[54] By evoking the language and spirit of equal protection long before the Fourteenth Amendment was written, Frelinghuysen offered a glimpse into the future and exposed the ugly discrimination embedded in Jacksonian Democracy.

The Defense of the Removal Act

Following this broadside against the bill, Senator John Forsyth of Georgia rose in rebuttal. He charged the other side with hypocrisy for ignoring the North's regular exercise of authority over Native Americans. Echoing Jackson's view in his Annual Message, Forsyth wondered why "Indians in New York, New England, Virginia are to be left to the tender mercies of those States, while the arm of the General Government is to be extended to protect the . . . Cherokees, from the anticipated oppressions of Mississippi, Alabama, and Georgia."[55] Similarly, Senator Robert Adams of Mississippi added that "everyone living within the boundaries of a particular state is subject to the laws of that state. Otherwise chaos reigns."[56] The act's proponents also challenged Frelinghuysen's reading of the Cherokee treaties. Forsyth pointed to the Treaty of Hopewell, which stated that "the United States in Congress assembled, shall have the sole and exclusive right of regulating trade with the Indians, and managing all their affairs in such manner as they think proper."[57] He said that this meant that the Tribe had no sovereignty and was subject to the will of Congress. Lastly, the senator maintained that the federal government had not met its obligation under the 1802 compact to extinguish the Cherokee title, and therefore Georgia's actions were justified.[58]

More broadly, Jackson's supporters scoffed at the idea that, in addition to federal rights and states' rights, there should be "Indian rights."[59] They claimed that the agreements with the Cherokees were not real treaties because "savages" did not have the dignity necessary to be a party to a treaty.[60] Representative

Lumpkin said that Knox's civilization policy was a concession that the Tribes were inferior:

> When gentlemen talk of preserving the Indians, what is it they mean to preserve? . . . Is it their barbarous laws and customs? No. You propose to furnish them with a code, and prevail upon them to adopt habits like your own. Their language? No. You intend to supersede their imperfect jargon, by teaching them your own rich, copious, energetic tongue. Their religion? No. You intend to convert them from their miserable superstitions to the mild and cheering doctrines of Christianity.[61]

Forsyth added that Native Americans were not "equal to the rest of the community" and therefore he did not "believe that this removal will accelerate the civilization of the tribes. You might as reasonably expect that wild animals, incapable of being tamed in a park, would be domesticated by turning them loose in the forest."[62] Congressman James Wayne of Georgia reiterated that "sovereignty over soil is the attribute of States; and it can never be affirmed of tribes living in a savage condition, without any elements of civilization."[63] Venom like this was frowned upon by traditionalists. In the new order, it was rewarded. Jackson later made Wayne a Supreme Court justice, where he remained long enough to join the majority in *Dred Scott*.

As the debate on the Removal Act drew to a climax, both sides pressed their efforts to the limit. Jackson told his supporters that he "staked the success of his administration upon this measure."[64] In the Senate, outnumbered opponents used parliamentary tactics to expose the injustice and illegality of the act. One amendment insisted that any negotiations on removal be legitimate; another required the federal government to guarantee the Cherokees' rights until they decided to leave.[65] Both proposals failed and the bill passed. In the House of Representatives, though, the fate of the act was in doubt. A substitute was introduced that would have delayed any action for a year while an independent commission inspected the new proposed tribal homeland. After considerable debate, the motion to table this poison pill passed by a single vote.[66]

THE MAYSVILLE TURNPIKE VETO

What separates theory from practice is that politicians must respond to events in real time and juggle many interests at once. As the Removal Act was moving toward a final vote in the House, Congress passed a bill authorizing $150,000 of government stock purchases in a corporation that would extend the National Road through Kentucky between Maysville and Lexington.[67] This project was typical of the internal improvements that rested on Marshall's reading of federal power. Thus, a Jacksonian would be inclined to veto the Maysville Turnpike.

Yet this impulse was tempered by the recognition that a Democratic Congress passed the bill. By vetoing the project, Jackson risked alienating members of his own party on the eve of the crucial vote on removal in the house.[68] The new movement was at a turning point. The president would be forced to choose between his two principal objectives—limiting federal authority and transforming the status of the Tribes—to save one of them. This is the kind of move that can splinter a rising political force and lead to its collapse. Even if that did not occur, such a decision would surely trigger a reaction and shift the constitutional change that the new regime would bring.

This doomsday scenario did not play out, though, because luck intervened and changed the equation. Article One, Section Seven, of the Constitution provides that the president has ten days (excluding Sundays) to decide whether to veto a bill.[69] The Maysville Turnpike passed less than ten days before the final vote on the Removal Act in the House of Representatives. Thus, Jackson did not have to walk the plank. He could wait until after the crucial vote and then issue his veto.[70] This was nothing more than chance acting in the president's favor. In those days, Congress lacked leaders who micromanaged the legislative agenda.[71] One can see a canny politician structuring the votes to give the president a way out of choosing between them, but in 1830 this did not happen. Luck took the place of cunning and temporarily saved the new generation from a schism. Aided by last-minute lobbying, the Removal Act passed the House 102 to 97.[72] Only after this vote did Jackson turn to the Maysville Turnpike issue.

The Madisonian Understanding of the Veto

Just as the president sought to overturn decades of practice on the autonomy of the Tribes, he faced equally powerful precedent in mulling over whether to veto the Maysville Turnpike. Prior to 1830, the consensus was that legislative precedents bound the other branches in their constitutional actions.[73] Put another way, the conventional view was that custom was a powerful source of authority, not just something that filled gaps between Supreme Court cases. One of the best expressions of this view was Madison's Bank Veto, discussed in chapter 1, where he swallowed his constitutional objections because Congress and the nation had repeatedly endorsed that institution.[74] While Jackson was issuing his vetoes, Madison expanded on his position by explaining that a veto would be inappropriate in the face "of all the obligations derived from a course of precedents amounting to the requisite evidence of the national judgment and intention."[75] Madison's Bank Veto therefore created an informal limit on the veto power—based on consistent practice—that became quite influential prior to Jackson's election.[76]

Institutional arrangements and constitutional substance were now merging, and what followed shows once again how the initial allocation of political resources directs the flow of events during a transitional period. In the 1820s, the Jacksonian movement gave no consideration to how the president should interact with Congress. If the Democrats had started with control of Congress, they probably would have used traditional arguments to advance their ideas. But that was not the situation. The president's plan to alter the law was confronted by the same contention across the board—the status quo was fixed by repeated acknowledgments of its validity by the political branches.[77] Recall that Senator Sprague stressed this point, citing Madison's Bank Veto, in opposing the Removal Act. Jackson could only achieve his aims by challenging the traditional view that legislative precedent was binding on the other branches.

To smash this consensus, the president turned to the veto. Jackson vetoed more bills than all of his predecessors combined, and these were crucial in mobilizing public support.[78] This tactic worked because it resonated with the deeper structure of the presidency. In a groundbreaking study of the executive branch, Stephen Skowronek writes that presidents are better at tearing things down than at building them up.[79] Vetoes capture this observation well, since they can only be used to end programs. This was no problem for Jackson, since he wanted to destroy the earlier generation's view of federal power. The place to start with was the Maysville Turnpike.

Jackson's Opening Bid

Boldness mixed with a dash of luck let the president veto the act as an "irregular, improvident, and unequal appropriation . . . of the public funds."[80] Both Madison and Monroe vetoed spending on "local" items that the states could not refuse to undertake.[81] Thus, the issue was not a black-and-white one about the existence of federal implied power—the question was how broadly that power should be construed.[82] In his argument against the Maysville Turnpike, Jackson relied on his predecessors' vetoes as a way of appealing to the more cautious elements within his caucus. Jackson claimed that this was a local project—and thus beyond the power of Congress—because it ran only within the confines of

Kentucky.[83] Since the bill sought to extend a national network of roads, clas-
sifying it as a local project was questionable, but the president's analysis of the
customary law was plausible. During such an early stage, the claims advanced by
the new movement always appear more modest than they actually are. Unsure
of the political support for radical change, the new leadership will try to set its
reforms in the context of existing principles. Just as the Removal Act claimed
to respect the Tribe's freedom on whether it would leave Georgia, in his first
veto Jackson claimed that he was doing nothing more than what past presidents
had done.

Although the "holding" of the veto was rather bland, Jackson's "dicta" undermined the idea of deferring to legislative and executive practice.[84] He spoke wist-
fully about Jefferson's narrow view of federal power on internal improvements,
noting its "deservedly high authority," and said, "The symmetry and purity of
the Government would doubtless have been better preserved if this restriction
of the power of appropriation could have been maintained."[85] He lamented
"the difficulty, if not impracticability, of bringing back the operations of the
Government to the construction of the Constitution."[86] That example was an
"admonitory proof of the force of implication and the necessity of guarding the
Constitution with sleepless vigilance against the authority of precedents which
have not the sanction of its most plainly defined powers."[87] It was the duty of all
officials, he said, "to look to that sacred instrument instead of the statute book"
when interpreting the Constitution.[88]

In this sense, the Maysville Turnpike Veto bridged the divide between the
competing generations. Jackson's action was within the parameters of constitutional tradition and drew on its precedents. Nevertheless, the rest of his statement took the assumptions of that regime to task. Practice was not an irresistible
rule of construction but a suspicious source of authority that must be watched
with "sleepless vigilance." Moreover, legislative precedent in "the statute book"
was unreliable in comparison with the constitutional text, which inverted Madison's notion that abstract opinion could not defeat consistent practice. With
these assertions, the president sought to undermine traditional principles and
prepare the nation for broad reform.

Notwithstanding the care that Jackson took to rest his veto on widely accepted
precedent, the response to his action suggested that the president's opponents
were not fooled. The *National Intelligencer*, a leading anti-Jackson newspaper,
held that the Maysville Veto threw the government back half a century.[89] Daniel
Webster charged that the only road that the administration wanted was a "road
to ruin."[90] And in a similar vein, another congressman said that "on the whole, I
consider this document artfully contrived to bring the whole system of internal

improvements into disrepute."[91] After touring the country and consulting with local politicians, Webster told Clay that "the passage of the Indian bill, and the rejection of the Maysville turnpike bill, have occasioned unusual excitement."[92] In part, that was because the Maysville Turnpike Veto was a herald for a challenge to the great pillar of the traditional constitution: the National Bank.

There is one postscript to this opening skirmish. Although most of the opposition to the Removal Act came from conservatives, another voice could be heard muttering in the background. A small group of radicals led by William Lloyd Garrison attacked the act not because the Tribes were sovereign, but because it violated the personal rights of Native Americans, just as slavery mocked the liberty of African Americans. Garrison praised Senator Frelinghuysen's efforts during the debate, stating that "if the dominant party in the Senate had not hearts more impenetrable than polar ice, his speech would have . . . rescued the American name from eternal infamy."[93] Thus, at the moment that the Jacksonians were achieving their first great victories, their constitutional successors were already beginning to stir in response.

3

Judicial Resistance: *Worcester v. Georgia*

> The judiciary is . . . the check of a preceding genera-
> tion on the present one; a check of conservative legal
> philosophy upon a dynamic people, and nearly always
> the check of a rejected regime on the one in being. This
> conservative institution is under every pressure and
> temptation to throw its weight against novel programs
> and untried policies which win popular elections.
>
> *Justice Robert H. Jackson,*
> The Struggle for Judicial Supremacy

During the initial phase of this collision between
traditionalists and reformers, the High Court sat on the sidelines. With the passage of the Indian Removal Act and the Cherokee Codes, however, the Court
got its chance to enter the fray as the inevitable lawsuits were filed. Although
justices do take a different approach toward constitutional questions from Congress or the president, during a generational confrontation those distinctions
almost completely disappear. The Court, as Justice Jackson said, represents the
established constitutional order. Justices are no less likely than their conservative counterparts in the political branches to express shock at the prospect of
radical change. In some respects, they are bound to get more upset, since their
training leads them to take a skeptical view of broad assertions that lack support in text or precedent. Accordingly, courts are apt to resist claims by a rising
movement that its legal vision should displace past wisdom.

The question that this chapter examines is how intense that resistance will
be. Thus far, the opposition to Jackson's platform was nothing remarkable: voting against the Removal Act and attacking the Maysville Turnpike Veto. After

failing to stop the first wave of reform, defenders of the status quo face a choice. They can conclude that change is inevitable and bow to the demands of youth by noting their objections while refusing to engage in further obstruction. Or they can escalate their resistance and hope that voters will see the folly of tampering with established principles. Constitutional conservatives almost always choose the latter path unless the costs of holding out are very high. This escalation does not happen all at once—it comes step by step as each side probes the other for weaknesses. In the Supreme Court, that resistance has a paradoxical effect. Instead of defending the traditional constitution, the justices end up inventing a new one in response to the reformers' perceived threat through a "preemptive opinion."

THE PRELIMINARY ROUND—CHEROKEE NATION V. GEORGIA

The wise men of the establishment took a dim view of the Removal Act's validity. At the urging of Daniel Webster, the Cherokees hired William Wirt, a distinguished former attorney general, to plan a litigation strategy.[1] Wirt took the unusual step of asking a friend to approach Chief Justice Marshall for his informal opinion on the case. Marshall wrote Wirt's contact and, although declining to address the "very interesting questions" involved, made it plain that he was paying a great deal of attention to what Jackson was doing: "I have followed the debate in both houses of Congress with profound attention, and with deep interest, and have wished, most sincerely, that both the Executive and Legislative departments had thought differently on the subject. Humanity must bewail the course which is being pursued, whatever may be the decision of policy."[2]

Marshall's interest in improving relations between whites and Native Americans was not new. Nearly fifty years earlier, as a delegate in the Virginia House of Burgesses, Marshall had proposed a bill to promote intermarriage between the groups.[3] When the measure was rejected, he said that "our prejudices oppose themselves to our interests, and operate too powerfully for them."[4] The chief justice did uphold the acquisition of tribal land in the past as a fait accompli, but told his colleague Joseph Story that "every oppression now exercised on a helpless people depending on our magnanimity and justice for the preservation of their existence, impresses a deep stain on the American character."[5]

Obstruction of Justice

Despite Jackson's assertion that Wirt's work on behalf of the Cherokees was "truly wicked," the lawyer began preparing a case that would challenge the

Georgia statutes.[6] A tribal leader said that "if we are removed . . . by the United States . . . we wish to leave in the records of her judicial tribunals, for future generations to read, when we are gone, ample testimony that she acted *justly* or *unjustly*."[7] The first opportunity involved a tribal member who was convicted by the State for the murder of another Cherokee on the Nation's land. Prior to the enactment of the repressive state laws, this kind of crime rested squarely within the jurisdiction of tribal courts. A writ of error was sought asking the Supreme Court to review the conviction because the State's assumption of jurisdiction was illegal. The justices granted the writ and ordered the State to appear, but Georgia had a different idea. Governor George Gilmer said that "so far as concerns the executive department, orders received from the Supreme Court for the purpose of staying, or in any manner interfering with the decisions of the courts of the State . . . will be disregarded."[8] The State ordered the sheriff to carry out the death sentence, and this was done before a large crowd that gathered for the occasion.[9]

This brazen lynching shocked political observers and was an early indication that the coming political battle would be intense. John Quincy Adams worried that "the Constitution, the laws and treaties of the United States are prostrate in the State of Georgia. Is there any remedy for this state of things? None. Because the Executive of the United States is in league with the State of Georgia."[10] The *Georgia Athenian* wrote that "the collision of authorities portends something serious. . . . [P]erhaps His Honor, Judge Marshall, may think it incumbent on him to arraign and punish (perchance he should possess the power) the State of Georgia for contempt of the Federal Court."[11] Even Martin Van Buren, who was Jackson's main supporter, showed his discomfort with this episode by omitting the details in his otherwise exhaustive autobiography. He noted only that "nothing further was done with the Writ of Error" after it was granted by the Supreme Court.[12] Since a hangman's noose deprived Wirt of his first plaintiff, he next sought relief in the Court's original jurisdiction, claiming that the Cherokee Tribe was a foreign state entitled to such a hearing against a State under Article Three, Section Two, of the Constitution.

What happened next demonstrated that this was not just one state defying the federal courts; it represented a fundamental split over whether traditionalists or reformers spoke for the people. After Wirt filed his petition, Jacksonians in Congress introduced a bill to repeal Section 25 of the Judiciary Act and deprive the Court of its power to review judgments from state courts.[13] This would not have altered its jurisdiction over Wirt's case, but the message was clear—the justices interfered with the president's agenda at their peril. Though this bill failed in the House, Story feared that this proposal and "the recent attacks in

Georgia . . . [were] but parts of the same general scheme, the object of which is to elevate an exclusive State sovereignty upon the ruins of the general Government."[14]

When a constitutional transition starts to unfold, reformers take an increasingly hostile attitude toward judicial review. In part, this rests on the simple fact that the courts are not yet under their control. The other issue, though, is legitimacy. Rising movements are filled with a righteous belief that the voters have given them a mandate for constitutional reform. On the other side, the justices generally believe that they represent the true voice of the people as set forth in the text of the Constitution and decades of precedent. These opposing views collide at every intersection between constitutional generations, and one result is that these are the points where calls for the abolition of judicial review reach a crescendo. Indeed, almost every major effort to restrict the Court's power has come during these brief but regular interludes, ranging from a Reconstruction-era statute that stripped the Court of jurisdiction to the constitutional amendments proposed during the New Deal to gut the Court's power to strike down statutes.[15]

Stating the Case

With this pall hanging over the Court, Wirt argued *Cherokee Nation v. State of Georgia* in March 1831.[16] It was a one-sided affair, as Georgia refused to recognize the Court's authority and boycotted the session.[17] Wirt asserted that the Cherokee Codes were contrary to the treaties with the Tribe and federal statutes governing tribal relations. Moreover, he maintained that the state laws were invalid because (1) the Commerce Clause gave exclusive authority over tribal affairs to Congress; and (2) the Contracts Clause barred States from interfering with a treaty between the United States and a tribe.[18] Wirt held that the Tribes were capable of entering into binding obligations, telling the Court that all people possessed "from their common parent equal rights."[19] John Sergeant, Wirt's co-counsel, added a strong plea for action, stating that otherwise "there will be no Cherokee boundary, no Cherokee nation, no Cherokee lands, no Cherokee treaties, no laws of the United States. . . . They will all be swept out of existence together, leaving nothing but the monuments in our history of [an] enormous injustice."[20]

This call fell on deaf ears, as the justices dismissed the suit for want of jurisdiction. While admitting that "if courts were permitted to indulge their sympathies, a case better calculated to excite them can scarcely be imagined," the chief justice held that a tribe was not a foreign state entitled to sue in the

Supreme Court.[21] Marshall gave three reasons for his conclusion. First, he said the Framers did not intend to allow the Tribes to sue in federal court at all, let alone in the High Court's original jurisdiction.[22] Second, he explained that the Commerce Clause was "divided into three distinct classes—foreign nations, the several states, and Indian tribes."[23] Since foreign nations and Indian tribes were distinguished there, the Court reasoned that they meant different things.[24] This distinction, Marshall said, threw light on the meaning of foreign state in Article Three, Section Two, and excluded the Tribes.[25] Lastly, the chief justice argued that the petition "requires us to control the legislature of Georgia. . . . The propriety of such an interposition by the court may well be questioned. It savours too much of the exercise of political power to be within the proper province of the judicial department."[26]

Cherokee Nation was the kind of cautious decision that people usually expect from courts, but Marshall did not stop there. Van Buren complained that he went on "as he did in the famous case of Marbury and Madison, to deliver an *extra-judicial opinion*" stating that the Cherokees were a distinct "domestic dependent nation."[27] Marshall even suggested how the case should have been brought, stating that the portion of the suit that "prays the aid of the court to protect their possession [of land] . . . might perhaps be decided by this court in a proper case with proper parties."[28] The comparison with *Marbury* was right on target. In both instances, the chief justice confronted the same problem—how should the Court respond to the challenge of a rising generation? The Court's strategy would be strikingly similar in each case—avoid a direct confrontation but do everything possible to influence public opinion against reform while setting down doctrines (for example, judicial review) that could defend and expand the traditional Constitution.[29]

The political strategy behind Marshall's thinking was revealed by what happened after the opinion was issued. On the day the case was announced from the bench, those present heard three opinions—one by Marshall for the Court, and one each by Justices Johnson and Baldwin, who concurred separately and argued against the Cherokee claims on the merits.[30] Tribal leaders were so discouraged by the fact that nobody supported their position that they thought of giving up their court fight. When Marshall heard this, he asked Justices Story and Thompson to dissent and support the Cherokee claims. Despite this flagrant disregard for the Court's procedures, that opinion appears in the reports as though it was an original part of the decision.[31] Story recalled that "neither Judge T[hompson] nor myself contemplated delivering a dissenting opinion, until the Chief Justice suggested to us the propriety of it, and his desire that we should do it."[32]

Accordingly, the first round of litigation led to a significant increase in tensions without resolving anything. Both Georgia and Chief Justice Marshall took dramatic steps to draw attention to their competing positions—including outright defiance of the law—but neither side climbed out so far on a limb that it could not retreat. As time passed, though, the logic of escalation would make it harder to act without consequences.

CIVIL DISOBEDIENCE AND RELIGIOUS FERVOR

At the same time that the Court was considering *Cherokee Nation*, the missionaries living among the Tribe faced their own decision as the deadline for taking the state loyalty oath drew near. Samuel Worcester of Vermont, the missionaries' leader, convinced his colleagues that "taking an oath of allegiance is out of the question."[33] Their objections were not religious in nature; they simply believed that Georgia's actions were "an invasion of the rights of the Cherokees and highly unjust and oppressive."[34] The inevitable showdown came one Sunday morning after church. Three of the American Board's missionaries, along with other whites living in the Cherokee homeland, were arrested for refusing to take the oath. But when they were brought to trial, a state court anxious to avoid creating a Supreme Court appeal ruled that, due to the public money they received, the defendants were federal employees and fell under an exemption in the oath statute.[35] In particular, the state court noted that Worcester was the federal postmaster to the Cherokee Nation. The missionaries had refused to raise their federal connection as a defense, but the court ordered their release anyway.[36]

The governor of Georgia, who was spoiling for a fight, now penned a revealing letter to the postmaster general. He began by arguing that the missionaries exerted "extensive influence over the Indians and [have] been very active in exciting their prejudices against the Administration of both the General and State Governments."[37] Thus, the governor stated:

> The object of this communication is to request that you dismiss Samuel Worcester from the office of postmaster. If Worcester is not now removed, he will, without doubt, consider himself authorized to conduct his seditious conduct. . . . It is due to the State, however, that those who, under the cloak of religious ministry, teach discord to our misguided Indian people and opposition to the rulers, should be compelled to know that obedience to the laws is both a religious and civil duty.[38]

Samuel Worcester, the head of the missionaries in the Cherokee Nation. Frontispiece from Althea Bass, Cherokee Messenger *(Norman: University of Oklahoma Press, 1936). Artist unknown.*

Shortly thereafter, Worcester was dismissed from his post and the president declared that the missionaries were no longer federal employees.[39] On May 16, 1831, Governor Gilmer wrote Worcester and told him that his "conduct in opposing the humane [removal] policy of the general government" would not be tolerated and that he and his friends had ten days "to take the oath to support the constitution and laws of the state."[40]

Worcester responded with an eloquent defense of traditional principles and vowed to sacrifice his body for the cause. Turning Gilmer's point around, he asked if opposing the humane policy of the federal government referred to "those efforts for the advancement of the Indians in knowledge, and in the arts of civilized life, which the general government has pursued ever since the days of Washington."[41] After noting that the oath would be "perjury for one who is of the opposite opinion," Worcester added that complying with the state order, given "the present state of feeling among the Indians, [could] greatly impair, or entirely destroy my usefulness as a minister of the gospel among them."[42] Worcester and the eleven whites who remained defiant were arrested and beaten.[43] Swiftly convicted this time and sentenced to four years at hard labor, the defendants were offered a suspended sentence if they took the oath.[44] Nine of the eleven accepted this deal. Worcester and his colleague, Elizur Butler, refused and applied for a writ of error. The stage was set for another showdown before the Supreme Court in *Worcester v. Georgia*.

As the Court prepared to consider this new challenge to the Cherokee Codes, the nation was plunged into another debate on the connection between faith and law. Religious groups opposed the removal of the Tribe, but they quaked with outrage at this attack on religious freedom in Georgia. Van Buren recalled that "it is scarcely possible now . . . to realize the extent to which many of our religious societies were agitated and disturbed by the imprisonment of those missionaries."[45] Opponents of Georgia's action emphasized that the prisoners were ministers engaged in "preaching the gospel to the Cherokee Indians, and . . . translating the sacred Scriptures into their language."[46] One paper wrote that this was the modern equivalent of a past constitutional struggle about whether "England had a right to make laws forbidding ministers to preach the gospel."[47] Worcester himself said that he and Butler were "martyrs in the cause of liberty."[48] Indeed, the American Board told them that their sacrifice "would rouse this whole country, in a manner unlike anything which has yet been experienced."[49] Furthermore, "the most intelligent members of Congress, are of opinion that the Supreme Court will sustain the Indians & that the people of the U.S. will yield & a settlement will be made."[50]

Georgia officials responded to this public relations offensive by denying that they were "disregarding the sacred character and holy functions of the missionaries of the Cross."[51] A special committee of the state legislature issued a widely publicized report asserting that "the laws of Georgia interfere not with the religious privileges, or conscientious opinions of men—and the State lends her aid to all efforts, for the dissemination of the truths of revelation."[52] The heart of the State's argument was that the oath statute did not discriminate against religion because it applied equally to all whites who wished to live in the tribal area:

> The law which has excited so much feeling among our brethren of the eastern states is not partial or exclusive in its operation. . . . Our law in this, as well as other cases, aims at no individual or individuals, and recognizes no exemptions. Your committee therefore declare that no objection can be urged against the State, with any propriety, upon the score of its inequality, for the State made all men "equal under the law."[53]

Supporters of the Removal Act said they were defending equality by ending the special privileges of the Tribes; now Georgia claimed that they were treating the faithful and unbelievers alike.

After reframing the issue as one of equal treatment, the State denied that religious activists could claim a special exemption. The committee report said that the missionaries bore the burden "to show that resistance to rightful civil authority is either a Christian duty or a Christian privilege—that things which are Caesar's are not to be rendered to Caesar, and that conscientious scruples can defeat the operation of laws."[54] The State said this request for an exception invited anarchy, for "if the opinion of every subject, as to the constitutionality of the laws under which he lives, can exempt him from their operation, then is Government a mockery, and Lawgivers, Judges, and Governors, the merest toys to be sported with according to the whims and caprices of individuals."[55]

Just as intergenerational friction led Jacksonians to question state funding for religious activity, Worcester's defiance sparked the broadest debate in our history on whether faith should compel the State to provide an exception from a neutral law. The language of the State's rebuttal anticipated a controversial modern Supreme Court opinion holding that no such exemption was required when a Native American tribe wanted to use the banned hallucinogen peyote in its religious ceremonies.[56] Echoing Georgia's view of 1832, the Court in 1990 said that making "an individual's obligation to obey [a neutral] law contingent upon the law's coincidence with his religious beliefs . . . permitting him, by virtue of his beliefs to become a law unto himself contradicts both constitutional tradition and common sense."[57] *Worcester* did not resolve this question because the First Amendment did not apply to the States at the time. Nevertheless, the memory of this religious dispute would be seared into the minds of the generation that succeeded Jacksonian Democracy.

WORCESTER V. GEORGIA AND PREEMPTIVE OPINIONS

Those who lived through 1832 thought they were seeing a turning point in constitutional law that rivaled the Founding. The first act of that dramatic year came in February, when the Court heard argument in *Worcester v. Georgia*. Once again, the State displayed its unwillingness to obey the Court by boycotting the session. Law and politics were on display, for while Wirt was making Worcester's plea he was also preparing a third-party bid for the White House.[58] In this charged atmosphere, Chief Justice Marshall issued his famous opinion striking down the Cherokee Codes and declaring that the Tribes "had always been considered as distinct, independent, political communities, retaining their original natural rights, as the undisputed possessors of the soil, from time immemorial."[59]

The conventional wisdom is that *Worcester* was a model of judicial integrity for reversing the missionaries' conviction in the teeth of intense political pressure.

Justice Hugo Black stated the Court's official position on the case in an opinion during the 1950s, calling *Worcester* "one of [Marshall's] most courageous and eloquent opinions."[60] In *Bush v. Gore*, Justice Stephen Breyer's dissent cited Marshall's defense of the Cherokees as a shining example of law transcending politics.[61] Academic commentary is just as complimentary, with one leading Indian law scholar stating that "to emulate Chief Justice Marshall in *Worcester* requires many things, including judicial courage."[62]

These tributes are misleading because they assume that the chief justice was merely restating existing doctrine, when in fact he was engaged in an act of massive resistance to the rising generation that I call a "preemptive opinion." This form of aggressive response is founded on the Court's willingness to create new doctrine that is specifically targeted at the reformers' agenda. In a preemptive case, the justices generally reach conclusions that are valid under existing precedent but restate those tenets in a grossly exaggerated manner that is more about negating the views of the rising generation than honestly evaluating the legal authorities. Naturally, these opinions are rare since they occur only when intergenerational tensions are at their peak; but when they do happen a fascinating mix of legal and political considerations comes into play.

Preemptive cases are the pinnacle of conservative resistance in the judicial branch, but they also mark the point where the escalation in the generational battle begins to warp the constitutional fabric. To achieve their sweeping political goals, preemptive opinions use three unusual tactics. First, the justices strain to decide every issue in the case rather than avoid ones that are unnecessary. Needless to say, decisive intervention and judicial restraint are not good partners. Second, the Court distorts the principles of the established generation in a way that hurts the opposition as much as possible. At this point, the justices throw off their blindfolds and actively join the political resistance. An opinion capable of accomplishing these goals, however, is hard to pull off because precedent generally (and thankfully) does not support such expansive and partisan reasoning. Thus, the third facet of a preemptive case is the development of some new theory of equality or fairness that can overcome this obstacle. All of these elements would be present in *Worcester*—the Supreme Court's first preemptive opinion.[63]

Deciding Unnecessary Issues

Reading *Worcester* for the first time, its most striking feature is Marshall's disregard for the issues on appeal. Although the case was about the oath statute, the Court focused its opinion—over twenty pages—on "an elaborate argument for

Cherokee independence."[64] Only at the end did the chief justice add a few para-graphs about the missionaries' plight.[65] In that brief analysis, though, he man-aged to hold all of the Cherokee Codes unconstitutional. Moreover, the Court used this as a *third* ground for reversal after concluding that the state statutes were preempted by federal law and by treaties with the Tribe.[66]

Despite this extraordinary effort to reach the constitutional issues, Marshall claimed that he had no choice because "those who fill the judicial department have no discretion in selecting the subjects to be brought before them."[67] This statement was false. The Court had at least three ways to avoid declaring that the Georgia laws were unconstitutional. For one thing, the petitioners did not get the lower court record properly certified—a pleading defect that could well have led to a dismissal of the suit if the Court was so inclined.[68] Next, the 1802 compact between the United States and Georgia stated that no person could enter Cherokee land without a federal license.[69] By adding conditions for en-try, the State was impeding federal policy and violating the compact.[70] Third, the Treaty of Hopewell said the Cherokees were "under the protection of the United States, and of no other sovereign whatsoever" and had the right to pun-ish trespassers "as they might think proper."[71] This language did not contem-plate a State playing a role in regulating the Tribe, and thus the Court could also have rested its judgment on that ground. All of this leads to an important point—there is no doubt that the conclusion in *Worcester* was correct. The prob-lem was how the Court got there.

Chief Justice Marshall did not stop with these reasons because such a narrow holding would not have had an impact on the broader constitutional debate. The Court wanted to turn public opinion against the Removal Act, not just against the Cherokee Codes. Moreover, Marshall wanted to counter the Jack-sonian argument that the Tribes had no sovereign rights and that the States should have the primary role in setting Native American policy. As the Court stated, "The Cherokees acknowledge themselves to be under the protection of the United States, and of no other power. Protection does not imply the destruc-tion of the protected."[72]

Reactive Legal Reasoning

After brushing aside the prudential concerns that counseled against deciding the sensitive issues, the chief justice proceeded to articulate a sweeping view of federal authority and tribal sovereignty that could not be squared with tradi-tional principles but did respond to the new generation's critique. The most remarkable example was at the end of Marshall's opinion. He wrote that "according to the settled principles of our constitution," control of tribal relations "are committed exclusively to the government of the Union."[73] This was the broadest assertion ever made by a Court that was always eager to proclaim federal supremacy. Holding that Congress had exclusive power over commerce with the Tribes was reasonable. Expanding that rationale to cover all interactions with Native Americans was not. Marshall's critics pointed out that the Commerce Clause, which was the only fount of authority available, could not provide Congress power over all noncommercial affairs with the Tribes when it did not grant such a police power elsewhere.[74]

The problem with the chief justice's emphatic (and distorted) assertion of federal authority is that it enhanced the credibility of the Removal Act, which explains why the rest of *Worcester* discussed the otherwise tangential issue of Cherokee rights. Mounting an effective challenge to the Jacksonian generation required the Court to explain why it was improper for Congress to use its exclusive power to pursue removal. Marshall's answer was to develop what were later characterized as "platonic notions of Indian sovereignty" that were unprecedented.[75] While Knox held that the national government should recognize some tribal rights, the Supreme Court said that Washington must respect Native American sovereignty in virtually all matters.[76]

Once again, this expansive interpretation was a fine political riposte to the Jacksonian assertion that the Tribes had no rights, but Marshall's legal position was weak. For instance, Marshall asserted that the European powers never claimed sovereignty over the Tribes, contending that "the extravagant and absurd idea, that the feeble settlements made on the sea-coast, or the companies under whom they were made, acquired legitimate power by them to govern the [Tribes] . . . did not enter the mind of any man."[77] The problem is that the Europeans did make this claim, as the concurring justices in *Cherokee Nation* pointed out.[78] Likewise, Marshall said that prior to the American Revolution the Crown respected the Tribes' sovereignty and "never coerced a surrender" of their land.[79] That claim was hard to sustain given the many brutal wars that had previously led to cessions of tribal land.

A more substantial problem with Marshall's view of Cherokee rights was that the main treaty between the Tribe and the United States did not seem to support the Court's holding. For example, Article Four of the Treaty of Hopewell defined the tribal region as "the boundary allotted to the Cherokees for their hunting grounds."[80] In *Cherokee Nation*, Justice Johnson argued that the word "allotted" "is the language of concession on our part, not theirs." He meant that the Cherokees "receive[d] the territory allotted to them as a boon, from a master or conqueror."[81] Furthermore, the description of the tribal land as hunting grounds was significant because hunters or nomads had no rights under international law. Most damaging of all was Article Nine of the treaty, which was cited in the congressional debates and gave Congress "the sole and exclusive right of regulating their trade and managing all their affairs in such manner as [Congress] shall think proper."[82] Justice Johnson concluded that this was "a relinquishment of all power, legislative, executive, and judicial, to the United States."[83] The chief justice responded with a long passage in *Worcester* citing other treaty provisions supporting his broader view of tribal sovereignty.[84] One leading scholar, though, observes that "rather than approach the interpretive questions as normatively neutral exercises, Chief Justice Marshall found some reason to work hard to counter the ordinary textual meaning of the treaty."[85] The Court's effort to articulate a persuasive response to the new generation's agenda could not be sustained without some special help.

A New Understanding of Equality

Since traditional precepts did not provide a firm basis for resisting Jacksonian Democracy, the chief justice changed the rules and fashioned a new constitutional principle of equality. He contended that the adverse text in the Treaty of Hopewell should be interpreted narrowly because the Tribe was a disadvantaged class. He asked if it was "reasonable to suppose, that the Indians, who could not write, and most probably could not read, who certainly were not critical judges of our language, should distinguish the word 'allotted' from the words 'marked out.'" Since "no chief was capable of signing his name," the Court said it was "probable the treaty was interpreted to them . . . [and that] it may very well be supposed, that they might not understand the term [allotted]."[86] The chief justice added that language giving Congress the right to manage Cherokee affairs should not be read as a relinquishment of sovereignty because it was "inconceivable that they could have supposed themselves, by a phrase thus slipped into an article . . . to have divested themselves of the right of self-government. . . . Had such a result been intended, it would have been openly avowed."[87]

Continuing in this vein, Marshall stressed that the treaties between the Tribes and the United States dealt in the "language of equality." For instance, the Court cited the first treaty ever made between Native Americans and the United States and said that "the language of equality in which it is drawn, evinces the temper with which the negotiation was undertaken, and the opinion which then prevailed in the United States."[88] In the Cherokee treaties, the chief justice emphasized that in most cases the rights and duties imposed by these agreements were the same for each side.[89] From these facts, the Court argued that "the only inference to be drawn . . . is, that the United States considered the Cherokees a nation."[90] Accordingly, he concluded that the Tribe must have sovereignty similar to that of the United States and could not be subjected to the discrimination of the Georgia statutes or (implicitly) the Removal Act.[91]

Viewed from a modern perspective, *Worcester* was the first case to state a crude equal protection principle in which the courts apply heightened scrutiny to laws because of their impact on an aggrieved minority. Not surprisingly, the nascent abolitionist movement was thrilled by Marshall's ruling and saw it as a beacon for the future.[92] To the extent that *Worcester* marks the birth of antidiscrimination law in this country, though, there are two rather surprising aspects to the opinion. One is that Native Americans, not African Americans, were the subject of the Court's first great pronouncement on equality. The other was that Marshall did not rest his analysis on the violation of individual rights. Although the Cherokee Codes and the Removal Act discriminated against individuals, he chose to base his opinion on the injury to the collective rights of the Tribe.[93]

Marshall's creation of an equality principle in *Worcester*, along with the debate over religious liberty discussed earlier, drives home a recurring theme of this study. Many of the constitutional principles that are now considered fundamental began as nothing more than offshoots of a generational conflict. The great engine of legal creativity is the primal desire to win. As a result, leaders caught up in the emotions unleashed by a fight for power often reach for unorthodox solutions to attract support. Innovations introduced in the heat of battle often become pillars of the constitutional order over time. This is nothing more than the common-law process at work, where intuitions drive the results and the deeper justifications come later.

And there was more to come. Following their denunciation of the constitutional upstarts, the justices ended their session for the year. The ball was now in the president's court, and he would soon offer a sharp rebuke to the chief justice.

4

The Bank Veto and the Election of 1832

A general discussion will now take place, eliciting new light and settling important principles; and a new Congress, elected in the midst of such discussion, and furnishing an equal representation of the people according to the last census, will bear to the Capitol the verdict of public opinion, and, I doubt not, bring this important question to a satisfactory result.

Andrew Jackson, Veto Message, July 10, 1832

Reform leads to resistance, and resistance leads to reform. That is the basic truth that underlies each transition from one generation to the next. The logic of escalation, though, creates a paradox for foes of the rising political tide. The more they resist, the more they intensify the depth and clamor for change. This boomerang effect came to pass following *Worcester*, culminating with the president's challenge to the traditional Constitution in his veto of the Bank. Of course, this battle does not occur in a vacuum. Each side seeks to frame its arguments in a way that resonates with voters. The cascade of events in 1832 was leading toward a verdict in the fall elections that would decisively alter the balance of power.

THE FALLOUT FROM WORCESTER

With a fresh Supreme Court opinion in hand, conservatives pressed their advantage. The chief justice's decision received enormous coverage in the press and was reprinted in full by major newspapers.[1] A few days later, John Quincy

Adams introduced a memorial in the House of Representatives requesting that a select committee be appointed to explore what measures could be taken to ensure that Georgia would comply with the Court's order.[2] Reflecting the divisions on this issue, an initial effort by Jackson's supporters to table the bill failed by one vote.[3] As the debate continued, Democrats vociferously attacked *Worcester* and declared that Georgia would not yield unless it "was made a howling wilderness" by federal troops.[4] Moderates eventually won the day by arguing that Congress should wait and see what the State did before taking any action.

Not surprisingly, Georgia refused to obey the federal mandate to release the prisoners, but the State came up with a clever solution to the problem posed by Marshall's opinion. Obviously, rejecting an order from the Supreme Court posed a big risk. To the extent that the establishment was trying to portray the reformers as a bunch of wild-eyed radicals, blatant obstruction by local authorities would aid that effort. Instead of affirmatively refusing to obey, the state court with jurisdiction over the missionaries simply did nothing. This presented a dilemma for Jackson's opponents because the Judiciary Act of 1789 said that the Supreme Court could order federal marshals to enforce a judgment only if the state court put its objections to the judgment in writing.[5] This form of passive resistance by the state had two implications, one of which is well known. The other, however, remains underappreciated.

First, notwithstanding the myth that Jackson said, "John Marshall has made his decision; now let him enforce it," in reality there was nothing to enforce.[6] One could say the president had a moral obligation to persuade Georgia to obey, with one congressman grumbling that "Jackson could by a nod of the head or a crook of the finger induce Georgia to submit to the law."[7] But the president had no legal duty to act. His supporters stressed this point, with one pamphlet noting that "when the Supreme Court assemble, and are officially informed that obedience to their mandate has been refused by the Court of Georgia, they must adopt some ulterior measure to enforce it. . . . Until they do decide, the President has no authority."[8] The problem was that even if Georgia put its refusal in writing, the Supreme Court was not in session and hence could not issue another order until it reconvened. As a result, historians who study this era agree that Jackson was right when he told a friend that "the decision of the supreme court has fell still born" and that no federal action was required.[9]

There is a second feature of this episode, though, that receives less attention. Why would Chief Justice Marshall and his colleagues issue an opinion without taking measures to ensure it would be obeyed? Since Georgia boycotted the oral argument in *Worcester* and *Cherokee Nation*, there could be little doubt that they would not accept the judgment. The justices may not have anticipated the decision of the state court to omit its objections from the record on remand, but by recessing for the year they left themselves in no position to act no matter what Georgia did. In this moment of constitutional drama, the casual air with which Marshall issued his opinion and then left town is perplexing. Unless, of course, the chief justice did not want to see his opinion enforced before the election.

The hidden element of *Worcester* is that it was an advisory opinion that affected no concrete rights at all. Through his artful stratagem of doing nothing to enforce the ruling, the chief justice avoided the embarrassing prospect of having the president refuse to carry out the judgment. That kind of open resistance would create a precedent that could have permanently harmed the judicial branch. Instead, the Court gave voters a chance to consider *Worcester's* indictment of the Jacksonian agenda and to change the political dynamic. The beauty of Marshall's trick is that *Worcester* looks like a real case rather than an advisory opinion that is, after all, prohibited under Article Three, Section Two, of the Constitution.[10] Courts have cited *Worcester* many times since then without realizing that they are relying on what was in reality an improper election manifesto.[11]

All of this demonstrates that the chief justice developed an elegant solution to the problem posed when courts join the resistance to reform. In *Worcester*, and to a lesser degree in *Cherokee Nation*, the justices offered a defense of tradition while minimizing the Court's institutional exposure. Georgia's refusal to put its resistance on the record only helped Marshall's cause. As long as the State took this position, the Court would not have to enforce its order and suffer the indignity of seeing its authority flouted by the president. Of course, this state of affairs could not be maintained indefinitely, because at some point it would be clear to all concerned that the Court was helpless.

In the meantime, the chief losers were the Cherokees and the members of Congress who wanted *Worcester* enforced. Once it was clear that Georgia would not acknowledge the judgment, the Tribe's sympathizers introduced another petition seeking "the most speedy and effectual measures to enforce the judgment of the Supreme Court of the United States, in the case of the missionaries Worcester and Butler, imprisoned under a judgment of a State court in Georgia."[12] A congressman outlined the State's unprecedented opposition and said that "surely the House will never consent to suffer the public justice to be defeated by such a trick as this."[13] Nevertheless, the petition was tabled and Jackson's supporters began to sense a change in the political momentum. A leading member of Georgia's congressional delegation countered: "Whenever a law or a judicial decision is of such a character that it does not receive the sanction of the moral feeling of the country, it is vain to hope to enforce it. . . . Sir, I may be permitted, without exhibiting an air of unbecoming triumph, to refer to the late decision of the Supreme Court as completely illustrative of these ideas."[14] With the fate in *Worcester* in doubt, generational tensions were near their peak. And the president was about to raise the stakes.

THE BANK VETO

In his veto of the Maysville Turnpike, Jackson argued against internal improvements in a restrained manner consistent with precedent. This cautious pursuit of reform was matched on the other side by *Cherokee Nation*, which launched a critique of the reform agenda while staying within the bounds of accepted practice. The spiral of escalation that drives the law in these transitional moments, however, was pushing both sides into a more extreme posture as the election neared. Marshall's preemptive opinion in *Worcester* articulated an extraordinary view of Federalism that shattered traditional principles in an attempt to discredit the new generation's policies. Now the president would act in kind with the most consequential veto of all time—a rejection of the National Bank that took out a central pillar of the old Constitution.[15] Casting aside his prior caution, Jackson offered the bold vision of limited federal power free from corruption that was the wellspring of his movement. At this critical time, the constitutional cycle reached the point where the Upstairs and Downstairs generations start changing places.

A Conservative Gamble

The Bank Veto was triggered by an attempt to open the rift within the Democratic Party that chance had so far concealed. Most of Jackson's supporters opposed the Bank, but some (largely those who voted for the Maysville Turnpike) backed the traditional approach to finance and federal spending. In 1830, the president barely held his coalition together. Now Henry Clay was bent on forcing Jackson to take a stand. The senator was the candidate running against the president in 1832, and he thought he saw a fantastic campaign issue. Clay requested a renewal of the Bank's charter even though it was not set to expire until 1836.[16] Conservatives hoped that no matter what Jackson did with the Bank bill, he would alienate one faction of his party. Indeed, Clay crowed that "should Jackson veto it, I will veto him."[17]

As the Bank recharter moved through Congress, it was not clear what Jackson would do. To placate the factions within his movement, the president had

Vice President John C. Calhoun, who split with Jackson over the issue of states' rights. Artist unknown. Library of Congress.

maintained an ambiguous position on the Bank question. And the consequences of an open rupture in the administration were dire. The vice president, John C. Calhoun, was already angry because he felt that the movement was not taking a strong enough position on states' rights. Accordingly, he broke with the president and even cast a tiebreaking vote in the Senate to defeat Martin Van Buren's nomination as ambassador to Great Britain.[18] Relations among the Democrats, in other words, were not great. No wonder Clay thought he could exacerbate these tensions by putting Jackson to the test, just as Chief Justice Marshall thought he was increasing the pressure on reformers with *Worcester*.

The Text of the Bank Veto

In response to this pincer movement, the president made an emphatic statement that Democrats hailed as a "Second Declaration of Independence" and conservatives called "a manifesto of anarchy, such as Marat or Robespierre might have issued to the mobs."[19] Jackson told his aide that "the Bank, Mr. Van Buren is trying to kill me, *but I will kill it!*"[20] Even before the recharter passed Congress in late June, he asked Amos Kendall to start drafting a veto message.[21] The draft was polished by others, particularly Attorney General Roger B. Taney and Levi Woodbury, who later joined Taney on the Supreme Court. This veto document would become a foundational text for the next constitutional regime and thus deserves careful scrutiny.

Policy Grounds

The opening portion of the veto message focused on Jackson's policy objections to the Bank. Alexander Hamilton explained that this financial institution was vital to "[link] the interest of the State in an intimate connection with those of the rich individuals belonging to it."[22] By contrast, Jackson described the recharter as an unwarranted "present" to the "opulent" shareholders of the Bank.[23] He wrote: "The bounty of our Government is proposed to be again bestowed on the few who have been fortunate enough to secure the stock and at this moment wield the power of the existing institution. I can not perceive the justice or policy of this course."[24] Furthermore, Jackson said that the increasing level of foreign ownership in the Bank posed a security threat in the case of a foreign war, as its "operations within would be in aid of the hostile fleets and armies without."[25]

This attack on foreigners was just a setup for Jackson's main point, which was that Hamilton's institution was dangerous because it created "a privileged order, clothed both with great political power and enjoying immense pecuniary advantages from their connection with the Government."[26] Since foreigners could not vote for bank directors under the charter, their growing role meant that "control of the institution would necessarily fall into the hands of a few citizen stockholders."[27] The president said that it was "easy to conceive that great evils to our country and its institutions might flow from such a concentration of power in the hands of a few men irresponsible to the people."[28] Jackson added that there was evidence that the Bank was abusing its authority, which was unsurprising since "the rich and powerful too often bend the acts of government to their selfish purposes."[29] This charter, the president concluded, furthered the "prostitution of our Government to the advancement of the few at the expense of the many."[30]

The other major policy ground for Jackson's veto was that the Bank violated principles of federalism. In a passage that Jefferson or Reagan would have loved, the president said that by "attempting to make our General Government strong we make it weak."[31] He went on to explain that our "true strength consists in leaving individuals and States as much as possible to themselves—in making itself felt . . . not in its control, but in its protection; not in binding the States more closely to the center, but leaving each to move unobstructed in its proper orbit."[32] Jackson was not saying that the Bank violated the Tenth Amendment by intruding on states' rights. He was instead asserting that traditional faith in federal action was wrong and should be curtailed because it was just a bad idea.

Constitutional Grounds

The president could have rested his veto on policy grounds, but he was not content with this rationale. Rather than follow Madison's precedent and waive the question of the Bank's constitutionality, Jackson decided to take on this issue. A movement bent on changing constitutional dogma cannot confine its objections to policy grounds alone. To bring about a more permanent shift, reformers need to delegitimize the deeper principles that sustain traditional policies. In part, this path was also taken to answer the opposition of conservatives who were using the Constitution to undermine Jackson's policies. Tit for tat is a powerful idea in intergenerational politics, and therefore the new movement took its opportunity to answer the charge that its agenda was barred by established authorities.

Wasting little time, the president opened his constitutional analysis by denying that the relevant precedents were binding. He explained that "it is maintained by the advocates of the bank that its constitutionality in all its features ought to considered as settled by precedent and by the decision of the Supreme Court. To this conclusion I can not assent."[33] The first observation about this quote is that Jackson distinguished "precedent" from court decisions. That was consistent with the standard method of analysis at the time that considered legislative precedents binding on all legal actors. Jackson discussed the congressional acts about the Bank, but he concluded that they did not limit his discretion.[34] The veto message said: "There is nothing in precedent . . . which, if its authority were admitted, ought to weigh in favor of the act before me."[35] With this statement, he went beyond his more cautious Maysville Turnpike Veto, which only questioned the wisdom of such authorities.[36]

It was Jackson's rejection of nonjudicial precedent, especially his refusal to cite Madison's Bank Veto, that raised the hackles of conservatives. Daniel Webster attacked Jackson's willful disrespect for precedent in a lengthy address on the Senate floor.[37] The Senator argued that "the legislative precedents all assert and maintain the power; and these legislative precedents have been the law of the land for almost forty years."[38] More important, "they settle the construction of the constitution, and sanction the exercise of the power in question so far as these ends can ever be accomplished by any legislative precedents whatever."[39] Thus, the leading Supreme Court advocate of his day was, ironically, less concerned about the veto message's implications for *M'Culloch* than with its disregard for congressional authority. When Webster said that "the President does

Senator Daniel Webster, the great orator who tried to stem the Jacksonian tide. Painting by Emile Lassalle. Library of Congress.

not admit the authority of precedent," he was talking mainly about legislative precedent.[40] Madison's idea that a veto could not be used to declare a bill unconstitutional in the face of settled precedent was abandoned and would never return.

In this collision over legislative precedent, there is a variation on a larger theme that runs through all generational transitions. As a rising movement challenges established tenets, conservatives always respond that it is unwise to undo the deeply rooted traditions of the law. What is unique about this era is that conservatives went further and, citing Madison's Bank Veto, argued that it was unconstitutional to change these customs. This view was the thread that connected the resistance to Removal with the opposition to Jackson's Bank Veto. Had this argument prevailed, future generations would have faced more pressure to seek a constitutional amendment to bring about reform, and the shape of our written Constitution would have looked quite different.

Following his rejection of legislative authority, the president addressed the relevance (or lack thereof) of *M'Culloch*. Jackson said that the opinion "ought not to control the coordinate authorities of this Government. The Congress, the Executive, and the Court must each for itself be guided by its own opinion of the Constitution."[41] In contrast to the analysis of tradition, which got lots of attention from contemporaries but is barely noticed now, the statement about the Court got relatively little notice from Jackson's peers but is the focus of modern analysts.[42] Part of this is due to our fixation on the Supreme Court. In Jackson's day, it was accepted that all branches of government could make their own constitutional judgments.[43] After all, the concept of legislative precedent would have been hollow if the justices could trump that consensus whenever they wanted. Moreover, Jackson noted that *M'Culloch* held that Congress could conclude that a Bank was a "necessary" means to execute its power, not that a president was required to concur.[44]

This discussion of the relationship between the Court and the president had a subtext that was not lost on contemporary observers. Read as a reply to *Worcester* rather than to *M'Culloch*, the Bank Veto takes on a different cast. In essence, Jackson was offering a justification for his refusal to back the justices on the Cherokee issue while laying the foundation for the more drastic step of not enforcing the judgment in *Worcester* if he was called upon to do so. The president did not go that far yet, but many in that era picked up on this coded message that each branch must "be guided by its own opinion of the Constitution."[45]

This was not an isolated example of lawlessness but represents a broader pattern of presidential response during a generational shift. The rise of the executive branch as the driving force for constitutional reform, which was contrary to the expectation of the Framers, is one of the most important institutional developments during the last two centuries.[46] Jefferson was the first to experiment with using his office as a focal point of the popular will, which explains why leaders in the 1830s often invoked his acts as a precedent for Jackson's decisions.[47] But Jefferson always publicly proclaimed his deference to Congress.[48] What makes Jackson unique is that he was the first president to declare that he was the tribune of the people and could assert an independent constitutional vision on their behalf. Webster typified the conservative reaction to this claim when he asked where "is the authority for saying that the President is *the direct representative of the People?* I hold this . . . to be mere assumption, and dangerous assumption."[49] Yet other presidents would follow Jackson's example when confronted by judicial resistance. Lincoln famously denied the authority of *Dred Scott*—the preemptive opinion defending Jackson's generation—and defied the case by signing a bill abolishing slavery in the territories.[50] Likewise, Franklin D. Roosevelt was prepared to give a speech in the midst of the New Deal stating that he would not obey a court order declaring his suspension of the gold standard invalid, but that crisis was averted when the justices upheld the president's action.[51] Such presidential radicalism is best viewed as the structural parallel to the preemptive opinion. In each case, the competing generations are pulled to their most extreme positions and turn precedent aside in an all-out effort to win.

The Bank Veto not only dismissed *M'Culloch* as irrelevant; it attacked the chief justice's reasoning supporting implied federal power. For example, the Court asserted that the Constitution did not restrict the means that Congress could use to carry out its power. The president disagreed. He explained that "on two subjects only does the Constitution recognize in Congress the power to grant exclusive privileges or monopolies. . . . Out of this express delegation of power have grown our laws of patents and copyrights."[52] Since Article One, Section Eight, said that this means was authorized only to support those ends, Jackson concluded that "it is consistent with the fair rules of construction to conclude that such a power was not intended to be granted as a means of accomplishing any other end."[53] That view oozed with bias against federal action. One could easily see Marshall taking the same text as proof that Congress was given this means and that it was not specifically withheld elsewhere.[54]

The Veto Message also argued that the Bank was an unconstitutional means because Congress could not delegate its authority to a private corporation without close public oversight. Invoking the text of the Necessary and Proper Clause, Jackson said that "the Government is the only '*proper*' judge where its agents should reside and keep their offices. . . . It can not, therefore be '*necessary*' or '*proper*' to authorize the bank to locate branches where it pleases to perform the public service, without consulting the government."[55] He also said that the Bank was not a valid way for Congress to exercise its power to "coin money," contending that this "was conferred to be exercised by themselves, and not to be transferred to a corporation."[56] At the core of this claim was the Jacksonian principle that personal freedom was jeopardized whenever the federal establishment passed into the hands of wealthy elites.[57]

This message of class equality, which fired the imagination of this generation of reformers, set up the Bank Veto's ringing peroration. Framing his campaign theme for the fall, Jackson characterized the traditional constitution as hopelessly corrupt:

> Many of our rich men have not been content with equal protection and equal benefits, but have besought us to make them richer by act of Congress. By attempting to gratify their desires we have in the results of our legislation arrayed section against section, interest against interest, and man against man, in a fearful commotion which threatens to shake the foundations of our Union. It is time to pause in our career to review our principles, and if possible revive that devoted patriotism and spirit of compromise which distinguished the sages of the Revolution and the fathers of our Union.[58]

58   *Chapter Four*

The battle lines were now drawn along generational, class, and regional lines. Closing his response to the Veto, Webster said: "It remains, now, for the people of the United States to choose between the principles here avowed and their Government. These cannot subsist together. The one or the other must be rejected."[59]

Submitting to the Verdict of the People

Although the parties in every transitional period escalate their demands out of an urge to win, the net effect of these escalations is to crystallize the constitutional issues for the electorate. As each camp is pushed into a more radical position, the voters get a clearer picture of the paths they must choose between. Thus, almost every generational collision is marked by a series of increasingly polarized elections that focus on first principles. In each of these moments, the people truly are the masters of their fate.

During the 1832 campaign, the dueling sides were represented by their respective texts—*Worcester* for traditionalists and the Bank Veto for reformers. Not coincidentally, these two great documents of state focused on the two lead issues of the campaign. The Bank's director, Nicholas Biddle, thought that Jackson's message was such a blunder that he paid for its distribution to the public. Later, he realized his mistake and started sending out Webster's Reply to the Veto.[60] While the Bank issue was more important during the campaign, the Cherokee Removal drew considerable attention as well. Senator Clay, Jackson's presidential foe, opened his campaign by discussing *Worcester* first and the Bank second, stating that "the Supreme Court is paralyzed, and the missionaries retained in prison in contempt of its authority, and in defiance of numerous treaties and laws of the United States . . . [and] that the veto has been applied to the Bank of the United States."[61] Hostile papers often ran debates on the issues side by side because in both cases Jackson "refused to recognize the supremacy of the Constitution as interpreted by the Supreme Court."[62]

Conservatives thought one path to victory involved splitting the rising generation through an appeal to religious voters upset by Georgia's imprisonment of the missionaries. The keynote address at the convention that nominated Clay for president pounded on this angle, stating that "few examples can be found, even in the history of barbarous communities, in which the sacred character of a minister of religion has furnished so slight a protection against disrespect and violence to the persons invested with it."[63] Indeed, the "inhuman and unconstitutional outrages committed under the authority of Georgia" motivated Van Buren's own niece to lecture him on the controversy when he was on a campaign swing through New York.[64] A paper asked whether "the Christian people of the United States [would] give their sanction . . . to the conduct of a President who treats the ministers of the Christian religion with open outrage . . . [and] commits them in defiance of law like common criminals to the penitentiary."[65]

Jackson's supporters sensed the danger and continued their impassioned defense against the charge that they were oppressing religious practice by allowing Georgia to jail Worcester and Butler. One Democratic pamphlet argued that "to connect the subject of the missionaries, now confined in the State of Georgia, with the election of the President, was altogether unwarranted. But as our opponents have chosen to do so—as they have assailed him for not having interfered and liberated them from their confinement" a reply was warranted.[66] The substance of their answer, once again, was that the missionaries had violated a neutral law that applied to everyone and thus it was wrong to say that ministers were being targeted or that they had any right to refuse the loyalty oath. In the president's view, "neither to him nor to any man does it belong, in this country, to step beyond the limits assigned by the laws, and to assume a power connected with religious concerns, not assigned nor authorized by our great constitutional charter."[67]

As the election results began to dribble in—in those days there was no national election day—the trend in Jackson's favor was unmistakable. The president carried the country by a clear margin, defeating Clay in the Electoral College 219 to 49 and winning 55 percent of the popular vote.[68] Jacksonians also seized control of the House of Representatives, bringing one more organ of federal power under their thumb.[69] Marshall fell into a gloomy mood and told Story that "I yield slowly and reluctantly to the conviction that our Constitution cannot last. . . . The union has been prolonged thus far by miracles. I fear they cannot continue."[70] The chief justice was right in a sense. His generation was passing away, and "our Constitution" would now belong to Jacksonian Democracy. Impressive as this victory was, though, conservatives still retained their hold on the Senate, led by the triumvirate of Clay, Webster, and Calhoun, who was elected after being replaced on the national ticket by Van Buren.[71] The constitutional cycle was about to enter a new phase.

THE CLOSING WHIMPER

Though the plight of the missionaries mesmerized the nation for most of 1832, the end of the story was anticlimactic. Shortly after the election, Calhoun and his South Carolina allies made good on a long-standing threat and declared a national tariff null and void in the state.[72] Now two states were defying federal authority. Yet while the president approved of Georgia's resistance to the Supreme Court, he was not a secessionist and saw Calhoun's doctrine of nullification as treason. In blunt fashion, Jackson issued a proclamation denying the right of a state to void a federal law and threatened to order in troops.[73] Faced with this tough prospect and offered a compromise by Clay, Calhoun backed down.

As part of Jackson's effort to settle the Nullification Crisis, he asked the governor of Georgia to pardon Worcester and Butler. The president worried that the continuing conflict between Georgia and the Court would inflame the situation and lead to the creation of a secessionist alliance with South Carolina.[74] Instead, the missionaries were freed and the Court was never called upon to enforce *Worcester*. Once again, chance had intervened to shift the dynamic. The Cherokees and the old constitutional tradition, however, would not be so lucky.

5

Triumph and Tears

We are . . . in the midst of a revolution, hitherto
bloodless, but rapidly tending towards a total change
of the pure republican character of the Government,
and to the concentration of all power in the hands of
one man.

Henry Clay

We are in the midst of a revolution—a happy and aus-
picious revolution, like the "civil revolution of 1800,"
which, according to Mr. Jefferson was "as real a revolution in the principles, as that of '76 was in the form, of
our Government." A like salutary revolution "in the principles of the Government," we have seen accomplished
during the past five years of this Administration.

William Rives

Once voters emphatically endorse a particular
movement, then the theme of the constitutional cycle shifts from conflict to
consensus. Outnumbered traditionalists resort to desperate tactics to slow down
the reform train, but eventually this fails. The insurgents now become the establishment, and they must confront the issue of how they should implement
their legal vision. There are two main alternatives—a constitutional amendment
or some form of Court-packing. In President Jackson's second term, his movement chose the latter path and inaugurated a new order in which Chief Justice
Marshall's great opinions, along with the freedom of the Cherokees, were abandoned.

Following his reelection, Jackson resumed his fight against the Bank by moving its federal deposits to state banks, thereby initiating a new confrontation with conservatives called the "Deposit Crisis." To carry out his plan, Jackson replaced two Treasury secretaries before settling on a recess appointee—Roger B. Taney, the former attorney general and future chief justice, whom Arthur M. Schlesinger Jr. described as the "spearhead of radicalism in the new cabinet."[1] When Congress reconvened in 1833, the question was whether the president had the authority to destroy an institution created by statute before its charter expired. As in the Bank Veto, the president resorted to a broad interpretation of his prerogatives. This was all he could do because he lacked control of the Senate and could not secure a new law repealing the Bank's charter. In announcing his withdrawal strategy, Jackson said that his actions were justified because he "consider[ed] his reelection as a decision of the people against the bank."[2] With this statement, he embraced the model that Jefferson pioneered by crushing the Federalist generation in 1800 and signaled his intent to use the presidency, instead of a textual amendment, to transform the Constitution.

Censure in the Senate

Reaction against the president's move was swift, as Clay introduced a censure resolution in the Senate declaring Jackson's actions unconstitutional.[3] This unprecedented remedy of censure, rather than impeachment, was again dictated by circumstance. Clay later said that "no Senator believed, in 1834, that, whether the President merited impeachment or not, he ever would be impeached . . . by a majority of his political friends in the House of Representatives."[4] Since no impeachment would be forthcoming given the balance of political forces, a censure resolution was the only way to express the Senate's views and frame the campaign for the 1834 elections. In Thomas Hart Benton's view, censure was "purely and simply for popular effect. Great reliance was placed upon that effect. It was fully believed . . . that a senatorial condemnation would destroy whomsoever it struck—even General Jackson."[5]

Debate on the Censure Resolution went on for three months, even while Jackson asserted that the proceeding was "unauthorized by the constitution, and in derogation of its entire spirit."[6] One of his main points was that this action, like internal improvements or the Bank, was not among Congress's enumerated powers.[7] With words that echoed the president's vetoes, Senator Forsyth dismissed the idea of a congressional power to censure, asking: "Where is that to be found? Nowhere. The right of the Senate rests upon implication."[8] True to form, Clay said he "supposed the right of the Senate to express its opinion, in any form, as to a violation of the constitutional power of Congress, would not be seriously questioned. What part of the constitution restrains it?"[9] Once again, the difference between the generations was on display in these instinctive reactions. Traditionalists like Clay held that any act not prohibited should be presumed valid, but Jacksonians responded that Congress was restricted to powers expressly listed in the document.

The two sides also clashed over the president's claim that his reelection was a mandate for constitutional reform. Clay rejected the idea that higher law could be changed without a formal amendment:

> I am surprised and alarmed at the new source of executive power which is found in the result of a presidential election. I had supposed . . . that the constitution could only be amended in the mode which it has itself prescribed. . . . But it seems that if, prior to an election, certain opinions, no matter how ambiguously put forth by a candidate, are known to the people, these loose opinions, in virtue of the election, incorporate themselves with the constitution, and afterwards are to be regarded and expounded as parts of the instrument![10]

Since Clay was responsible for putting the bank issue at the center of the 1832 campaign, his claim that the issue was "ambiguously put forth" was open to criticism. Forsyth replied that "the issue, the Senator well knows, is made by the two parties. . . . they presented the question distinctly and intelligibly to the people."[11]

There is deeper insight lurking behind Clay's dismissal of Jackson's mandate for constitutional change. Instead of challenging the popular support for the new generation, the senator was shifting the ground to the issue of whether reformers could legitimately change the Constitution without an Article Five amendment. In one sense, this could be the honest response of a formalist concerned with the legality of any shift that occurs outside of the rules. In another sense, the emphasis on the need for an amendment was a way of raising the bar. Getting a majority is one thing; getting a supermajority is something else. Conservatives could no longer say, as they did on the Cherokee Removal and Bank issues, that a majority could not overturn established practice. They could say, though, that the only way to alter doctrine in the courts was with a textual amendment. Beleaguered traditionalists in every era make this assertion whenever the fight appears lost from their perspective.[12]

By contrast, Democrats in the Senate offered a different vision of democracy, which held that elections rather than formalities were the key component for assessing the legitimacy of constitutional change. Senator Benton, rising in reply to Clay, made this point:

> The senator from Kentucky calls upon the people to rise, and drive the Goths from the capitol. Who are those Goths? They are General Jackson and the democratic party,—he just elected President over the senator himself, and the party just been made the majority in the House—all by the vote of the people. It is their act that has put these Goths in possession of the capitol to the discomfiture of the senator and his friends.[13]

In this same vein, another senator added that "the people was the tribunal to which the bank appealed; it was the tribunal of the bank's choice. The decision was against the bank."[14]

The Jacksonians, in other words, saw the problem as legal realists. Their focus was on the depth and breadth of enthusiasm for the new program, not on whether that desire for reform was channeled through the formal amendment procedures outlined in Article Five. Once again, this pragmatic view could reflect a broader take on the law, but rising movements are more likely to hold this philosophy because it plays to their strengths. Fresh from a series of electoral victories in which constitutional issues played a big part, reformers are apt to claim that "the people" are behind them and that arguing about the legal niceties is an attempt to thwart the national will.[15]

The Protest Message

Just as the Senate resorted to an unconventional measure by passing the Censure Resolution, so Jackson responded with an equally unprecedented Protest Message that symbolically vetoed the Censure. In defending his removal of the deposits from the Bank, the president said that he was acting as "the direct representative of the American people" and appealed for the rejection of a government of "powerful monopolies and aristocratic establishments."[16] Upon receipt of the message, Clay remarked: "This protest is but a new form of the veto. That conservative provision of the constitution has been most remarkably expanded and employed under the present administration."[17] Another senator remarked: "An appeal of the President to the American people against the Senate, with a view to accomplish, or even to suggest a change, formal or informal, in the constitution of the latter, through the direct intervention of the people, is, in its very nature, of a revolutionary tendency."[18] Political competition had again forced Jackson to match the innovations of his opponents and develop new powers in his office.

The object of the censure debate was the same as what drove the discussion of the Bank Veto—the quest for an electoral decision that would break the stalemate. Benton noted that, whether the Senate liked it or not, the protest "will be compared with speeches delivered for three months in this Capitol, against this President, and an enlightened and upright community will decide between the language of the defense, and the language of the accusation."[19] Ever the optimist, Webster vowed that "we shall hold on, sir, and hold out, till the people themselves come to [the Senate's] defense."[20] Yet the cavalry did not show up to defend Webster's Alamo. Jacksonians achieved a rare sixth-year surge in congressional strength in the 1834 elections, as the Democrats swept into control of the Senate and kept the House of Representatives.[21] The generational transition, for all intents and purposes, was over. Only the Supreme Court remained in the hands of traditionalists.

TRANSFORMING THE COURTS

Once a movement gains complete control of the political branches, the focus turns to the implementation and cementing of their long-term constitutional agenda. One popular strategy for doing this involves changing the members of the Supreme Court. The most famous example, of course, is the New Deal, when Franklin D. Roosevelt selected a new set of justices to extend his generation's view that the Depression required a major expansion of federal power and a commensurate reduction in property rights. Lawyers acknowledge that the five years following FDR's first Court pick saw changes as great as any imposed by an amendment.[22] The tactic of altering the composition of the bench rather than the constitutional text, which was also employed by Jefferson, Jackson, and Reagan, is used for a good reason—it's easier. A constitutional generation only needs to control the presidency and the Senate over a sustained time to remake the Court. Jackson was better at this than most presidents, as he pushed through a statute that expanded the Court's size.[23] This exercise in "court-packing," though, only happened after his foes tried a dose of "court-tampering." The pattern of tit-for-tat retaliation still held even though the balance of power had shifted.

The Floating Justice

The Supreme Court was a central issue of the lame-duck congressional session of 1835. While the Democrats racked up big victories in the midterm elections, a conservative majority still held power in the Senate. Justice Johnson passed away in the autumn of 1834, and Jackson nominated Representative Wayne of Georgia as his replacement.[24] Notwithstanding Wayne's vote for the Removal Act, he won bipartisan support with his Unionist stance during the Nullification Crisis and was confirmed. A few weeks later, Justice Duvall resigned and Jackson selected Taney as his successor.[25]

In contrast to the Wayne appointment, the Taney nomination created a donnybrook. His central role in removing the deposits from the Bank made him a symbol of radicalism. One opposition paper complained: "The pure ermine of the Supreme Court is sullied by the appointment of that political hack, Roger B. Taney."[26] The Senate previously rejected his nomination to be Treasury secretary—he was only a recess appointment—and was determined to block his new promotion. Rather than oppose Taney outright, Webster developed a clever strategy that demonstrated how far Jackson's opponents were willing to go to stop his constitutional bandwagon.

Reform of the Circuits

To understand how the Taney nomination unfolded, some background is necessary on how the judiciary was organized in the 1830s. As is true today, the nation was divided into different judicial circuits. At this time, though, the circuit courts were composed of a district judge and a Supreme Court justice. Each justice was assigned to a circuit and required to spend most of the year "circuit-riding" to hear cases. The justices were assigned to a circuit where they lived and practiced to ensure they understood the relevant state law.[27] Thus, when a vacancy occurred on the Court, there was also an opening on the circuit where the previous justice had circuit-riding responsibilities. Since each circuit needed a justice, the number of circuits had to equal the number of justices. Circuit-riding, therefore, placed a federalism roadblock in the way of informal constitutional change by the president. He was not free to choose anyone he wanted to fill a vacancy. A nominee had to come from the circuit where the prior justice was assigned. Otherwise, that circuit would be deprived of someone knowledgeable in its state law. Though a president could find supporters everywhere, a particular nominee could not be chosen unless the right geographic vacancy developed.

As the nation grew, there was a need for new circuits. By the 1830s, one-quarter of the states, mostly in the West, were outside of the circuit system.[28] In these states, Congress provided a temporary remedy by allowing a single district judge to exercise the jurisdiction of both the district and circuit courts. Needless to say, this was not a good solution because that lone judge wielded tremendous and, in many instances, unreviewable power.[29] Attempts were made to correct this problem by creating new circuits for the western states, but they foundered on the fact that doing so would require an expansion of the Supreme Court. As Senator Frelinghuysen noted: "The great and serious obstacle that has stood in the way of the claims of the West, have been the difficulties and dangers of enlarging the Court to the number that was desired."[30] These difficulties were as much political as logistical. Opponents did not want to give Jackson a windfall of extra justices.

Court-Tampering

Faced with Taney's nomination to replace Justice Duvall, Webster introduced a bill that would merge two of the smaller eastern circuits, including the one Duvall represented, and add a new western circuit.[31] This would keep the number of circuits and Court seats unchanged while extending the circuit system to those who did not have access. In this respect, it looked like a reform measure. Under Webster's proposal, though, the Court vacancy would no longer be in the East; it would be in the West. Thus, if the measure passed, the president would be forced to withdraw Taney's nomination—both Taney and Duvall were from Maryland—which is what Webster was after. He told a friend: "Mr. Taney's case is not yet decided. A movement is contemplated to annex Delaware and Maryland to Judge [Henry] Baldwin's circuit, and make a circuit in the West for the judge now to be appointed. If we could get rid of Mr. Taney, on this ground, well and good; if not, it will be a close vote."[32] The proponents of this bill, therefore, could hide their constitutional politics behind a rationale of improving judicial efficiency.

"Court-tampering" is a tactic that both rising and falling generations use depending on the circumstances, but what ties these choices together is that they are almost always justified by a technical argument rather than by politics. When the Jeffersonians repealed the Judiciary Act of 1801 and eliminated hostile Federalist judges, that act of "court-shrinking" was justified on the ground that there was no need for these new judges given the modest size of the federal docket.[33] During the New Deal, an analogous plan of court-packing was defended on the opposite ground—that the justices had too much work and could not keep up. Only in rare instances, such as Reconstruction, is court-tampering proposed without any efficiency rationale. These extraordinary measures come to pass, though, only during generational transitions.

Despite Webster's profession of disinterested statesmanship, Jacksonians in Congress knew what was going on and killed his bill. Benton explained that the proposed western circuit encompassed all of the states up and down the Mississippi and was too big for circuit-riding by a single justice.[34] As for the real purpose of the measure, Benton used some colorful metaphors: "There is an old-maxim, that 'there are many ways to kill a dog;' and 'there are two ways to drown a man.' One is to throw him overboard, and another is to 'scuttle the ship and let him go to the bottom.' He might speak in enigmas, but they would be perfectly intelligible to Senators at least."[35] Adding to Benton's description of this as a crude attempt to scuttle Taney's nomination, Representative Carmichel said that "whilst [the bill] professes to sink a district, its effect is to despatch a judge. . . . [T]he obvious effect of it is to affect injuriously the interests of Maryland, and to crush one of her most valued citizens."[36] Though the circuit reform bill failed, the conservative majority in the Senate did manage to filibuster Taney's nomination and prevent a vote.[37]

Court-Packing

Parliamentary magic could only work for so long, and when Congress reconvened later in 1835 its members reflected the public support for Jackson and his party. When Chief Justice Marshall died that summer, the president nominated Taney for that post, and this time he was confirmed by the new Democratic Senate.[38] Having placed his right-hand man in the center chair, Jackson next flexed his political muscle and pushed through a circuit reform bill. The 1837 Act created two new western circuits and expanded the number of justices from seven to nine. There is no doubt that this reform was necessary to address the dilemma created by leaving states outside of the circuit system. Jackson also saw this as an opportunity to seize control of the only branch that remained in conservative hands. Sure enough, the president and his handpicked successor, Martin Van Buren, filled the new seats with loyal supporters.[39] Webster told a friend that the Court was "gone."[40]

This was the first successful example of Court-packing in our history and a major milestone for the Jacksonian generation. Reformers would henceforth pursue their vision of change through the courts rather than through textual amendments. Indeed, there is no evidence that Jackson ever thought seriously about moving an Article Five amendment through Congress. It would be a mistake, however, to conclude from this that his movement was not interested in altering the Constitution. The issue was the means by which this change would occur. In a sense, the reformers' decision to take a pragmatic course was logical because, as was said earlier, their power rested on popular acclaim rather than on legal formalities. As a result, they may well have felt no need to enshrine their work in a textual amendment even if they could have done so.

THE TREATY OF NEW ECHOTA AND THE FALL OF WORCESTER

The final resolution of the Cherokee conflict also suggests that Jackson's generation could have mustered the votes to pass an Article Five amendment if they had wanted to. At the same time that Jackson was packing the Court, he was making aggressive efforts to negotiate a treaty with the Tribe that would end its stay in Georgia. After years of resistance, an agreement called the Treaty of New Echota was reached in 1835 with a tribal offshoot that wanted removal.[41] The full tribal assembly voted this proposal down, 2,225 to 114.[42] Georgia responded by invading the tribal area and jailing the Cherokee leadership. Shortly thereafter, a second assembly was called. Most Cherokees boycotted this meeting, and the treaty was approved there by a paltry vote of 79 to 7, which clearly represented only a tiny fraction of the Cherokee government.[43]

Conservatives in the Senate, who needed only one more than one-third to defeat a treaty, attacked this transparent fraud when it was submitted for ratification. Clay introduced a resolution stating: "That the instrument of writing, purporting to be a treaty concluded at New Echota on the 29th of December, 1835, between the United States and the chiefs, head men and people of the Cherokee Tribe . . . were not made and concluded by authority, on the part of the Cherokee tribe, competent to bind it; and, therefore, . . . the Senate cannot consent to and advise the ratification thereof, as a valid treaty."[44] After a fierce debate, the Democrats managed to get the required supermajority and ratified the Treaty of New Echota by one vote.[45] There is a cruel irony in this result. Both the Removal Act and this "treaty" were passed by the narrowest possible margin, which shows beyond dispute that what happened to the Tribe was not inevitable.

Just as the Senate overturned *Worcester* through this "treaty," similar rumblings of discontent could be heard in the state courts. When Cherokees living in Tennessee mounted a challenge to that state's version of Georgia's repressive laws, the state attorney general replied that Marshall's opinion did not bind the Tennessee Supreme Court.[46] That extraordinary claim was justified because the case "involved a political as well as a legal question, and was made at a time when high political excitement prevailed . . . was heard upon an ex parte argument . . . [and] has been assailed by many of the ablest politicians and legal characters of the age."[47] As a result, the attorney general said that the state supreme court should give the justices an opportunity to revisit *Worcester*. Judge John Catron, whom Jackson would later name a justice, agreed with this reasoning and upheld the state statute. Without attacking *Worcester* by name, Judge Catron contested its analysis and said that the contrary conclusions of the president and Congress expressed in the Removal Act "ought to have great weight with the courts of justice."[48]

The Tennessee Supreme Court added one other note that was a harbinger of how abolitionists would use the Cherokee Removal and *Worcester* in their coming critique of Jacksonian Democracy. Catron made the following observation about the relationship between Native American rights and African American rights:

> We dare not say the unconverted heathen was not a perpetual enemy to the Christian, or that he had political rights independent of us, without saying to the red man of this continent: "Take your own, we are your subjects; the country is yours, and the right to govern it is yours;" without saying to the enslaved black man of Africa: "Go in peace! You was enslaved by superstition and fraud, and are free as we are."[49]

Putting aside the Tennessee court's use of a slave dialect, which shows what African American litigants were up against, the point of this passage was that Marshall's vision of tribal autonomy was in tension with the practice of slavery. Indeed, even though the subjugation of the Tribes was "in conflict with our religion and with our best convictions of a refined and sound morality," it was the basis for all title claims, and "the title of every slave in American, North and South, rests on no better or different foundation."[50] In the coming years, abolitionists would hammer this point home to argue that slaves and tribes both deserved the fruits of freedom.

Accordingly, the Senate and the state courts pronounced *Worcester* dead almost simultaneously. This was no coincidence. With a new generation in power, the landmarks of the old regime could no longer stand. Indeed, the effect of the two-thirds vote for the "treaty" was the same as a two-thirds vote for an amendment overruling *Worcester*. America stood on the brink of a new era.

EPILOGUE

While 1835 marked the beginning of the Jacksonian majority, the constitutional implications of the shift became readily apparent in 1837. Fresh from another electoral success in 1836, the Democrats spent the lame-duck congressional session reflecting on the meaning of their achievements as their leader prepared to retire. Some actions taken during this period were concrete, like the passage of the Court-packing law. Others were more symbolic, such as Chief Justice Taney's first session presiding over the Court.[51] The two issues that filled the agenda in 1837, though, were still the Bank and the Cherokee Removal.[52]

The Fall of M'Culloch

Shortly before President Jackson's retirement, the Senate moved to expunge the Censure Resolution of 1834.[53] This measure was introduced by Thomas Hart Benton, who capped his years of service in the cause of reform with a remarkable statement of what he thought his generation's legacy would be. The relevant passage is lengthy, but should not be paraphrased:

> [Jackson] has demonstrated, by the fact itself, that a national bank is not "necessary" to the fiscal operations of the Federal Government, and in that demonstration he has upset the argument of [Alexander] Hamilton, and the decision of the Supreme Court of the United States, and all that has ever been said in favor of the constitutionality of a national bank. All this argument and decision rested upon the single assumption of the "necessity" of that Institution to the Federal Government. He has shown it is not "necessary". . . . In this single act he has vindicated the constitution from an unjust imputation, and knocked from under the decision of the Supreme Court the assumed fact on which it rested. *He has prepared the way for the reversal of that decision*; and it is a question for lawyers to answer, whether the case is not ripe for the application of that writ of most remedial nature . . . which was invented lest in any case there should be an oppressive defect of justice—the venerable writ of audita querela defendentis—to ascertain the truth of a fact happening since the judgment, and upon the due finding of which the judgment will be vacated.[54]

Thus, the Jacksonian leader in the Senate argued that M'Culloch, like *Worcester*, would be overruled as a consequence of this generation's rise to power.

The problem that Benton focused on was how to bring a case challenging *M'Culloch*'s continuing vitality before the new-and-improved Court. This was hard because the Bank no longer existed and thus the justices could not easily be compelled to take up this issue. Benton's solution, seen in this light, was brilliant. He wanted someone who had lost a case to the Bank to seek a writ

Senator Thomas Hart Benton, the captain of the new generation in Congress. Painted by Ferdinand T. L. Boyle. National Portrait Gallery, Smithsonian Institution.

of *audita querela* and claim that an intervening change in the "facts" justified overturning that judgment and *M'Culloch*. Of course, this was strictly a legal fiction. Marshall based his analysis on the idea that Congress had the discretion to determine whether a Bank was necessary, not on whether a Bank was necessary. Conservatives sharply criticized Benton's reasoning, with one offering this comment:

> We are told by the Senator from Missouri that the President has corrected and repealed the decision of that court in relation to the constitutionality of the Bank of the United States; and that, in his opinion, all that remains to be done is to issue an audita querella [*sic*] to ascertain the fact, have it entered on the record, and the judgment reversed. Here is at once a new attribute of power, and a most extraordinary mode of proceeding.[55]

Benton's approach was unconventional at best and disingenuous at worst, but this approach would have brought *M'Culloch* before the Court and memorialized this central element of Jacksonian constitutionalism.

Nobody followed up on Benton's suggestion, so the issue of how to dispose of *M'Culloch* remained. There was another option. If the Bank was resuscitated by the political branches at some point and its validity was challenged, then Chief

Justice Taney and his comrades in arms would have to revisit Marshall's analysis. In 1837, however, this seemed pretty far-fetched.

Exile

Since the high-toned quality of constitutional discourse can often dull its cruelty, it is important to end this chapter by exploring what the reversal of *Worcester* meant to its victims. The Cherokees were now prey caught in the open. General Winfield Scott informed the Tribe's leaders that "the President of the United States has sent me, with a powerful army" to enforce removal.[56] As federal and state troops swarmed into the Cherokee homeland, "families at dinners were startled by the sudden gleam of bayonets in the doorway and rose up to be driven with blows and oaths along the weary miles of trail that led to the stockade" where they were locked up like cattle.[57] On their way out, "they saw their homes in flames, fired by the lawless rabble that followed on the heels of the soldiers to loot and pillage."[58] Of the 18,000 Cherokees who were shipped west along the "Trail of Tears," about 4,000 died.[59] One militiaman later said that "I fought through the civil war and have seen men shot to pieces and slaughtered by thousands, but the Cherokee removal was the cruelest work I ever knew."[60]

Looking back on the Removal, Martin Van Buren wrote that "unlike histories of many great questions which agitate the public mind in their day [this issue] will in all probability endure as long as the government itself, and will in time occupy the minds and feelings of our people."[61] In the short term, he was wrong. *Worcester* followed the Cherokees into exile. Its ideas received no hearing in the halls of power, and the Taney Court would never cite the case in its opinions on Native American law. Yet this would be an exile to Elba instead of St. Helena. The resistance of Chief Justice Marshall would remain alive among one tiny, but increasingly vocal, group of dissenters—the abolitionists. Their turn in the constitutional wheel was not far off.

6

Chance and the Whig False Positive

Suppose [the Bank] question goes before the Supreme
Court, and they take it up as an original question,
what will be the result? I say then to you wait—there is
a lion in your path. It is time that you have the power
to remove that lion by increasing the circuits, and
appointing new judges enough to have a majority of
them in favor of the Bank; but will you incur so fear-
ful a responsibility—will you agitate the country for
such a purpose?

Representative Henry Wise

Once a new constitutional generation wins over-
whelming popular support, the remnants of the old establishment usually just
throw in the towel. Conservatives often gnash their teeth in the process, but
they recognize that their first principles are obsolete and can no longer survive.[1]
To preserve their political viability, they must accept the core objectives of their
foes and redirect their critique into more fruitful areas. This choice is often
described as a "switch-in-time," which was the term applied to the Court's sudden embrace of the New Deal in the face of FDR's Court-packing plan.[2] Other
generational transitions are marked by similar retreats made under institutional
duress, most notably President Andrew Johnson's capitulation to the Reconstruction generation discussed in chapter 9.[3]

Jacksonian Democracy stands as the most notable exception to this pattern.
Members of the old generation like Clay and Webster kept on fighting through
their election defeats in 1832, 1834, and 1836. They remained resolute and did
not acknowledge the futility of further resistance. That steadfastness was finally

rewarded in 1840, when the newly christened Whig Party swept the Democrats from the presidency and Congress.[4] Just as conservatives were on the cusp of undoing Jackson's work, though, chance intervened again. The new Whig president, William Henry Harrison, fell ill and died a few weeks after his inauguration.[5] He was replaced by Vice President John Tyler, a states' rights Democrat who was put on the ticket to attract crossover votes.[6]

This dramatic turn of events rendered the Whig resurgence one of the many false starts in the constitutional cycle. More important, Harrison's sudden death deprived Jackson's supporters of their one great chance to overrule *M'Culloch* in the Supreme Court. Only the president's demise prevented the Bank's return—a return that would have led to the test case that Senator Benton wanted. Instead, President Tyler vetoed a bill creating a new bank in a message that served as the functional equivalent of that missing Taney Court opinion. Although Tyler's successors denounced Chief Justice Marshall's logic in other vetoes of legislation they deemed beyond Congress's powers, there was never any judicial declaration to that effect. This crucial omission deprives lawyers of a record documenting *M'Culloch*'s reversal by the Jacksonian generation.

A LOOMING RESTORATION

In many respects, the Whig victory in 1840 looked like a rerun of the Jacksonian triumphs in the 1820s. At that time, reformers drew popular support from the hardships created by the Panic of 1819. The late 1830s saw another severe panic, which conservatives blamed on Jackson's destruction of the Bank.[7] Likewise, reformers in the 1820s railed against the corruption of elites who had been in power too long. By 1840, though, the Democrats were the establishment and were the ones being depicted as arrogant and out of touch. Thus, contemporaries had every reason to think they were seeing a repeat of recent events—just running in the opposite direction.

To the extent that anyone remembers our ninth president, it is for having the shortest administration in history. Yet William Henry Harrison did manage to make a significant contribution in his Inaugural Address, which spelled out how he planned to break with Jackson's precedents. Ghostwritten by Webster, the Address said: "The great danger to our institutions does not appear to me to be in a usurpation by the Government of power not granted by the people, but by the accumulation in one of the departments of that which was assigned to others."[8] Harrison identified part of this danger as Jackson's use of the veto, since "it is preposterous to suppose that a thought could for a moment have been entertained that the President, placed at the capital, in the center of the country, could better understand the wants and wishes of the people than their own immediate representatives."[9] Finally, the new president confirmed his revisionist ambitions by invoking a quote that Jacksonians hated: "I believe with Mr. Madison that 'repeated recognitions under varied circumstances in acts of the legislative, executive, and judicial branches of the Government, accompanied by indications in different modes of the concurrence of the general will of the nation'" settled constitutional questions.[10]

This Inaugural Address therefore laid down two ominous markers for Democrats and their hard-won constitutional accomplishments. First, Harrison's use of Madison's quote on the Bank's constitutionality was a signal that he intended to sign a new financial charter into law and reinstate the deference to legislative precedent that was a hallmark of the previous legal regime. Second, Harrison was sending a message that he would not stand in the way of the Whig legislative program. This was a scary prospect for Democrats because that agenda was being readied by none other than Senator Clay, Jackson's archenemy.[11] And rather than waiting until December, which is when a new Congress usually began, Clay convinced Harrison to summon a special session that would start in May.[12]

DRESS REHEARSAL FOR A PREEMPTIVE OPINION: *GROVES V. SLAUGHTER*

At the same time that Democrats in Congress were expressing concerns about the Whig revival, the justices heard argument in *Groves v. Slaughter*.[13] This case is not well known by modern scholars, but the decision speaks volumes about the generational pattern in constitutional law. *Groves* represents the Jackson Court's first nod in the direction of a preemptive opinion. In essence, *Groves* was the equivalent of *Cherokee Nation*—a case in which the justices criticized their generational foes but stopped short of a head-on confrontation. And just as *Cherokee Nation* gave a preview of what *Worcester* would look like, so *Groves* provided a glimpse of the arguments that would shape the great Jacksonian preemptive opinion—*Dred Scott*. Furthermore, *Groves* marked the turn from the issues that dominated the 1830s—Indian Removal and the Bank—to the one that drove the next intergeneration collision—slavery.

The Arguments of Clay and Webster

Groves raised the issue of Congress's authority over domestic slavery for the first time. In 1832, the State of Mississippi adopted a new constitution prohibiting

President William Henry Harrison, whose untimely death redirected the path of constitutional law. Lithograph by Chas Fenderich & Co. Library of Congress.

the import of slaves from other states.[14] This was not an abolitionist provision. It was a protectionist measure designed to stem the outflow of capital caused by the purchase of "foreign" slaves. The issue presented was whether a note given for the purchase of out-of-state slaves after the ratification of this clause was valid, and, if so, whether a state provision favoring local slavers was consistent with the Commerce Clause.[15] Clay and Webster were retained to defend the note's legality, and Washington society turned out to watch the great orators in action.

Over the next seven days of argument, the Whig leaders mixed orthodox legalisms with a subtle challenge to Jacksonian tenets. Clay and Webster said that the state constitutional provision was not self-executing at the time the transaction took place and therefore the sale was lawful.[16] One objection to this argument, though, was that state courts held that the constitutional clause barring the purchase of out-of-state slaves was self-executing.[17] Clay and Webster replied that these cases were ambiguous, but Clay adding the following radical argument against following these holdings:

Who are the judges of the courts of Mississippi, and what is the tenure of their offices? They are elected by the people; and the judges so elected form the court of errors; and a court thus constituted are called upon to decide a case affecting a large portion of the citizens of the state, in which strangers to the state, and who have no influence in their appointment, are the claimants! The judges of Mississippi are sitting in their own cause; in the cause of those around them; of those who gave and can take away their offices![18]

This was the first (and only) constitutional argument ever mounted against the election of state judges, which was a part of Jackson's efforts to increase popular democracy.[19] Basically, Clay was inviting the Court to say that elected judges did not deserve the deference given to appointed judges because community pressures would prevent elected judges from impartially applying the law. If this argument prevailed, states would face a strong disincentive to have elected judges, and such a precedent might have eventually led to a declaration that an elected state judiciary was unconstitutional.[20]

In the alternative, Webster focused on the point that if the state constitutional provision on slaves was self-executing, then it violated Congress's exclusive power to regulate interstate commerce. He said there was no doubt that the State was interfering with the interstate slave trade, and hence to rule in the State's favor "the court will be obliged to find out something in the introduction of slaves, different from trading in other property. This will be difficult."[21] Traditional Jacksonians were hostile to this broad assertion of federal power because it raised the prospect of a return to Marshall's position in *M'Culloch*. Another faction of Democrats, though, was concerned about the more specific implication that Congress could ban the interstate trade in slaves under the commerce power.[22] This was a fear that had not played a major role in Jackson's rise to power.[23]

It was clear by now that the premises of the Jacksonian generation were under severe assault in Congress and in the Supreme Court. With this shift in political fortune, conditions were ripe for the resumption of the tit-for-tat retaliation that frames each generational clash. Chief Justice Taney and his colleagues would now have a chance to weigh in on these ominous trends.

The Justices Hold Their Fire

The Court that considered *Groves* was already engaged in the complicated task of integrating Jacksonian ideas with the precedents laid down by the Framers and by the Jeffersonian generation. That effort began almost as soon as Taney arrived on the bench. In *New York v. Miln*, the Court held, over a dissent by Justice Story, that a state law requiring shipowners to report all persons on their vessels upon entry did not violate the Commerce Clause.[24] *Miln* distinguished

Marshall's commerce rulings and sounded the trumpet for states' rights by explaining that "all those powers which relate to merely municipal legislation, or what may, perhaps, more properly be called *internal police*, are not thus surrendered or restrained; and that, consequently, in relation to these, the authority of a state is complete, unqualified and exclusive."[25] Likewise, in *Charles Warren Bridge v. Warren Bridge*, the Court refused to strike down a state legislature's revision of a contract involving a toll bridge and limited the broad reading of the Contracts Clause in *Dartmouth College*.[26] As Chief Justice Taney said, "While the rights of private property are sacredly guarded, we must not forget that the people also have rights."[27] In both cases, the Court expressed its support for a new set of first principles at odds with the priorities of earlier generations.

Nevertheless, in *Groves* the Court passed on its chance to endorse Jacksonian tenets. In a brief opinion, the majority held that the state provision on the slave trade was not self-executing and hence the note was valid.[28] Accordingly, there was no need to address the federal questions raised by Clay and Webster. As in *Cherokee Nation*, the result of *Groves* was unremarkable. And like *Cherokee Nation*, there were strong forces bubbling under the surface brought on by the expected sequel to the generational confrontation. A telling indication of the tense backdrop to *Groves* came from two Jacksonian justices who were not satisfied by this exercise of restraint in the face of the new Whig threat. They issued opinions that reached out to decide the issues the Court avoided and ruled on them in a sweeping fashion using unprecedented theories. These concurrences not only displayed the traits of a preemptive opinion, but they closely tracked the approach that the justices would later take in *Dred Scott*.

The chief justice focused on the point that Congress had no power to bar the interstate slave trade as Webster implied. Without much explanation, Taney stated that "the action of the several states upon this subject cannot be controlled by congress, either by virtue of its power to regulate commerce, or by virtue of any power conferred by the constitution of the United States."[29] In *Dred Scott*, he carried this conclusion to its logical extreme by arguing that Congress also had no power to prohibit slavery in the territories.[30] The chief justice was taking a genuine Jacksonian principle (limited federal implied power) and expanding it beyond all recognition to say that federal officials possessed absolutely no power over domestic slavery. Taney's aggressive interpretation was novel, but can be compared to Marshall's equally aggressive dictum in *Cherokee Nation* that the Tribes were domestic dependent nations. The root of both unprecedented claims is that they were a prelude to unbridled judicial resistance.

Meanwhile, Justice Henry Baldwin stated that Congress could regulate the interstate slave trade but that slave owning was a right that could not be abridged unreasonably. In his view, because slaves were property "the owners are protected from any violations of the rights of property by congress, under the fifth amendment."[31] He illuminated his analysis with the following hypothetical: "If . . . the owner of slaves in Maryland, in transporting them . . . should pass through Pennsylvania or Ohio, no law of either state could take away or affect his right of property."[32] This was an accurate prophesy of the issue presented in *Dred Scott*, which involved a slave who passed through Illinois and resided in a federal territory and a free state before returning to a slave state.[33] Moreover, Baldwin's opinion in *Groves* was the first statement of the highly controversial doctrine of substantive due process, which the Court uses to protect unwritten rights. Once again, the friction from a generational clash was the source of constitutional creativity.

The point of this comparison between *Cherokee Nation* and *Groves* is to show that the generational collision played out in the same way in the early 1830s and early 1840s. A Court committed to one set of first principles faced a dire challenge from a political movement with a sharply different philosophy. That threat led the justices to suggest that there were constitutional deficiencies in the opposition, but the Court initially rested its decision on modest grounds before moving on to a preemptive opinion.[34] Yet before this pattern could repeat itself in full, Harrison dropped dead and the cycle was cut short.

AND TYLER TOO

John Tyler was the first vice president to become president, and contemporary observers thought that this transition would not alter the constitutional dynamic. Senator Clay was optimistic about the new president, telling a friend that "I can hardly suppose that V.P. Tyler will interpose any obstacle to the adoption of measures on which the Whigs are generally united."[35] There was some basis for this hope. Although Tyler supported Jackson's vetoes of the Maysville Turnpike and the Bank, he opposed the president's actions during the Deposit Crisis.[36] Senator Tyler, a proud Virginian, said that those comparing Jackson and Jefferson as great reformers were mistaken and that any invocation of Jefferson's "name in justification, or even in excuse, of these proceedings, is to do his memory the greatest injustice."[37] As a disgruntled Democrat, Tyler seemed like a good balance to Harrison on the ticket.

The Vice Presidential Exception

Unfortunately for conservatives, Tyler did not agree with Harrison's view of the veto power or with his support for the Bank. The moment of truth came when the special congressional session passed a bill to create a new Bank. The president promptly stamped this with a veto. Stating that "the country has been and still is deeply agitated by this unsettled question," Tyler explained that he was elected vice president by the people "with a full knowledge of the opinions . . . entertained and never concealed" that he considered a Bank unconstitutional.[38] In particular, he said the power of the Bank to keep its branches within a state even after that state's consent was withdrawn violated principles of federalism.[39] Thinking that these objections could be met, Congress passed an amended charter. This was also vetoed, with the president stating that "mere regard to the will of a majority must not in a constitutional republic like ours control this sacred a solemn duty of a sworn officer."[40]

As one commentator put it, "The ensuing outburst of fury against the President at this second veto has probably been equaled only by the merciless attack on Andrew Johnson and his supporters by the Radical Unionists after the Civil War."[41] With the exception of Webster, Tyler's entire cabinet resigned in protest.[42] Furthermore, the Whigs in Congress passed a manifesto expelling the president from the party and declaring that an amendment abolishing the veto was necessary to end the "suffering inflicted during the last twelve years by the maladministration of the Executive Department."[43] No matter how much they denounced Tyler, though, the Whigs lacked the numbers to override his vetoes or reverse the precedents supporting executive authority. One Whig paper suggested that a way out of the deadlock was for "'an overgrown Whig ruffian' to choke [Tyler] to death," or if that was unpalatable, perhaps "he ought to be shot down in his tracks, as he walks along."[44]

The replacement of Harrison by Tyler is a prime example of the role chance plays in constitutional politics. Indeed, in these transitional times chance is often a critical factor. Given the emphasis so far on the regularity of reform, this statement may seem counterintuitive. There is also something a little distressing about the thought that law—the vessel of our collective values and reason—is subject to the whim of fortune. Nevertheless, every clash of constitutional generations is littered with quirky breaks that shift the outcome.[45] In this sense, law looks a lot like war. The great military theorist Carl von Clausewitz said that "no other human activity is so continuously or universally bound up with chance" as armed conflict.[46] The plans of generals are often laid waste by bad weather,

President John Tyler, who refused to support the Whig program. Artist unknown. Lithograph by Chas Fenderich & Co. Library of Congress.

equipment failure, or another freak accident. Constitutional law displays similar traits. Although there is a cyclical pattern that frames the law's evolution, once a generational clash puts first principles on the table a wide range of possible outcomes emerge. In such unsettled times, chance has plenty of room to wreak havoc.

Tyler's promotion illustrates a systemic weakness that allows chance to come into play more frequently than we might like. In essence, the problem is that presidents and vice presidents often hold very different views on the direction of constitutional law. This division of opinion flows from the fact that vice presidents are picked to balance tickets by appealing to different segments of the electorate.[47] As a result, when a president dies the expectations of all political actors are upset.[48] One implication of this observation is that the generational cycle can easily be thrown out of whack.[49] Think about what would have happened if Jackson had died in 1831 following *Cherokee Nation*. The office would have passed to John C. Calhoun, a vice president who had already broken with administration policies. Though it would be too much to say that Calhoun would have differed with Jackson on every point, there can be little doubt that the path of the law would have moved in another direction. Perhaps the confrontations of 1832, such as *Worcester* and the Bank Veto, would not have occurred. It is even more probable that the Nullification Crisis would have played out in a different fashion under President Calhoun. Unlike this hypothetical, though, the substitution of Tyler for Harrison was a historical event with serious consequences.

Whither Conservatism?

With this unexpected loss of the presidency, conservatives led by Senator Clay pursued the only strategy open to them, which was to launch a campaign focused on gaining a supermajority in Congress following the 1842 midterm elections.[50] The Whigs thought they saw a winning issue in Tyler's abuse of executive power, particularly since he was unelected. To pound this message home, Clay introduced a constitutional amendment to abolish the veto and used the debate to bash Tyler.[51] The senator was confident in his plan notwithstanding its failure to work against Jackson, stating that Democrats stood "for Executive supremacy—for the arbitrary principle that the will of one man shall prevail against the will of the whole country. We are willing to go before the people upon that issue."[52]

The most controversial tactic employed by Whigs to break Tyler's resistance is one that Newt Gingrich tried in the 1990s—a government shutdown. In setting fiscal policy for the 1842 budget, the Whigs loaded the tariff bill with conditions that Tyler could not accept so that he would be forced to issue a veto and deprive the federal government of operating revenue.[53] When he did veto the legislation, Congress passed a second and even more objectionable bill that the president also vetoed.[54] Following this second veto, the House of Representatives took the unusual step of committing the bill to a select committee.[55]

Just as conservatives in the Senate passed the unorthodox Censure Resolution in 1834 to seek popular support before the midterm election, now conservatives in the House of Representatives sought a way to overcome the president's resistance before another midterm election. John Quincy Adams said that a select committee was necessary because "the executive and legislative branches of the Government are placed in a state of civil war, and for which there was, in his opinion, no remedy, but that remedy which the people must take in their own hands."[56] The Committee Report was issued right before the election and read just like a campaign manifesto. Getting right to the point, the committee explained that "the case has occurred . . . contemplated by the founders of the Constitution by the grant to the House of Representatives of the power to impeach the President."[57] Since obtaining a conviction in the Senate was impossible, the committee concluded that "the irreconcilable difference of opinion and of action between the legislative and executive departments of the Government is but sympathetic with the same discordant views and feelings among the people. To them alone the final issue of the struggle must be left."[58]

Tyler's response to this challenge was to follow Jackson's precedent and issue a protest. Conceding that he was "a President without a party," Tyler denounced the Select Committee for going beyond the four corners of the veto "to arraign the motives of the President for others of his acts since his induction into office."[59] He called upon the people to sustain his actions and "protest[ed] against every attempt to break down the undoubted constitutional authority of this department without a solemn amendment of that fundamental law."[60] Thus, Tyler adhered to Jackson's substantive precedents by vetoing the Bank and also accepted his institutional precedents by invoking the protest.

Once again, the nation faced a fundamental choice between going back to the generation led by Clay or sticking with the ideas articulated by the Jacksonians. When the votes came in, the verdict was clear. The Whigs suffered a catastrophic defeat in the House of Representatives, going from a 133 to 102 advantage to a 142 to 79 deficit, which was "one of the most staggering reversals in off-year congressional elections ever witnessed in American history."[61] Even this dreadful setback did not deter the Whigs from continuing their resistance, and they nominated Clay for president in 1844. His defeat in that election, however, ended the conservative effort to displace the Jacksonian generation, for the Whigs were soon supplanted by a new vehicle for reform—the Republican Party.[62]

The Missing Jacksonian Opinion

The Tyler interlude shows how luck can jolt the constitutional cycle, but these events also reveal the limits of chance in the law. Crucial as Harrison's death was, it did not alter the ultimate outcome of this generational confrontation. Moreover, the scope of the Whig defeat in 1842 suggests that even had Harrison lived the conservative program would ultimately have failed.[63] A minority party sometimes wins elections, but if its leaders are wise they do not challenge the core principles of the generation in power unless they sense that a temporal transition is at hand.[64] If they do so based only on a single victory, then they are likely to suffer a severe defeat. Thus, chance cannot change the overall result of the constitutional cycle just as it cannot overturn the outcome of a war.

Nevertheless, Harrison's death does prove that chance can alter the form of a constitutional transformation much like fortune often determines the winner of a single battle in a war. Early in the Whig administration when most political

observers were convinced that a Bank bill would pass, one congressman pre-
dicted what would happen next:

> There was another mode of deciding this question, besides repeal, and that
> was before the Supreme Court. God forbid that he should say any thing
> disparagingly of that sacred tribunal; but he would ask, if the distinguished
> gentleman, who removed the public deposites from the Bank of the United
> States was not at the head of it, and if a majority of its members, was not
> of that school of politicians, who believed a Bank of the United States to
> be unconstitutional?[65]

In other words, the president's signature of the Bank bill would create a test case
for those who wanted to challenge *M'Culloch*. And the Court that would hear
that case was packed with justices appointed by Jackson and Van Buren—some
of whom had already indicated their willingness to resist a Whig comeback.

This leads to the unavoidable, if somewhat surprising, conclusion that only
William Henry Harrison's death prevented *M'Culloch* from being overruled by
the Supreme Court. Like any counterfactual, this cannot be proven beyond
doubt. The evidence for this view, however, is powerful. Not only were Democrats trying to get a case before the Court, but most of the justices were chosen
because of their adherence to that generation's constitutional ideas.[66] Besides,
the Bank was not a side issue for this movement; it was a central issue. All of
this explains why there was a widely held expectation that when such a case was
argued the result would be an opinion striking down the Bank.[67]

No such opinion was ever issued, of course, and the ironies surrounding this
omission are almost too good to be true. For one thing, the chief supporters
of Tyler's vetoes were Democrats, so the Jacksonians effectively sabotaged their
constitutional legacy by blocking the test case for *M'Culloch*. Likewise, Jackson's
development of the veto power into a potent weapon was what gave Tyler the
tool he needed to block the creation of the case that would have written Jackson's main substantive achievement into doctrine. Finally, had Whigs gotten
their way and passed the bill, they would have inflicted terrible damage on
the long-term viability of their principles. Instead, their failure saved Marshall's
logic from being voided and made it easier for the Republicans to revive that
decision during Reconstruction.

Rather than setting a precedent that one generation would use the Court to
overrule a central precedent of the prior one, Harrison's death established that
presidents would veto legislation that rested on a broad understanding of federal implied power. The veto messages of the Jacksonian era, which stated that

Congress had no authority over education, internal improvements, or health care, read exactly like opinions repudiating *M'Culloch*.[68] For instance, Tyler rejected an internal improvements bill by saying: "The inferential power, in order to be legitimate, must be clearly and plainly incidental to some granted power and necessary to its exercise. To refer it to the head of convenience or usefulness would be to throw open the door to a boundless and unlimited discretion and to invest Congress with an unrestrained authority."[69] President James Polk vetoed another such bill because "it is not enough that [the action] may be regarded by Congress as *convenient* or that its exercise would advance the public weal. It must be *necessary and proper* to the execution of the principal expressed power to which it is an incident, and without which such principal power can not be carried into effect."[70] Even as late as 1860, President James Buchanan said that "we must . . . inquire, [i]s its exercise 'necessary and proper'?–not whether it may be convenient or useful."[71] All of these vetoes relied upon an implied power test that flatly contradicted Marshall's interpretation in *M'Culloch*, which said that "necessary" did mean convenient or useful.

Since the justices never got the chance to overrule Marshall's opinion, they did the next best thing and simply refused to recognize the holding of *M'Culloch* as binding authority.[72] Given that this is one of the most revered constitutional cases, it may be shocking to learn that the Taney Court never cited Marshall's discussion about the validity of the Bank, the Necessary and Proper Clause, and the implied power of Congress. Like *Worcester*, *M'Culloch* was left to wither away. Jackson's triumph seemed complete.

7

The Rise of Abolitionism

Georgia's resistance to the appellate jurisdiction of
the supreme court first sprung from jealousy of in-
terference with the "peculiar institution." . . . And I
think I shall be borne out by the memories of those
who remember the controversy, that the legislation
of Georgia on that occasion, although ostensibly for
another purpose, was in fact to prevent the civilization
and christianizing of the Cherokee Indians, whom . . .
it could not otherwise enslave and make subservient
to the propagation of slaves.

Abolitionist pamphlet of the 1850s

During the rise of the Jacksonian generation, abo-
litionists barely registered in the public debate. Like rodents scurrying around
during the dinosaur age, they were the most unlikely candidates for future success. Consequently, up until now their appearances in this book have been fleet-
ing and insignificant, which is exactly how they looked to their contemporaries.
Yet since we know the abolitionists and their Republican heirs would forge
some of our most powerful legal landmarks, the focus now turns to their story.

In chronicling the rise of the Reconstruction generation, the cyclical pattern
underlying constitutional law will become even more vivid. From this point
on, all of the fundamental issues raised by the collision between the abolitionists and Jacksonian elites will have a counterpart in the prior struggle between reformers and traditionalists. The only difference is that the role played
by the Democrats switches—now they are the Upstairs establishment and not
the Downstairs rebels. Roger Taney, who was the leading radical in the 1830s,

became the head reactionary in the 1850s as the abolitionist juggernaut gathered.[1] And in a final twist, the abolitionist generation would mount their assault by using the transformative precedents of their Jacksonian predecessors.

Once again, each constitutional generation is strongly influenced by the preceding one. A legal consensus exists while the next group of reformers comes into its own, and part of what shapes their views is a reaction against the flaws (as they see it) in the ruling order.[2] In personal and political life, people often respond to their parents whether they realize it or not. Understanding that "feedback effect" was helpful in showing how Jacksonian thought evolved in response to the great precedents of the Marshall era. The same technique can shed light on how the abolitionists were shaped by the major events of Jackson's rise to power.

BAPTISM BY FIRE

Although there were abolitionists from the day that the first slave arrived on our shores, there is a consensus among historians that the abolitionist movement did not become a significant political force until the 1830s.[3] Prior to that time, the foes of slavery were poorly organized and generally endorsed the far more limited approach of colonizing (i.e., deporting) slaves back to Africa. In fact, virtually all of the great abolitionist leaders supported colonization during the 1820s.[4] In the span of a few years, however, these people became the backbone of a movement that advocated immediate abolition. As Ronald G. Walters writes, the attack on colonization by its old supporters in the 1830s is inexplicable and "haunts everything written on the subject."[5] One school of thought is that a profound religious revival under way at the time heightened awareness of the injustice of slavery.[6] Another explanation is that southerners overreacted to the presence of a few abolitionists by attacking the freedom of speech about slavery, which created a backlash among moderates.[7]

Although these arguments hold part of the answer, there is a crucial element that most commentators overlook: the flowering of abolitionism coincided with the Cherokee Removal.[8] Explaining why these developments might be connected is easy when one considers the similarities between Removal and colonization. The argument on behalf of each policy assumed that the best way to resolve a racial or cultural conflict was by shipping the minority off to another region. They were also both coercive policies that did not recognize the autonomy of the affected individuals to stay where they were. This geographic segregation may have seemed like a good idea, but when colonization supporters were confronted with the harsh reality of the Cherokee Removal things looked rather different. Indeed, the one thread linking the folks who abandoned colonization for abolitionism in the early 1830s was their opposition to the Indian Removal Act. This group included the leading lights in the antislavery struggle, such as Roberts Vaux, Angelina Grimke, Arthur Tappen, Lydia Maria Child, Benjamin Lundy, William Lloyd Garrison, Charles Storrs, Beriah Green, Elizur Wright, James Birney, and Theodore Weld.[9]

Fortunately, there is no need to speculate about whether a link existed between the Removal and the surge in abolitionist feeling, since many leaders in the cause actually said there was one. Consider the example of William Lloyd Garrison, who is perhaps the most famous antislavery activist. As late as 1829, he was expressing support for repatriating slaves.[10] When Jackson proposed the Removal Act, however, Garrison was outraged and wrote several articles criticizing the measure. Shortly thereafter, he modified his position on slavery to the radical bent for which he is now known. Denouncing colonization in the strongest terms, Garrison argued that slaves were "as unanimously opposed to a removal to Africa, as the Cherokees from the council-fires and graves of their fathers."[11] In a similar vein, he said that proslavery attitudes were "answerable" for the Removal, asserting that both were the fruit of "this wicked distinction of color in our land."[12]

Garrison's view that there was a relationship between the Removal and the need for abolition was made clear in the pages of his new newspaper—the *Liberator*. Responding to the dismissal of the Tribe's challenge in *Cherokee Nation*, he changed the *Liberator*'s masthead into the famous engraving of a slave auction conducted on top of trampled sheets of paper entitled "Indian treaties."[13] The *Liberator* became legendary for its uncompromising pursuit of abolition, but Garrison's mouthpiece also continued to focus attention on the plight of the Cherokees and on the relationship between that issue and slavery.[14]

James Birney, another antislavery leader who helped develop the ideas behind the Fourteenth Amendment, agreed that Removal was the catalyst for the abolitionist cause.[15] Birney left the Colonization Society of Kentucky in the early 1830s, explaining in an open letter that the Cherokee crisis had changed his mind.[16] He noted the "very great resemblance [colonization] bears, in its most prominent features, to that of the Indians, who have been moved upon, in nearly the same manner to 'consent' to leave their lands."[17] After comparing the two issues, Birney said both posited that "it was easier to remove from the country those who were the subjects of this degradation, than to successfully

William Lloyd Garrison, the abolitionist firebrand and foe of the Cherokee Removal. Artist unknown. Library of Congress.

combat and overthrow the prejudices and false principles which produced it."[18] A comrade in arms said that Birney realized that "from the Indian to the Negro, the transition was easy and natural. . . . He could hardly fail to see, when the wrong of the Indians had thoroughly aroused him, that the sufferings of the Negro flowed from the same bitter fountain."[19]

The experiences of Garrison and Birney were typical of a trend within activist circles following the Cherokee Removal. One sign of the Removal's impact can be seen in the first meeting of the American Anti-Slavery Society, held soon after *Worcester* came down. The leaders of this abolitionist group once supported colonization.[20] In the interim, they all agitated against the Removal and changed their views on slavery. When the Massachusetts Anti-Slavery Society issued its annual report in 1838, it focused on the Removal rather than on slavery.[21] Commenting on the Trail of Tears, the report explained that "the primary object of the South, through the instrumentality of the national government, is doubly atrocious: first, to get forceful possession of [tribal] lands—and the next upon these lands to establish slavery."[22] Following the congressional debate on appropriations for the Removal, Charles Francis Adams wrote that "it is slavery that is at the bottom of this. I am more satisfied of the fact every day I live."[23] This view that discrimination against the Tribes was motivated by a desire to further slavery would become a common refrain.

Detail of The Liberator *masthead following the passage of the Indian Removal Act. The Library Company of Philadelphia.*

TRIBAL RIGHTS AND THE PROMISE OF ABOLITION

In the minds of this new generation of reformers, the bond between African American and Native American rights continued to resonate long after the 1830s.[24] Abolitionists often harked back to the Removal and to Marshall's landmark-in-exile. While they clearly focused more on slavery, "few comments are more common in their speeches than that their goal was that both blacks and Indians be secured in their rights as men."[25] As the abolitionist John Beeson said, slavery was but "an extension of the unneighborly, unchristian, and destructive practice which for generations has been operating against the Aborigines."[26]

This duality in abolitionist thinking was reflected by the debate within the civil and political institutions they created. Following the approach of the *Liberator*, radical papers often linked Native American and African American issues.[27] In the Quaker meetings and the Philadelphia lyceums where antislavery activists gathered, the two main issues for discussion were almost always abolition and tribal freedom.[28] And when Birney was offered the presidential nomination of the Liberty Party, which was the first attempt by this generation to organize into a national force, he wrote that its platform should be shaped in recognition of the fact that "we have so long practiced injustice . . . in the treatment of the colored race, both negroes and Indians, that we must begin to regard injustice as an element—a chief element—the chief element in our government."[29]

Moving into the public square, the connection between slaves and Tribes remained a powerful theme for reformers. Perhaps the best illustration of this tie involved the "gag rule" against antislavery petitions in the House of Representatives. In response to the increasing number of these requests, the House adopted a rule, at the behest of southerners, that all petitions concerning slavery be tabled without discussion.[30] Concerned about this challenge to the First Amendment's right of petition, abolitionist members led by John Quincy Adams and Joshua Giddings decided to attack the gag rule by introducing petitions on Removal and Native American rights. Their view was that these issues were sufficiently related to slavery to allow debate on its substance while avoiding the gag rule.[31] During his tenure in the House, Giddings continued to focus attention on tribal issues and use them as a vehicle to challenge slavery.[32] Later on, he became the mentor of another congressman who would expressly link the Cherokee Removal with the Fourteenth Amendment—John Bingham.[33] Another example of this tactic came when John Quincy Adams introduced a petition for a constitutional amendment to redefine the status of the Tribes. Passed initially by the Massachusetts legislature, the proposal stated that the allocation of congressional seats among the states should be made "according to their respective number of free persons, including Indians not taxed," which altered the original text by including Indians not taxed as free persons and eliminating the infamous Three-Fifth's Clause that counted slaves as less than a person.[34] The amendment had no chance of passing, but the proposal reinforced the bond between the two minority groups.

Throughout the antebellum era, *Worcester* also remained a major part of abolitionist thought. For instance, in the 1840s, Salmon P. Chase, the antislavery lawyer and future chief justice, attended a service at which the pastor "asked for the deliverance of the land from Slavery among other sins & evils & in Sermon spoke of the imprisonment of Butler & Worcester in Geo[rgia] Penitentiary."[35] On the eve of the Civil War, the abolitionist pamphlet quoted at the start of this chapter gave a rich summary of the case and argued that Georgia's resistance to the Court grew out of a desire to defend slavery.[36] Soon we shall see how John Bingham used *Worcester* to challenge Chief Justice Taney's analysis in *Dred Scott* and as an example of what the Fourteenth Amendment was designed to prevent.[37]

The problem with this abolitionist reading of *Worcester* was that the case had nothing to do with slavery, unless that term is defined in an extremely broad way. If the abolitionists were so sensitive to the lessons of the 1830s, how could they make this mistake? One answer is that this was no mistake since these leaders correctly saw that the basic issue behind *Worcester* and slavery was the

same—irrational prejudice—and that the cure was the same—extending fundamental rights to all. Another answer is that every movement needs symbols to
rally around, and at this time *Worcester* was the most egalitarian Supreme Court
opinion available.[38] A similar process was at work in the 1920s and 1930s, when
progressives searching for a hero ended up lionizing the dissents of Justice Oliver Wendell Holmes Jr., who was an odd choice given his illiberal views.[39] The
crucial point is that abolitionists saw *Worcester* as a force for justice, just as they
saw the Cherokee Removal as an antiprecedent that represented everything that
was wrong with the law.

In sum, the views of the emerging constitutional generation of abolitionists were shaped in part by its reaction against the landmarks of Jacksonian
Democracy. That course paralleled the evolution of the Democrats themselves,
who drew their constitutional inspiration from hostility toward *M'Culloch* and
its broad reading of federal authority. Thus, Van Buren was right when he said
that the lessons of the Removal "will in time occupy the minds and feelings of
our people."[40]

THE CRITIQUE AND THE RESPONSE

The same people who converted to abolitionism because of the Removal re-
sponded by developing the ideas that would later become the Fourteenth
Amendment. Most scholars trace that text's tripartite structure of the Privileges
or Immunities, Due Process, and Equal Protection Clauses to the work of James
Birney and Theodore Weld.[41] Based mainly in Ohio and Pennsylvania, the
Birney-Weld school began its attack on slavery in the 1830s with pamphlets that
demanded basic rights for all Americans.[42] Many of the leaders who gave us the
Fourteenth Amendment, such as Thaddeus Stevens and John Bingham, were
disciples of this line of thought, especially its focus on equal protection.[43] Indeed, Bingham's hostility to slavery can be traced to his exposure to the Birney-
Weld views when he was a college student in Ohio during the mid-1830s.[44]

Rights Backed by National Power

The new generation's focus on fundamental rights was based on the view that
the Jacksonian principle of majority rule was, in Horace Greeley's words, a
rule of "might makes right."[45] If that was the problem, then one solution was
the creation of a legal order in which popular prejudice was checked not by a
benevolent elite—the Federalist innovation that Jackson attacked as aristocracy—

but with a more robust definition of personal liberty that a majority could not touch.[46] This strategy, though, would succeed only if the focus on rights was coupled with a rule that they would apply to all citizens equally. In a very real sense, abolitionists were just building upon the Jacksonian belief in egalitarianism for whites by extending it to the groups that the Democrats excluded. Republicans believed that they could, in Lincoln's stirring turnabout, create a universe where "right makes might."[47]

As for the content of these universal rights, the rising generation looked primarily to the Bill of Rights and concluded that they should be extended to the states. Though this inclination was already evident in the outrage directed at Georgia's attack on religious freedom in *Worcester*, the impulse toward incorporation was more a reaction against efforts by the establishment, which abolitionists referred to as the "Slave Power," to crush dissent.[48] Along with the aforementioned gag rule on antislavery petitions, officials in the South were aggressive in banning the speech of anyone who advocated ending slavery.[49] Reformers said that this represented a repudiation of the Bill of Rights for blacks and abolitionist whites.[50] Accordingly, they held that slavery could never be abolished until these guarantees were applied to the states.[51] Once again, concrete grievances were driving the ideology of reformers, just as it did in Jackson's era.

To correct the abuses that the Jacksonian regime heaped on African Americans and Native Americans, the ascending generation was by necessity also driven to reject their predecessors' narrow view of federal authority. Applying the Bill of Rights to the states required a significant expansion of national power. Likewise, the abolition of slavery required a broad reading of Congress's reach since slavery was a creature of state law. Abolitionist tracts, including an influential one by Birney, spilled a lot of ink arguing why Congress possessed the power to abolish slavery and enforce rights secured by the Constitution.[52] Just as *Worcester* was the best Supreme Court case on equality at the time, *M'Culloch* was the best one supporting the exercise of national power that the abolitionists wanted. It should come as no real shock, therefore, that Republicans referred to the decision as "the celebrated case of McCulloch v. The State of Maryland" and often cited Marshall's opinion to support their efforts to fight discrimination.[53]

No Rights at All: *United States v. Rogers*

While the rising generation was formulating a new set of constitutional answers, the establishment was busy implementing its contrary policies. The discussion thus far has focused on what the Taney Court did not do, namely, recognize *M'Culloch* or *Worcester* as binding authority. Nonetheless, Chief Justice Taney and his colleagues also acted to write their generation's views into law. The best example was *United States v. Rogers*, a case that addressed the status of the Cherokees in the new order.[54]

Rogers brought the relationship between Jacksonian Democracy and the Tribe full circle by showing the impotence of Marshall's logic as compared to Jackson's political success. The case involved a white man who was indicted for murdering another white in the territory of Arkansas, which is where the Tribe was sent after the Removal.[55] The defendant argued that he and his alleged victim were under the Cherokees' jurisdiction, not the federal government's, since they had both renounced their citizenship, married Cherokee women, and been accepted as tribal members.[56] The first issue for the justices was whether a tribe had the power to make American citizens into tribal members and remove them from the grasp of Congress. Answering with an emphatic no, Chief Justice Taney wrote: "Whatever obligations the prisoner may have taken upon himself by becoming a Cherokee by adoption, his responsibility to the laws of the United States remained unchanged."[57] The chief justice ended this part of his discussion with the following summary of the law: "The Indian tribes residing within the territorial limits of the United States are subject to [Congress's] authority, and where the country occupied by them is not within the limits of one of the States, Congress may by law punish any offence committed there, no matter whether the offender be a white man or an Indian."[58] Thus, as Jackson had always maintained, Congress and the states could govern Native Americans without restriction. Although in this case that authority rested with Congress because the alleged crime was committed in a territory, the clear implication of Taney's statement was that if the crime had occurred within a state then the power to punish would rest there. There was no mention of tribal sovereignty.

After setting this piece of the puzzle into place, the Court added a racial gloss on the question of tribal identity. The next issue in *Rogers* was whether federal law covered the alleged crime. Under a statute passed in Jackson's second term, no federal jurisdiction existed over "crimes committed by one Indian against the person or property of another Indian."[59] Taney rejected Rogers's submission that he was an Indian for purposes of this law by reading the statute in racial terms. The chief justice said that "the exception is confined to those who by the usages and customs of the Indians are regarded as belonging to their race. It does not speak of members of a tribe, but of the race generally."[60] In this case, the defendant "was still a white man, of the white race, and therefore not within the exception in the act of Congress."[61] Such reasoning, of course, was fully in accord with the discriminatory ideas that were behind the Removal Act in the first place.

The sharp contrast between *Rogers* and the abolitionist philosophy framed the debate that would fuel the next generational collision. From the perspective of the Democrats, nonwhites had no rights and the implied power of Congress was carefully limited to give the states maximum autonomy. Reformers countered that the liberties in the Bill of Rights were the birthright of all Americans and that the federal government was empowered to enforce them against their leading abusers—the states. These dueling narratives reached their apex in *Dred Scott*, the Jacksonian preemptive opinion, and in the Fourteenth Amendment, which overruled *Dred Scott* and set the Republican ideology into the legal firmament.

A New Party Explodes on the Scene

The growth of the Republican Party from nothing in 1854 to complete control of the federal government six years later seems astounding by modern standards.[62] Put in context, however, the abolitionists' path to power was similar to the one taken by their predecessors. In both cases, the arrival of the new generation was heralded by the collapse of the existing party structure and the creation of a fresh party committed to profound change.

One thing that distinguishes the 1850s from the 1820s is the slower pace at which the new generation got organized. It took only five years for Jackson to ride the *M'Culloch* decision and the Panic of 1819 to a popular vote plurality. It took more than two decades after the Removal for abolitionists to coalesce into a similar force and three for them to get a plurality. This delay resulted from the abolitionists' greater ambition. Ending slavery involved a wrenching shift in our institutions along with a credible threat of civil war. Mobilizing support for that platform naturally took more time than it did to convince voters to follow Jackson's more modest program. The rising movement also faced institutional resistance from the two parties that emerged from the generational collision of the 1830s.[63] This made forming a new party or taking over an existing one harder than it was for the Jacksonians, who arose in an era when party identity was weaker.

Nonetheless, once the Republican Party was born, its charge to power was just as fast as Jackson's. The leading event that caused the extinction of the Whigs was the Kansas-Nebraska Act.[64] This act undid the Missouri Compromise and its slavery ban in the northern territories by allowing any territory to have slavery if its residents so desired.[65] By expanding the potential scope of the slave system, the act convinced many voters that maybe there was something to the "extreme" claim that there was a Slave Power bent on extinguishing freedom everywhere. This sentiment was crystallized by Lincoln's refrain that the Union "cannot remain permanently half-slave and half-free. . . . It will become all one thing or all the other."[66] Certainly the great compromisers on slavery, such as Henry Clay or the Framers, would not have agreed with this statement.

Here we begin to see a pattern first described by Richard Hofstadter, which is that in moments of crisis people tend to blame social ills on elite conspiracies.[67] That tendency is especially pronounced for a rising constitutional generation. Republicans blamed the Slave Power, Jackson attacked a sinister aristocracy, Jefferson feared monocrats bent on bringing back the monarchy, New Dealers denounced economic royalists, and modern conservatives are haunted by a cultural elite.[68] These caricatures all describe a real issue that drives a new generation and exposes faults in existing arrangements. There is a fine line, however, between saying that the Slave Power is a threat and engaging in a paranoid rant that points fingers at the Masons or Skull and Bones.[69] Something must convince voters that the radicals have a case, and hence each winning constitutional generation is the beneficiary of some lucky break that gives them a leg up on the other pretenders. Jackson's good fortune was the coincidental timing of the 1819 Panic and *M'Culloch*. Republicans reaped the whirlwind from the Kansas-Nebraska Act.[70]

One might wonder why the Whig Party did not benefit from this hostility to the Democratic establishment, or why reformers did not just take over that party. Historians explain the disappearance of the Whigs by noting that they were tainted in the eyes of antislavery forces because of their repeated compromises on the issue.[71] Another factor was that, by the 1850s, professionals in the Whig organization were demoralized. Not only were they tired of being smacked around by Democrats, but in 1852 the two titans who held the party together since its inception—Henry Clay and Daniel Webster—died.[72] Consequently, by 1854 the Whig Party was an asset that nobody wanted. In the 1820s, President Monroe's party collapsed in just four years. In the 1850s, the Whigs went from the second-largest party in 1852 to almost nothing in four years. This was the signal that a generational transition was at hand.

Republicans established their first national platform in 1856 and began turning their constitutional ideas into concrete proposals. As its main plank, the party declared that the Constitution conferred upon Congress "sovereign powers over the Territories of the United States for their government" and would use that power "to prohibit in the Territories those twin relics of barbarism—Polygamy and Slavery."[73] This was a repudiation of the Kansas-Nebraska Act, and the platform was beginning to flesh out the rising generation's view that federal power should be used to secure basic rights. In the general election, Republican

John C. Fremont lost the White House but carried eleven states and about one-third of the popular vote.[74] This strong showing shook the Jacksonian establishment to its core.

It is difficult to understate the panic that gripped Democratic ranks when Republicans appeared on the horizon. President Franklin Pierce used his Annual Message in 1855 to denounce the "passionate rage of fanaticism and partisan spirit" that gripped the slavery issue and attacked abolitionists for their "wild and chimerical schemes of social change which are generated one after another in the unstable minds of visionary sophists and interested agitators."[75] Taking their cue from the president, other Jacksonians argued that "Republicans posed a particular threat to the nation's safety. . . . As such, they had no legitimacy, posed a massive danger to the Union, and had to be put down."[76] This cry of alarm should sound familiar. It echoed the gloom-and-doom sentiments expressed by Chief Justice Marshall about the demise of "our Constitution" in the event of a Jacksonian takeover.

Of course, every campaign is filled with claims about the ghastly consequences of an opposition win. What differentiates a generational transition from an ordinary election is that the alarmist talk from conservatives is matched by massive acts of resistance. In the 1850s, conservatives did not wait around to see what reformers would do in office. They decided to strike first.

8

Judicial Resistance:
Dred Scott v. Sandford

An Act of Congress which deprives a citizen of the
United States of his liberty or property, merely because he came himself or brought his property into a
particular Territory of the United States, and who had
committed no offense against the laws, could hardly
be dignified with the name of due process of law.

Dred Scott v. Sandford

It is useless to dwell upon a proposition so absurd;
it has no sanction in the Constitution or in reason.
The extra-territorial legislative power of every State
is limited to its own citizens and subjects. That is the
decision of the Supreme Court, in the great case of
Worcester *vs.* the State of Georgia. . . . I conclude,
therefore, that the Territories are not under the dominion and sovereignty of the States severally. . . . The
Constitution is based upon the EQUALITY of the human race.

Representative John Bingham

Chief Justice Taney's signature opinion is one of
the most hated and misunderstood decisions in our jurisprudence. In declaring
that African Americans could not be citizens because they were "beings of an
inferior order, and altogether unfit to associate with the white race, either in
social or political relations; and so far inferior, that they had no rights which
the white man was bound to respect," the Court clearly reached the nadir of its

99

moral authority.[1] Moreover, by ruling that Congress lacked the power to bar slavery in the territories under the Missouri Compromise, the Court precipitated a crisis that led to a horrific bloodbath.[2] Surely there is nothing good that can be said about such a decision.

Once we recognize that constitutional law moves in a cyclical fashion, however, *Dred Scott* appears in a different light. The case was an act of massive judicial resistance in favor of Jacksonian Democracy—the mirror opposite of Marshall's preemptive opinion in *Worcester*.[3] In both situations, the justices reached out to decide unnecessary issues in order to make a political statement.[4] On each occasion, the Court essentially invented a new constitution designed to blunt the momentum of the oncoming generation. While Chief Justice Marshall tried to stop Jackson's movement by enhancing federal power and the rights of minorities, Chief Justice Taney labored to halt the Republican juggernaut by sharply limiting federal authority and ensuring that African Americans had no rights. Finally, in both cases the pressure of political competition forced the justices to propose a new concept of fairness to support their opinion. In *Worcester*, the novel contribution was group equality; in *Dred Scott* it was substantive due process.[5] All of these connections vindicate Thomas Hart Benton's claim that *Dred Scott* was "the child and champion of party, and itself a touchstone of party," just as *Worcester* was in its time.[6]

The only difference between *Worcester* and *Dred Scott* is that one comports with modern concepts of federal power and civil rights while the other does not. Indeed, it is not even clear that *Dred Scott* was legally incorrect from the limited perspective of which side should have won the lawsuit, just as it is wrong to say that Marshall reached an incorrect judgment in *Worcester*. This suggests a crucial point about constitutional doctrine, which is that values determine the status of judicial decisions more than reason. Although some opinions are more logical than others, that is not what usually distinguishes the landmarks from the losers.[7] The true distinction is whether an opinion's core ideals are accepted by the nation. *Dred Scott* is not wrong because it is unprofessional; it is wrong because its premises are no longer shared by our country.[8] In the end, Chief Justice Taney's effort to declare the Republican Party's main plank invalid failed. The fierce resistance of the establishment only deepened the yearning for reform.

THE SECOND PREEMPTIVE OPINION

Dred Scott involved a suit by a Missouri slave who claimed that his stay in Illinois and in a federal territory where slavery was barred made him a free man.[9]

Dred Scott, the slave who dared to be free. Library of Congress. Wood engraving by Century Magazine.

He brought an action in state court and a jury returned a verdict in his favor.[10] (Thus, the only body that ever ruled in Dred Scott's favor was an all-white jury.) The state supreme court reversed and held that Missouri law controlled his status.[11] This was in accord with a case from the U.S. Supreme Court, *Strader v. Graham*, in which Chief Justice Taney ruled that each state could apply its own choice-of-law rule to slaves.[12] Petitioners in that case argued that the Northwest Ordinance of 1787, which barred slavery in the existing territories, trumped any state choice-of-law decision. In dicta, the Court said this "could not influence the decision upon the rights of the master or the slaves in that State, nor give this court jurisdiction upon the subject."[13]

Accordingly, any attempt by Scott to seek a writ of error from his state court judgment was bound to fail. The claim that his stay in Illinois set him free was barred by *Strader*. Moreover, the dictum in that opinion was specific in saying that federal law did not trump a state's choice-of-law rule either. Of course, Scott could have argued that *Strader*'s discussion of federal law was dicta that should not be followed, but that contention was not promising. Nevertheless, when Scott filed a federal lawsuit, he asserted the same substantive claims as in his failed state suit. In the federal circuit court, the defendant answered with a plea in abatement, which challenged the jurisdiction of the court on the ground that Scott was an African American and thus, not a citizen capable of bringing an action.[14] Though that argument was rejected, Scott lost anyway. He could prevail on appeal only if he persuaded the Supreme Court to reverse itself and fashion a national choice-of-law rule for slavery. The chances of this were remote, and hence one can hardly call Taney on the carpet for ruling against Scott.[15] The problem was that he did not stop there.

Deciding Unnecessary Issues

Dred Scott is famous for rejecting the presumption that courts should not decide issues that are not before them. In a critique of the opinion, Thomas Hart Benton accused Taney of "hunting for errors [and] making a bridge to get from a case of personal rights to a question of political power."[16] Just as in *Worcester*, this grasping behavior was necessary if the Court was going to take a stand against the next generation.[17]

To begin with, the Court could have avoided the jurisdictional issue entirely and simply ruled against Scott on the merits, relying on *Strader*. Three justices noted that Scott's master did not challenge the jurisdiction of the court on appeal, and hence the issue was waived.[18] Chief Justice Taney responded with an argument that is familiar to modern lawyers, which is that a jurisdictional defense could not be waived because the constitutional authority of the federal courts is limited.[19] The problem that may have been on the Court's mind was that conceding jurisdiction would set a precedent for slaves who wanted to attack their detention under the Fugitive Slave Act.[20] Even though those suits were very unlikely to succeed, the resulting flood of litigation would have troubled any reasonable court, just as Marshall was not keen in *Cherokee Nation* to allow the Tribes free rein to sue in the Supreme Court's original jurisdiction.

A more plausible way to dispose of Scott's suit was by relying on the Missouri Supreme Court opinion, which held that Scott was not a state citizen, and dismissing his attempt to invoke the jurisdiction of the federal courts. Basically, Scott was trying to relitigate the issue of whether he was a citizen of Missouri—a claim that was a loser in state court. Ordinarily, under the doctrine of res judicata this sort of redundant claim would be barred. While Scott's master did not assert res judicata as a defense, one justice wrote that the Court could use the doctrine in an independent inquiry of the jurisdictional issue.[21] The reason Scott's state citizenship mattered was that his action was based on diversity jurisdiction under Article Three, Section Two, of the Constitution, which requires state citizenship.[22] Thus, if the state supreme court decision was followed, Scott's claim would fail.

Next, even if the justices felt compelled to examine whether Scott was a U.S. citizen as part of its jurisdictional inquiry, that was a far cry from Taney's gratuitous decision to ask whether any African American could ever be a citizen.[23]

It is not clear why national citizenship was relevant for purposes of bringing a lawsuit in federal court, since the Constitution contains no such requirement. Yet both the chief justice and the lead dissenter, Justice Benjamin R. Curtis, seemed to agree that this was a necessary element.[24] In spite of this conclusion, the Court could have confined its analysis to whether a slave was a citizen, even though this question probably answered itself. Instead, Taney reached back to the original plea of abatement filed by the defendant, which posed the broader issue about African American citizenship.

Finally, there was no need for the Court to address the issue of whether the Missouri Compromise was constitutional. The hook for this inquiry was that Scott claimed he was free because he lived for a time in a territory where slavery was banned by that act. *Strader* said that this type of argument could not supersede a state choice-of-law rule, but if the act was completely invalid then Scott's claim would also fall. By this point, though, the Court had ignored four other ways of resolving the case. This behavior is reminiscent of *Worcester*, where the justices overlooked the statutory and treaty-based grounds for decision so that they could declare Georgia's acts unconstitutional and condemn the Removal Act. In *Dred Scott*, Chief Justice Taney wanted to take up the issue of congressional power over slavery because that was the central creed of the Republican Party. As an integral figure in the rise of the prior constitutional generation, he wanted to defend its achievements by all available means.[25]

REACTIVE LEGAL REASONING

Let us now turn to the Court's analysis of the merits, which proceeded to resolve the gratuitous questions at a towering level of generality that brushed aside all contrary precedent. In the process, the chief justice elevated the principles of white supremacy and limited federal authority associated with the Jacksonian regime in an attempt to discredit the attack being mounted by the constitutional insurgents.[26]

African American Citizenship and the Tribes

By adopting the plea of abatement, the Court framed the first issue as whether any African American could be a citizen. Chief Justice Taney began by looking for guidance from the closest analogy he could find from his experience, which was the status of Native Americans. Although some commentators see this step as illogical, we know better.[27] Since the Jacksonian generation was largely defined by the struggle over Cherokee rights, any principled analysis of minority rights in that era had to start with a comparison to the Tribes. Here is what the chief justice said about that connection:

> The situation of this population was altogether unlike that of the Indian race. . . . Although they were uncivilized, they were yet a free and inde-pendent people, associated together in nations or tribes, and governed by their own laws. . . . These Indian Governments were regarded and treated as foreign Governments. . . . It is true that the course of events has brought the Indian tribes within the limits of the United States under subjection to the white race; and it has been found necessary for their sake as well as our own . . . to legislate to a certain extent over them and the territory they occupy. But they may, without doubt, like the subjects of any other foreign state, be naturalized by the authority of Congress, and become citizens of a State, and of the United States.[28]

With a nod toward the Cherokee Removal—which Taney described with the euphe-mism "the course of events"—the chief justice argued that the previous autonomy of the Tribes distinguished them from African Americans. Thus, he concluded that Native Americans could be citizens and African Americans could not.[29]

At first glance the chief justice's description of the Tribes seems at odds with Jacksonian principles. For instance, he said that they were "a free and indepen-dent people," even through *Rogers* held that Congress governed them. Similarly, the Court called them "foreign governments," but *Cherokee Nation* held that they were not foreign states.[30] On the other hand, these statements were all in the past tense or qualified by the observation that Congress now had the power to legislate over the Tribes. Since no constitutional amendment changed their rights, the justices needed to explain how the current degraded status of the Tribes could be reconciled with the Framers' contrary views. The solution was to concede that Native Americans once had rights, but that "the course of events" had changed things. That euphemism was broad enough to include a professional view that gradual change occurred, or the more accurate view that a generational transition was the culprit.[31] Furthermore, the Court's view that Na-tive Americans could be citizens was not inconsistent with Jacksonian dogma. Some tribes were, in fact, naturalized during this era and the Court upheld these acts.[32] Accordingly, the reference to the Tribes as being "foreign govern-ments" is best read as applying to naturalization alone.

The central point is that Chief Justice Taney interpreted the Native Ameri-can precedent to say that the Constitution created a racial caste system. *Worces-ter* used a group rights analysis to argue that the Cherokees were equal to the

Chief Justice Roger B. Taney, the pillar of the legal establishment. Artist unknown. Library of Congress.

United States, but *Dred Scott* used the same approach to deny equality to African Americans. In response to the dissent's argument that there were free blacks at the time of the Founding (including some who voted for delegates to the state conventions that ratified the federal Constitution), Chief Justice Taney said that this observation was irrelevant.[33] The reason was that "the number that had been emancipated at that time were but few in comparison with those held in slavery; and they were identified in the public mind with the race to which they belonged, and regarded as a part of the slave population rather than the free."[34] In other words, *Dred Scott* held that group membership defined a person's status. Ironically, the Court agreed with the abolitionist mantra that the freedoms of Native Americans and African Americans were bound together. The difference was that Taney used this parallel to reinforce legal barriers rather than to expand rights.[35]

Having drawn what wisdom he could from the best available precedent, the chief justice proceeded to support his conclusion by reading the rest of our history through a racist lens. Just as *Worcester* bent over backward to interpret treaties and the history of tribal relations in generous terms, *Dred Scott* gave an incredibly narrow construction to anything that could support African American citizenship. In a line that still sends chills up the spine, Taney said that "the enslaved African race were not intended to be included" in the Declaration of Independence's claim that all men are created equal.[36] This assertion was followed by a lengthy discourse on all of the racist legislation enacted by the states and by the federal government since the Founding.[37] Justice Curtis wrote that the idea that the Constitution "was made exclusively for the white race is, in my opinion, not only an assumption not warranted by anything in the Constitution, but contradicted by its opening declaration, that it was ordained and established by the people of the United States, for themselves and their posterity."[38] His dissent also pointed out a flaw in Taney's analysis, which was that there were just as many state court decisions, state constitutions, and federal laws that disavowed racial classifications and supported equal citizenship.[39]

In sum, Taney's review of the citizenship issue was intended to defend his generation's views by erecting a constitutional obstacle to reformers. This was the culmination of a belief in white supremacy that started with the effort to end Native American sovereignty in the 1830s. The fact that there was no clear principle set down by the Framers against African American participation in the polity was immaterial. Though Taney claimed he was interpreting their intent, a careful examination shows he was doing no such thing.[40] The chief justice was, in fact, applying the Jacksonian generation's values at the expense of precedent and the rising generation's critique.

The Missouri Compromise

The breadth and distortions in the Court's discussion only got worse when the inquiry turned to the Missouri Compromise. In striking down this act, the chief justice read the implied power of Congress narrowly and held that barring slavery in the territories was beyond its scope.[41] This was consistent with Jacksonian views, but Taney would inflate that concept beyond all recognition in an attempt to declare the Republican Party's key plank invalid. Just as Marshall gave an unprecedented construction to federal authority in *Worcester*, Taney now did the same thing from the opposite direction.

Dismissing Legislative and Judicial Precedent

The first problem with the chief justice's conclusion that the powers of Congress were limited in the territories was that an opinion by Chief Justice Marshall said that Congress possessed plenary power there.[42] In *American Insurance Company v. Canter*, the petitioner challenged a ruling from a Florida territorial court because that court did not have a judge with life tenure as mandated by Article Three of the Constitution.[43] In rejecting this claim, Marshall wrote: "In legislating for [territories], Congress exercises the combined powers of the general, and of a state government."[44] Consequently, Scott argued that just "as a State may unquestionably prohibit slavery within its territory, this sentence decides in effect that Congress may do the same in a Territory of the United States."[45] Chief Justice Taney disagreed, contending that the statement "has no reference whatever to the power of Congress over rights of person or rights of property—but relates altogether to the power of establishing judicial tribunals to administer the laws constitutionally passed, and defining the jurisdiction they may exercise."[46] This was a narrow reading of the opinion, in part because it is hard to say why Article Three did not bind Congress while other constitutional provisions did. One theme that was beginning to emerge from the Court's opinion, though, was intense hostility to congressional power.

The next hurdle for the justices was that the aforementioned Northwest Ordinance of 1787, which was supported by the Framers, barred slavery in those original territories. Scott contended that this illuminated the scope of Article Four, Section Three, of the Constitution, which says that "Congress shall have power to dispose of and make all needful Rules and Regulations respecting the Territory or other Property belonging to the United States."[47] The Court responded by holding that the Territory Clause referred only to territories existing at the Founding, and that the power to govern anything acquired afterward was implied.[48] Since the area covered by the Missouri Compromise was part of the Louisiana Purchase, under Taney's analysis the Territory Clause did not apply there. This might seem like a tortured reading of the provision, but the Court had always maintained a studied ambiguity in prior cases over whether Congress's power to govern the territories came from the Territory Clause or was implied from the government's authority to acquire territory as a sovereign power.[49]

The Echo of M'Culloch

To ascertain the scope of this implied power, Scott's lawyers next tried to resuscitate M'Culloch.[50] This case seemed relevant not only because it was the leading judicial pronouncement on implied power, but because Marshall actually compared the Territory Clause with the Necessary and Proper Clause in his opinion. M'Culloch explained that "the power to 'make all needful rules and regulations respecting the territory or other property belonging to the United States,' is not more comprehensive, than the power 'to make all laws which shall be necessary and proper for carrying into execution' the powers of the government."[51] In drawing this analogy, Marshall focused on the obvious parallel between the words "needful" and "necessary."[52] As the dissenters noted, the broad definition of "necessary" in *M'Culloch* informed the scope of the territo-rial power.[53] Justice Curtis stressed this point, arguing that "whether a particular rule or regulation be needful, must be finally determined by Congress itself. Whether a law be needful, is a legislative or political, not a judicial, question. Whatever Congress deems needful is so, under the grant of power."[54]

The majority's answer to this argument was silence. An opinion that we now consider fundamental was simply ignored just as it was in every implied author-ity case and presidential veto issued after the Bank Veto. That omission was not just an oversight. *Dred Scott* repudiated *M'Culloch*'s admonition that courts should defer to legislative judgments about the appropriate means for exercising its authority. So much for the staying power of Marshall's dazzling reasoning.

A New Understanding of Fairness

Although Chief Justice Taney's fidelity to the principle of limited federal power was impressive, it left him with two problems. The first was that there was no sovereign governing body in the territories. If Congress could not take certain actions in the territories, then nobody could. Consequently, the Court needed a very strong justification to set aside congressional authority here. Second, the Court did not explain how it would analyze the issue. After all, the justices were not willing to use the Territory Clause, *McCulloch*, or any other Marshall Court precedent. Moreover, Taney refused to consider the Northwest Ordinance or any statutes pertaining to the governance of those territories as precedent.[55] Much as *Worcester* needed special help to support its exceptionally broad reading of tribal sovereignty, *Dred Scott* developed (or, more accurately, adopted Justice Baldwin's suggestion from *Groves* on) the doctrine of substantive due process to explain its unprecedented holding narrowing the scope of territorial governance.

Specifically, the chief justice argued that the Due Process Clause suggested a limit on the implied authority of Congress.[56] He said that the due process protection given to property counseled "against any inroads which the General Government might attempt, under the plea of implied or incidental powers" against slavery.[57] This is different from the modern version of substantive due process, which creates rights that restrict the express and implied powers at all levels of government, rather than just suggesting how these powers should be construed. The past and present doctrines are similar, though, in that they end up inserting the ruling generation's values into the Constitution rather than reasoning from the constitutional text. Indeed, most unwritten rights begin as desperate efforts to ward off a generational challenge. The most notable example is the "liberty of contract" doctrine invented by the Court in the 1890s as the Populist generation was on the march and threatening to institute sweeping redistributive programs.[58] This "creativity" is problematic because it strains the fine line that separates the rule of law from judicial tyranny. In Justice Curtis's words, "when a strict interpretation of the Constitution, according to the fixed rules which govern the interpretation of laws, is abandoned, and the theoretical opinions of individuals are allowed to control its meaning, we have no longer a Constitution; we are under the government of individual men."[59]

One of the reasons why innovations in cases such as *Dred Scott* and *Worcester* are greeted with disdain by segments of the legal establishment is that the "countermajoritarian difficulty" is at its greatest strength in the transitions between generations. This core premise of constitutional theory holds that there is a tension between judicial review and democracy because unelected judges can invalidate the acts of elected officials.[60] Naturally, this problem is most acute when there is a sharp division between the principles being articulated by the two branches, as is the case during a generational clash. Unorthodox solutions to substantive legal issues are an inevitable product of political combat, but when those novelties are proposed by elected leaders, as was true with the debate over religious freedom or the authority of legislative precedent, they can be tested quickly by the electorate to establish their legitimacy. The same cannot be said about doctrinal novelties, which take more time for the electorate to overturn if they disagree.

This helps explains why many of the most reviled cases in the Court's history are clustered at the boundaries between constitutional generations. Just as volcanoes rise on the fault lines of tectonic plates, the heat of a political confrontation sparks preemptive decisions that seize the nation's attention and bring forth accusations that the rule of law is being undermined.[61] It would be overstating matters to say that contentious decisions come only during a generational collision, but there is a good reason for thinking that they are likely to be found within these discrete periods. When the justices void an action of the new movement by applying traditional principles in a distorted way, their ruling retains its power only if conservatives in the political branches win the battle for public opinion. If that does not happen, then that same judicial resistance will be declared ill-advised activism, which is what eventually happened to *Dred Scott*. *Worcester* held this dreaded label while Jacksonian Democracy was the ruling orthodoxy, but when the abolitionist generation came to power, Marshall's opinion would be transformed into an enduring landmark and, in effect, switch places with *Dred Scott*.

The Battle Is Joined

Chief Justice Tancy's defense of his ideals marked the latest escalation in the fight between the Jacksonian and Republican forces. His contemporaries recognized that *Dred Scott* was a direct attack on the new generation, as "it sweeps away every plank of their platform, and crushes into nothingness the whole theory upon which their party is founded."[62] Like *Worcester* and the Corrupt Bargain in the prior era, however, these attempts to squash reform only redounded to the advantage of the challengers.

The counterattack against *Dred Scott* began before the decision was issued, and the fight was led by Congressman John Bingham, a leading Republican who would later be the primary drafter of the Fourteenth Amendment.[63] Responding to the argument that excluding slavery in the territories was unconstitutional, Bingham said that this was "absurd."[64] In a speech that was reprinted in papers throughout the nation, he anticipated Taney's due process interpretation and said that just because citizens could enter the territories did not mean they had a right to take their state's law with them.[65] Then, in a passage quoted at the beginning of this chapter, he cited "the decision of the Supreme Court, in the great case of Worcester v. State of Georgia" as support for the proposition that state law could not operate beyond its own legitimate borders and that "the Constitution is based upon the EQUALITY of the human race."[66] Bingham's reading of *Worcester* as an antislavery case is consistent with the construction put on the opinion by the abolitionist movement. Moreover, he was suggesting that one object of the rising generation was the restoration of the Marshall decisions that were swamped in the 1830s.

Building on Bingham's position, *Dred Scott* became a rallying cry for reformers who argued that the case was the next step in the Slave Power's quest to make slavery legal everywhere.[67] Though most Republicans criticized Taney's reasoning by calling it dicta, Lincoln offered a more sophisticated analysis. When asked how he justified his criticism of this judicial precedent, he said:

> If this important decision had been made by the unanimous concurrence of the judges, and without any apparent partisan bias, and in accordance with legal public expectation, and with the steady practice of the departments throughout our history, and had been in no part, based on assumed historical facts which are not really true; or, if wanting in some of these, it had been before the court more than once, and had there been affirmed and re-affirmed through the course of years, it then might be . . . factious, nay even revolutionary, not to acquiesce in it as a precedent.[68]

*President Abraham Lincoln, the leader
of the rising generation. Currier & Ives.
Library of Congress.*

What is notable about Lincoln's lawyerly criticism is its similarity to the argument made against *Worcester* by the Tennessee attorney general twenty years
earlier.[69] In both instances, foes of the Court's extraordinary resistance stressed
that there was a political component to the decision that counseled against its
acceptance. And in neither case did they just flout the Court's authority and
urge a curtailment of judicial review. Lincoln viewed the Court's preemptive
opinion not as a final blow, but as an opportunity to engage the electorate in a
dialogue about what the Constitution should be.

It is wrong to say, as Charles Warren did, "that Chief Justice Taney elected
Abraham Lincoln to the Presidency," but there is no doubt that *Dred Scott*
ultimately energized Republicans.[70] Just as the forces unleashed by reformers
destroyed the Whig Party, by 1860 those same spirits were tearing the Jacksonian coalition apart. A new generation was about to assume power, and Senator
William Seward proclaimed that Republicans would follow the path of their
predecessors to "reorganize the court, and thus reform its political sentiments
and practices."[71] The sun was setting on Jackson's America.

9

The Fourteenth Amendment in Jackson's Shadow

Under the Constitution as it is, not as it was, and by
force of the fourteenth amendment, no State hereafter
can . . . ever repeat the example of Georgia and send
men to the penitentiary, as did that State, for teaching
the Indian to read the lessons of the New Testament,
to know that that new evangel, "The pure in heart
shall see God."

Representative John Bingham

Reform leads to resistance, and resistance leads to
reform. That is a central theme of the constitutional cycle.[1] When the preemptive opinion in *Dred Scott* backfired and helped bring Lincoln to the White House, Southern Democrats chose to escalate their resistance by following the precedent of the Framers and declaring independence. Needless to say, their effort failed. One consequence of that futile resistance, however, is that it greatly deepened the support for radical change. In 1861, Lincoln stressed that he had no intention of interfering with slavery in the states.[2] Four years and hundreds of thousands of deaths later, voters were in no mood to accept such a modest position, and by 1865 Republicans were ratifying a Thirteenth Amendment barring slavery everywhere. With the conclusion of the Civil War, the new generation was poised to implement its constitutional mandate.

Then a curious thing happened—Lincoln was assassinated. His successor, Vice President Andrew Johnson, was a hard-core Jacksonian who was put on the ticket to attract crossover votes. This turn of events was shocking, but the same scenario had played out twenty-four years earlier with the death of William Henry Harrison and his replacement by John Tyler. As in that interlude, Lincoln's death did not change the ultimate outcome of the generational transition. What this substitution did do was rearrange the form of the new constitutional ideas, just as Tyler's accession prevented *M'Culloch* from being overruled by the Supreme Court. Because Republicans could not reshape the Court with new justices, they were forced to write the Fourteenth Amendment to overcome President Johnson's resistance.[3]

In assessing the debate on this central constitutional text, this chapter shows how its drafters looked to the precedents of Chief Justice Marshall—*M'Culloch* and *Worcester*—for guidance. This is a somewhat unconventional approach to an amendment that focused on racial justice.[4] Nevertheless, there is a strong continuity between the birth of the abolitionist generation in the fight between Jackson and the Whigs, the development of their ideas in response, and the revival of those reference points during Reconstruction. Accordingly, looking to these facets of the Fourteenth Amendment not only brings the story of Jacksonian Democracy full circle but also reveals some "missing links" in interpreting its fundamental guarantees.

THE LAST JACKSONIAN

After struggling in vain since Lincoln's election, the previous generation was handed a golden opportunity for redemption by the rise of one of its own to the White House. Central casting could not have come up with a more perfect representative of traditional ideals than Andrew Johnson. After all, Johnson was named after Jackson (his full name was Andrew Jackson Johnson), spent his political life representing Jackson's home state of Tennessee, and considered Jackson his hero.[5] Like Jackson, Johnson was a states' rights supporter but opposed secession. In fact, he was the only southern senator who stayed loyal to the Union during the Civil War.[6] Like Jackson, Johnson was committed to white supremacy and fought to preserve executive power against Congress.[7] As Johnson's lawyer said during his Senate impeachment trial: "Who is the President of the United States? A democrat of the straightest of strict constructionists; an old Jacksonian."[8]

The leaders of the rising generation also saw Johnson as the standard bearer for the prior constitutional regime. James G. Blaine, a Republican member of Congress at the time, described his colleagues' view "that one of [Johnson's] especial weaknesses was an ambition to be considered as firm and heroic in

President Andrew Johnson,
the leader of the conservative
resistance. Photograph by Jesse
Harrison Whitehurst. Library of
Congress.

his Administration as General Jackson had proved in the Executive chair thirty years before."[9] One Republican even mocked the president by reciting a poem that made the same point:

> Where Jackson stood now doth another stand—
> The favored ruler of our favored land.
> With heart as pure and patriotism as great,
> A second Andrew steers the ship of state. . . .
> Entwined in laurel wreaths two names shall be
> Together joined as champions of the free—
> The name of Andrew Jackson men shall find
> With that of Andrew Johnson closely twined.[10]

The circumstances behind Johnson's impeachment also reinforced the idea that he and Jackson were "closely twined." In the 1830s, the president's dismissal of a Treasury secretary who refused to carry out his Bank policy led to Jackson's censure. In the 1860s, the president's dismissal of a War secretary who refused to carry out his Reconstruction policy led to Johnson's impeachment.[11] These parallels between Jackson's and Johnson's behavior were often invoked during the impeachment trial.[12]

Given the other similarities between the rise of the Jacksonian and abolitionist generations, the bond between the two Andrews is not surprising. Just as the only difference between *Worcester* and *Dred Scott* is their connection with modern values, the only reason why Jackson is on the twenty-dollar bill and Johnson is seen as one of our worst presidents is a difference in constitutional time.[13] Voters saw states' rights and ethnic exclusion as a solution to the problems of the 1830s, but these same policies were not the cure for the ills of the 1860s.[14] Yet Johnson was not willing to give up his lifelong beliefs without a fight. Like his illustrious predecessor, the president appealed to the people for support against his foes in Congress.

THE CYCLE OF ESCALATION REKINDLED

The comparison between Jackson's censure and Johnson's impeachment points up a broader theme that links these events, which is that both were unorthodox measures brought on by a generational turnover. Republicans hoped that the president would back their approach to Reconstruction, but Johnson was unwilling to go beyond the abolition of slavery. And when Congress passed a Civil Rights Act in 1866 to guarantee the freedmen their basic liberties, he answered with a veto. The president sounded the well-worn theme of the dangers of broad federal authority, observing that the bill represented "an absorption and assumption of power by the General Government which, if acquiesced in, must sap and destroy our federative system of limited powers and break down the barriers which preserve the rights of the States."[15] Moreover, he inveighed against the racial implications of the act, arguing that the "distinction of race and color is by the bill made to operate in favor of the colored and against the white race."[16] In general, Johnson took a dim view of African American citizenship reminiscent of *Dred Scott*, asking whether the freedmen "possess the requisite qualifications to entitle them to all the privileges and immunities of citizens."[17]

The defection of President Johnson left the abolitionist generation with a quandary not unlike the one that faced the Whigs when Tyler replaced Harrison. One critical difference, though, was that Republicans (barely) held a two-thirds majority in Congress and were therefore able to override Johnson's veto of the Civil Rights Act and overcome his resistance.[18] Of course, the only reason that they had such a supermajority, as Johnson stressed in his veto, was that Congress was excluding the South's representatives while Reconstruction proceeded.[19] This fragile state of affairs was threatened by the coming midterm elections, particularly since the president was now publicly denouncing the new generation's transformative ambitions. More important, his resistance meant that reformers could not depend on the support of the Supreme Court, since Congress could not compel the president to appoint justices friendly to the military occupation of the South.

In response to this acute dilemma, the Republicans passed the Fourteenth Amendment to secure their constitutional mandate and frame the campaign against the Democrats. Unlike their Jacksonian forebears, the new generation did not have the luxury of choosing between writing an amendment and filling the courts with supporters. Their decision might look like the conventional choice, but that was not how it appeared to President Johnson. In true Jacksonian fashion, he urged the electorate to reject the Fourteenth Amendment in a Protest delivered to Congress.[20] His concern was "whether any amendment to the Constitution ought to be proposed by Congress and pressed upon the Legislatures of the several States for final decision until after the admission of such loyal Senators and Representatives of the now unrepresented States."[21]

As a result, the Fourteenth Amendment embodied the division between the generations on substantive and procedural grounds. The Jacksonian establishment, led by President Johnson, held that the end of slavery did not require a broader reconsideration of federalism and white supremacy. Part of that solicitude for states' rights was demonstrated by the president's insistence that a constitutional amendment could not be passed by Congress unless all of the states were represented. Republicans, on the other hand, combined their nationalistic views on the scope of federal power and the Bill of Rights with a shift in emphasis to national institutions in the amendment process.[22]

In sum, Lincoln's death shifted Reconstruction's center of gravity from judicial opinions to the Fourteenth Amendment, just as the passing of President Harrison redirected the meaning of Jacksonian Democracy from judicial opinions to presidential vetoes.[23] Yet the substance of each generation's agenda did not change. Republicans now stood ready to draw on their long experience in Jackson's shadow.

THE MEANING OF THE FOURTEENTH AMENDMENT

The legitimacy of proposing a constitutional revision without the southern states was a primary concern during this intergenerational struggle, but modern lawyers are more interested in the ends that the Fourteenth Amendment was designed to achieve. Drafted primarily by Congressman John Bingham, Section One of that amendment reads as follows:

> All persons born or naturalized in the United States, and subject to the jurisdiction thereof, are citizens of the United States and of the State wherein they reside. No State shall make or enforce any law which shall abridge the privileges or immunities of citizens of the United States; nor shall any State deprive any person of life, liberty, or property, without due process of law; nor deny to any person within its jurisdiction the equal protection of the laws.[24]

[handwritten margin note: Makes ay born/nat. ind. citizens + States can't infringe on ruct]

Two purposes of this language are relatively clear. First, the text was intended to overrule the preemptive opinion in *Dred Scott* by making all African Americans citizens. Next, Section One protected the basic rights of all citizens from infringement by the states, including the protections of the Civil Rights Act and the Bill of Rights.[25] In these respects, the Fourteenth Amendment tracked the objectives of the abolitionist movement since the 1830s.

Another goal of the amendment was the restoration of Marshall's discarded landmarks, and the most obvious example was *M'Culloch*. Section Five of the text stated that "the Congress shall have power to enforce, by appropriate legislation, the provisions of this article."[26] Scholars and judges agree that this formula, which was repeated in the Thirteenth and Fifteenth Amendments, was intended to incorporate Chief Justice Marshall's construction of the Necessary and Proper Clause into the new constitutional text.[27] Indeed, an 1866 circuit court case upholding the Civil Rights Act as appropriate legislation under the Thirteenth Amendment explained that "in McCullough v. Maryland, Chief Justice Marshall used the phrase 'appropriate' as the equivalent and exponent of 'necessary and proper.'"[28] This embrace of *M'Culloch* was consistent with the new generation's generous view of federal authority and disdain for the Jacksonian philosophy of states' rights.[29]

What is often overlooked, however, is that the Republicans were just as determined to salvage *Worcester* and use it as a source of guidance for the Fourteenth Amendment. This insight emerges more clearly once the cyclical nature of constitutional law is given its proper recognition. The influence of *Worcester* on the Framers of the Fourteenth Amendment is significant because it sheds new light on the meaning of phrases like "due process" and "equal protection" that are at the heart of contemporary legal discourse. Accordingly, the evidence surrounding this issue must be examined with care.

The Expansion of Native American Rights

The link between African American freedom and Native American freedom continued to inspire abolitionist thought during the 1860s.[30] In 1864, Senator Charles Sumner issued a report on "a bill to secure equality before the law" that would guarantee the right of all citizens to testify in federal court.[31] At the time, state law governed federal testimonial rights, and many states barred nonwhites from providing evidence in cases involving whites. Sumner stressed in his report on the bill that these discriminatory policies acted against African Americans and Native Americans.[32] Writing in support of Sumner's proposal, the chief justice of the Maine Supreme Court asked, "If the black man or the Indian is to have his rights as against the white man, is he not entitled to the same witnesses against the white man which the latter has against the former?"[33] Otherwise, "a white man may commit any and all conceivable outrages upon the persons and property of the negro and Indian . . . with entire impunity."[34] What is eye-opening about this statement is that it is virtually identical to the criticism made by Senator Frelinghuysen against Georgia's exclusion of Cherokee testimony in the 1830s, which helped inspired the growth of abolitionism in the first place.[35]

As Reconstruction got under way, the new generation expressed strong support for tribal rights. As the *National Anti-Slavery Standard* explained, one of the "good results of the abolition of chattel slavery, and of the increasing recognition of the equal rights of the victims of that iniquitous system, [is] that a more just policy is now sought and recommended in relation to the Indians."[36] Elaborating on this theme, members filled the *Congressional Globe* with statements that wrapped Native American and African American rights together.[37] For example, one said that "the Indian is a man, and he is entitled to protection, and I never will consent to legislate on any other theory than that."[38] Another commented that the Republicans rejected the doctrine that the Declaration of Independence "was applicable alone to white men, and not to the black man, the red man, or any other than the white man."[39]

The more telling point is that Congress and the states backed these words with vigorous action. For instance, while Massachusetts was busy removing disabilities from African Americans, it was simultaneously declaring all Native Americans "citizens of the Commonwealth . . . entitled to all the rights, privileges and immunities of citizenship."[40] And at the same time that the Committee on Reconstruction was investigating the conditions of African Americans and proposing the Fourteenth Amendment, a similar Committee on the Indian Tribes was looking into their appalling treatment and proposing sweeping reforms.[41] The rampant corruption in the Indian Bureau exposed by this committee led Congress to enact legislation that barred government agents with commercial interests from negotiating treaties with the Tribes and required tribal agreements to be approved by the House of Representatives.[42] President Ulysses S. Grant would remove these corrupt bureaucrats and—in a move that directly evoked the civilization policy that Jackson overthrew—replace them with missionaries.[43] With the prior generation's policies now in retreat, Congress renewed appropriations to these groups in a move that one scholar calls "the most extensive state and church interlocking at the federal level in the nation's history."[44]

Critics of this sunny view of tribesmen and freedmen marching together toward freedom might note that the Fourteenth Amendment did not treat both groups alike on the question of citizenship. Section One says that only persons "subject to the jurisdiction" of the United States are citizens, and this phrase was intended to exclude Tribes that maintained their independence from the United States.[45] Senator Lyman Trumbull, the chairman of the Judiciary Committee, told his colleagues that "of course we cannot declare the wild Indians who do not recognize the Government of the United States at all . . . to be the subjects of the United States in the sense of being citizens. They must be excepted."[46] On the other hand, Republicans stressed that Native Americans who did not belong to a tribe were now all citizens and had the same rights as everyone else. When the Senate rejected an effort by radical Republicans to make all tribesmen citizens, it led to this revealing exchange:

MR. HENDERSON: One word in reply. It used to be supposed that this Government was made exclusively for the white man, and it was so decided. We are deciding to-day that it was made for the white man and the black man, but that the red man shall have no interest in it.
MR. TRUMBULL: We are not deciding any such thing.[47]

It is easy to minimize the importance of this extension of citizenship, but Justice John Marshall Harlan later said this was "the first general enactment making persons of the Indian race citizens of the United States."[48] Democrats hoping to defeat the Fourteenth Amendment agreed, with one senator telling his constituents that "this section will confer citizenship on the negroes and the Indians. . . . Senator Doolittle's amendment to exclude Indians from its operation was rejected. . . . Are we prepared to go so far, and to bring the negroes and Indians into political association with ourselves?"[49]

More important, members of Congress held that a distinction between African Americans and Native Americans was required by *Worcester*. To the extent that the Tribes held treaty rights that exceeded the rights of citizens, the imposition of citizenship would be a violation of those treaties.[50] Likewise, "an act of Congress which should assume to treat the members of a tribe as subject to the municipal jurisdiction of the United States would be unconstitutional" under *Worcester* because the Tribes were sovereign.[51] Indeed, a reasonable reading of *Worcester* was that it mandated special treatment for the Tribes that was inconsistent with citizenship. This point is worth stressing because it shows that, notwithstanding the influence that the Cherokee Removal had on Reconstruction, John Marshall's opinion and John Bingham's amendment are not alike in all respects. The Reconstruction Framers reconciled this intergenerational tension by holding that the Tribes were not entitled to citizenship.[52] Thus, the distinction drawn by the Fourteenth Amendment on this issue does not undermine the connection drawn in this era between African American and Native American liberty.

The Cherokee Removal in Congress

The respect accorded to *Worcester* in the text of the Fourteenth Amendment reflected a broader awareness of the Cherokee Removal in Congress. As one congressman said, "Every student of American history must remember the excitement which this treaty [of New Echota] produced throughout the country and the influence it exerted upon our national politics."[53] Another noted that "there are men here who can certainly recollect twenty-five or thirty years ago when the whole country rang with moral indignation against the treatment of those Indians by citizens of Georgia."[54] When Thaddeus Stevens took a brief break from the debate on the Civil Rights Act of 1866, he reminded his colleagues about this injustice and its implications:

> I remember, sir, when a law was passed by the State of Georgia extending the jurisdiction of that State over the Indian lands within the State. . . . In a short time, under those State laws, a system of persecution was carried on against those Indians. . . . [The first] case was carried to the Supreme Court of the United States, and when that tribunal was about to reverse the decree of the State court, the [petitioner] was hanged, and that ended the case. That is the manner in which the Indians are treated whenever they are put out of the protection of the United States, and placed under the control of the State laws. I trust that we shall never disgrace the national legislation by any act which will give the sanction of law to such an outrage as I have cited.[55]

Although Stevens made this point in a discussion about tribal rights, his statement shows that he was well aware of the Cherokee litigation and its role as a negative precedent for future actions.

These statements about the Removal were not specifically focused on the Fourteenth Amendment, but there were many others that were. First, *Worcester* was discussed during the debate on the Civil Rights Act, which was the direct antecedent to Section One.[56] Later in that same debate, Senator Trumbull relied on a provision of the "Treaty" of New Echota that gave some Cherokees citizenship as proof that Congress could make African Americans citizens without a constitutional amendment.[57] A more explicit example of the impact of the Removal on the amendment came during debate on legislation to enforce the guarantees of Section One. Congressman George Hoar of Massachusetts observed that "the principal danger that menaces us to-day is from the effort within the States to deprive considerable numbers of persons of the civil and equal rights which the General Government is endeavoring to secure to them."[58] He then made this illuminating comparison:

> The history of the Indian tribes within our jurisdiction is an instructive lesson. It is a history of violence, injustice, [and] rapine, committed often under the direct authority of the States. Whatever resistance, feeble and impotent as it has been, has been made to all this has been by the United States. In the famous case of the Georgia Indians, the judiciary of the nation went to the extreme of its power in protecting the rights of the weak and defenseless.[59]

This characterization of *Worcester* as a civil rights case reinforces the point made earlier about why abolitionists clutched it to their breast even though the opinion had nothing to do with slavery. Chief Justice Marshall's ruling was the best authority available for their values, in part because it was spawned by intense opposition to the contrary views of Jacksonian Democracy.

John Bingham: The Author Speaks

The strongest evidence of the connection between the Cherokee Removal and the Fourteenth Amendment comes from the leading drafter of Section One— John Bingham. He was last heard arguing that *Worcester* and *Dred Scott* were linked by their contrasting views on equality. In 1871, Bingham went to the well of the House and made his most comprehensive remarks on what Section One was intended to accomplish. After explaining that one key object of the text was

Congressman John Bingham, the author of Section One of the Fourteenth Amendment. Artist unknown. Library of Congress.

the application of the Bill of Rights to the states,[60] he used *Worcester* as a prime example of what he was worried about: "Under the Constitution as it is, not as it was, and by force of the fourteenth amendment, no State hereafter can . . . ever repeat the example of Georgia and send men to the penitentiary, as did that State, for teaching the Indian to read the lessons of the New Testament."[61]

Just as Bingham once used *Worcester* as a touchstone for equality, he now used the case to illuminate the scope of basic liberties. Bingham also made the same point to his constituents in a series of addresses during the 1866 campaign. In one stump speech, he appealed to the voters for support against the president: "If you rally at the fall . . . depend upon it that every State South will rally to the lead of Tennessee, and ratify the Amendment. Is not that worth striving for? Then hereafter, in Georgia, men shall not be imprisoned, as in the past, for teaching the lowly to read in the New Testament of another and a better life."[62] It is notable that, in his public comments on Section One, the abuse of the Georgia missionaries was the only example that Bingham always used to explain why we desperately needed the Fourteenth Amendment.

Though this book has thus far avoided the temptation to discuss current controversies, Bingham's comments do undermine the Supreme Court's holding in *Employment Division v. Smith* that a neutral law does not violate free exercise even if it imposes a significant burden on religious practice.[63] This was the same argument that Georgia made in the 1830s to explain why its oath law was not a violation of religious freedom. That argument, though, was rejected by Bingham just as it was rejected by religious activists at the time.[64] His point also came in a specific discussion on the Fourteenth Amendment's purpose, which is the text through which the Free Exercise Clause was extended to the states.[65] Thus, the only broad public discussion of this constitutional question cuts against the decision in *Smith*.[66] Yet nobody has ever discussed either the debate about the missionaries' imprisonment or Bingham's response when considering that case.[67]

That oversight is not surprising, because unless one takes a generational approach to constitutional law, the relevance of the Cherokee Removal (or the 1830s for that matter) is far from obvious. When that perspective is adopted, though, a new dimension of the Fourteenth Amendment comes into view. The text expressing the values of the Reconstruction generation was shaped by the lessons its members learned by dint of their experience with Jacksonian Democracy. And part of that crucible was the Cherokee Removal and the repudiation of *Worcester*. In framing their intergenerational contest with Andrew Johnson, reformers drew upon that legacy and thereby pulled Native Americans into the heart of Fourteenth Amendment analysis.

THE FINAL RESTORATION AND THE NEXT RENEWAL OF THE CYCLE

President Johnson's resistance to reform and the abolitionist generation's escalation by creating a new constitutional text set the terms for the midterm elections in 1866. Despite Johnson's unprecedented personal campaign for Democratic candidates around the country, the Republicans won the decisive victory that eluded the Whigs in 1842.[68] Increasing their already-healthy majorities, reformers could now override presidential vetoes at will. And when Johnson later tried to use his prerogatives as commander in chief to prevent the southern states from ratifying the Fourteenth Amendment, Congress retaliated by playing its ultimate trump card—impeachment.[69] The president was acquitted by the Senate, but his survival was assured only when he pledged to halt his active resistance to the new generation's agenda.[70] Following this surrender by the old guard, the amendment was ratified and Republicans corrected the anomaly created by John Wilkes Booth with the election of one of their own, Ulysses S. Grant, as president. A new period of consensus under Republican rule began that was every bit as stable as the prior generation under Democratic rule.

Though the articulation of this new regime's principles would evolve over the next few decades, the most immediate impact was the restoration of *Worcester*

Chief Justice Salmon P. Chase, the new pillar of the legal establishment. Artist unknown. Library of Congress.

and *M'Culloch* as sound law. In 1835, the Jacksonians consolidated their rejection of *Worcester* through what amounted to a joint declaration by the Senate—in the "Treaty" of New Echota—and by the Tennessee Supreme Court that the decision was no longer valid. In 1870, the Senate took the lead in altering *Worcester*'s status on behalf of the abolitionist generation. Issuing a report on the relationship between the Tribes and the Fourteenth Amendment, the Senate Judiciary Committee showered praise on the "prose of the 'greatest of our Chief Justices'" and said that his ruling was something "no man acknowledging the authority of reason can gainsay."[71] The conclusion of this analysis was that *Worcester* was "the unquestioned law of the court to-day."[72] Since the case was never overruled or even criticized by the Taney Court, this statement seems innocuous. But given the history that this book lays out, this quote is astonishing. The key to the Judiciary Committee report was that it ignored any intervening Jacksonian cases, such as *Rogers*, as if they did not exist.[73] A new constitutional generation was smoothing over the clash between the Marshall Court and Jacksonian Democracy to suit its own interests. There is a wonderful irony in this strategy, of course, because willful ignorance was the same stance that the Taney Court took toward Marshall's landmarks as part of that generation's formula for success.[74]

At the same time that the Senate was raising *Worcester* from the dead, the Court was performing the same ritual on *M'Culloch*. In *Hepburn v. Griswold*, a case decided in 1870, Chief Justice Salmon P. Chase addressed the question of whether the implied power of Congress included the imposition of paper money upon unwilling citizens.[75] As the starting point for his analysis, Chase wrote that "the rule for determining whether a legislative enactment can be supported as an exercise of an implied power was stated by Chief Justice Marshall, speaking for the whole court, in the case of McCullough v. The State of Maryland."[76] Moreover, "the statement then made has ever since been accepted as a correct exposition of the Constitution," and this "must be taken then as finally settled, so far as judicial decisions can settle anything."[77]

Once again, from a conventional legal perspective this states a truism, because *M'Culloch*, like *Worcester*, was not challenged by the Taney Court. From this book's perspective, however, Chase's statements read like an extraordinarily artful act of construction that masks a major turning point.[78] A hint of the sleight of hand at work appears when he says that the *M'Culloch* test "is finally settled, so far as judicial decisions can settle anything."[79] "Finally settled" implies that the issue was once in doubt. Likewise, the Court's emphasis on the ability of judicial decisions to settle these issues looks like a sly reference to the political forces that buried and then revived *M'Culloch* in successive generations.[80]

With these twin acts by the Senate and the Supreme Court, the abolitionist generation reached the mountaintop. While this movement was busy implementing its legal principles, a tiny group of agrarian activists was growing restless. The currency issue decided in *Hepburn* would become the main concern for those who were troubled by a decline of the rural values that Jefferson and Jackson celebrated. These radicals formed the core of the Populist generation, led by William Jennings Bryan and his demand that "you shall not crucify mankind upon a cross of gold," which challenged the Republican establishment in the 1890s.[81] That contest is a compelling story, but one that would take another book.

Conclusion:
In Search of the
Missing Constitution

There is a mysterious cycle in human events. To some
generations much is given. Of other generations much
is expected. This generation of Americans has a ren-
dezvous with destiny.

Franklin D. Roosevelt's acceptance speech
at the 1936 Democratic National Convention

This book has focused on one turn of the constitu-
tional cycle. The Jacksonian era contained some of the most vivid illustrations
of the themes that shape the evolution of the law in every generation. For all
that Jacksonian Democracy contributed, however, this period gets less attention
than any other successful constitutional movement. We pay a price for that ignorance. In *Smith*, the Supreme Court would have learned a great deal about the
free exercise of religion issue by focusing on the link between the transition of
the 1830s and the drafting of the Fourteenth Amendment. And this is just the
start of what a generational model can tell us about modern legal problems.

One powerful lesson that emerges from applying this approach is that the
meaning of the Fourteenth Amendment cannot be fully grasped without considering the role of Native Americans. The Framers of that text formed their
ideas in reaction to the Cherokee Removal and maintained that African American and tribal rights were intimately linked. Just as their liberties rose together
during Reconstruction, they fell together in later decades. Yet the connection
between these groups was severed during the twentieth century. The cruel discrimination against African Americans became a central part of constitutional
lore, but tribal doctrine was soon reduced to "a tiny backwater of law inhabited
by impenetrably complex and dull issues."[1] This split was the product of many
forces, but the result is that civil rights lawyers do not pay much attention to this
important aspect of antidiscrimination law.

126

This omission from our past is most unfortunate because it diminishes the meaning of constitutional equality in ways that even this author cannot fully appreciate. For example, there are many great cases that cried out for a comparison with the abuses of the Cherokee Removal, most notably the internal exile of Japanese Americans during World War Two.[2] Likewise, recent scholarship suggests that the future of equal protection analysis lies in evaluating how far demands for assimilation can go when minorities seek to express their distinct cultural values.[3] If this assessment is correct and cultural choices become the new legal frontier, then Native Americans will become the critical source of useful analogies. After all, the history of the Tribes is largely a story about their efforts to preserve their distinctiveness in the face of pressure to conform to Western practices.[4] Far from being a dull backwater, Native American law should be on the cutting edge for antidiscrimination advocates.[5]

The interpretive resources revealed by holding the Jacksonian years to the light is part of a larger theme about the value of paying attention to every legal generation, not just the ones that produce new constitutional text. Our failure to do so is understandable. Text is easily accessible, but changes in practices or institutions are harder to detect. Nevertheless, the siren song of text creates legal distortions by encouraging judges and scholars to cram meaning into that text that was never there instead of attributing changes to their true source in the unwritten customs of a subsequent generation.[6] Furthermore, blindness to the creativity of nontextual generations sometimes masks the meaning that is in the text by cutting off our ability to understand the experiences that influenced its authors. Finally, the examination throughout this book indicates that the creation of text is usually a product of chance rather than deliberation. Legal generations follow the path of least resistance in their race for power, and thus the form of any change they initiate is dictated more by fate (i.e., the balance of political forces or the sudden death of a leader) than by any abstract concern about the legitimacy of using unwritten customs rather than text.

Once these nontextual movements are incorporated into our constitutional narrative, the regular and predictable cycle proposed by this book moves from a hypothesis to a theory. During the 1890s, the Populist generation tried and failed to supplant Republican rule. This unsuccessful transition, not unlike the Whig failure of the 1840s, moved the law in a more conservative direction without any textual amendment. In the 1930s, New Deal Democrats overcame the bitter opposition of the Supreme Court and established a new order—again without a constitutional amendment. Move ahead to the 1960s, and we find a generation that left a rich legacy of civil rights grounded on statutes and cases rather than constitutional text. Finally, we arrive at the present generation, led to power by Ronald Reagan, which is still putting through significant doctrinal reforms without an amendment. In each of these creative periods, the constitutional cycle unfolded in a similar way, though of course that claim cannot be proved here.

In all of these generations, the wellspring of constitutional meaning was the electorate rather than judges. The assertion that citizens and the political branches play a role in determining what the Constitution requires is not novel. What may be surprising is that the vaunted stability of higher law rests on majority opinion instead of being threatened by it. Under the conventional account, "courts stand against any winds that blow as havens of refuge for those who might otherwise suffer because they are helpless, weak, outnumbered, or because they are non-conforming victims of prejudice and public excitement."[7] Although judges sometimes defend constitutional tenets against momentary passions, in most cases the voters are the ones defending precedent from revisionist politicians or judges.[8] During the reign of a particular generation, the first principles applied by all branches are sustained by the control of one political party based on some unique collective experience. If elected officials try to challenge that consensus, as the Whigs did in the 1840s, they are usually punished by the electorate for straying from settled law. By contrast, intense confrontations between the Supreme Court and majority opinion, which consume the attention of law professors and critics of judicial review, generally occur only during those brief interludes when one generation is supplanting another. In this sense, judges are less important than people think.

Nevertheless, the question of how the Constitution should be interpreted by courts stirs immense interest. The problem is that the text and precedents created by previous generations are always being construed by the current one. If contemporary values are contrary to these authorities, there is an inevitable temptation for judges to read the past selectively. Sometimes this must be done, but unless there are limits, constitutional government would crumble. Stare decisis, a principle everyone likes but nobody can define with precision, helps mediate this temporal dilemma. One insight about stare decisis that flows from the generational model is that cases on different subjects could be linked by their place in constitutional time. For instance, a set of Supreme Court opinions might share a theme of conservative resistance. This is relevant because it suggests that the viability of each decision in this group can be judged in relation to the others, which provides a new tool to ascertain whether certain precedents should be retained or overruled.[9] The next stage of this project will explore that thought, along with other interpretive puzzles, in depth.

I share the sentiment of Lincoln's First Inaugural when he said, "I am loath to close."[10] This book offered some fresh ideas about our constitutional past and tried to sketch out fruitful lines of research for others to pursue. That inquiry cannot begin soon enough, for in some nondescript place the band of rebels who will lead the next generation is already meeting and asking, "What if?"

Notes

Introduction

1. The Declaration of Independence, para. 2 (U.S. 1776).

2. See Richard Primus, *The American Language of Rights* (Cambridge, UK: Cambridge University Press, 1999) (exploring how rights emerge in response to concrete harms rather than from a philosophical framework).

3. See Gerard N. Magliocca, "Constitutional False Positives and the Populist Moment," *Notre Dame Law Review* 81 (2006): 821–88 (describing the effort of the Populist generation to reshape constitutional doctrine on economic matters).

4. Thomas Hart Benton, *An Examination of the Dred Scott Case* (New York: D. Appleton, 1857), 123.

5. For example, this was what shaped the jurisprudence of Justice Oliver Wendell Holmes, who is frequently mischaracterized as an Olympian figure. Biographers of Holmes have noted that the youthful idealism that led him to volunteer for the Union Army was shattered by multiple injuries in war. After that traumatic experience, he became a skeptic who saw the law as nothing more than a struggle for power. See Albert W. Alschuler, *Law without Values* (Chicago: University of Chicago Press, 2000), 41–51; see also Louis Menand, *The Metaphysical Club* (New York: Farrar, Straus and Giroux, 2001) (examining how the Civil War influenced a generation of intellectuals, including Holmes).

6. See, e.g., Norman Ryder, *The Cohort Approach: Essays in the Measurement of Temporal Variations in Demographic Behavior* (New York: Arno Press, 1980); and David B. Bernstein and Ilya Somin, "Judicial Power and Civil Rights Reconsidered," *Yale Law Journal* 114 (2001): 615 (noting that generational cohorts do not get enough attention in legal analysis). The most interesting analogy outside of politics comes from Thomas S. Kuhn, who describes how science develops in a cyclical rather than a linear fashion, with leaders like Newton or Einstein shattering the old paradigm and creating a new orthodoxy. See Thomas S. Kuhn, *The Structure of Scientific Revolutions* (Chicago: University of Chicago Press, 1996).

7. See Richard Hofstadter, *The Idea of a Party System* (Berkeley: University of California Press, 1969) (providing a fine treatment of the origins of the party system); and James L. Sundquist, *Dynamics of the Party System* (Washington, DC: Brookings Institution, 1983) (describing each of the electoral realignments from the Founding until the Reagan Revolution); cf. Stephen Skowronek, *The Politics Presidents Make*, rev. ed. (1993; repr., Cambridge: Harvard University Press, 1997) (describing this pattern in the context of the presidency).

8. To avoid any confusion, I am not saying that all people born at the same time think alike. Nor I am saying that the period in which people are born is the sole factor that shapes

their political identity. The point is that there are observable tendencies in society that can be useful in analyzing legal issues and tracing the course of constitutional development.

9. There are some constitutional scholars that make time a focus of their analysis. See Bruce Ackerman, *We the People: Foundations* (Cambridge: Harvard University Press, 1991), 94–99 (noting the distinction between lived experience and remote knowledge in judicial behavior); and Jed Rubenfeld, *Freedom and Time* (New Haven: Yale University Press, 2001), 101–44 (arguing that constitutional principles should be conceived in temporal terms). My analysis is different because it stresses how temporal factors create a regular and predictable pattern of legal development.

10. "Constitutional generation" is a term of art that refers to the bundle of substantive views and institutional arrangements that characterize a particular era (e.g., the Founding, Reconstruction, Jacksonian Democracy, etc.). The word "generation" is used to indicate the important role that time plays in creating and destroying these regimes that tracks the turnover of distinct generations in the population.

11. See Joseph A. Schumpeter, *Capitalism, Socialism, and Democracy* (New York: Harper and Row, 1976), 81–86.

12. This work joins a recent trend in the literature, which is often called "popular constitutionalism," that addresses the importance of constitutional law outside of the courts. See Larry D. Kramer, *The People Themselves: Popular Constitutionalism and Judicial Review* (New York: Oxford University Press, 2004); Mark V. Tushnet, *Taking the Constitution from the Courts* (Princeton: Princeton University Press, 1999); and Gary D. Rowe, "Constitutionalism in the Streets," *Southern California Law Review* 78 (2005): 401–56. For a criticism of the stronger form of this argument, see Larry Alexander and Lawrence B. Solum, "Popular? Constitutionalism?" *Harvard Law Review* 118 (2005): 1594–1640.

13. 17 U.S. (4 Wheat.) 316 (1819).

14. 31 U.S. (6 Pet.) 515 (1832).

15. 60 U.S. (19 How.) 393 (1857).

16. Nelson F. Adkins, ed., *Common Sense and Other Political Writings* (New York: Bobbs-Merrill, 1953), 51 (quoting Paine's landmark 1776 pamphlet *Common Sense*).

Chapter 1: The Rise of Jacksonian Democracy

1. 17 U.S. (4 Wheat.) 518 (1819); see R. Kent Newmyer, *John Marshall and the Heroic Age of the Supreme Court* (Baton Rouge: Louisiana State University Press, 2001), 244–53.

2. 17 U.S. (4 Wheat.) 122 (1819); see Arthur M. Schlesinger Jr., *The Age of Jackson* (Boston: Little, Brown, 1945), 31.

3. M'Culloch v. Maryland, 17 U.S. (4 Wheat.) 316 (1819).

4. See Richard S. Arnold, "How James Madison Interpreted the Constitution," *New York University Law Review* 72 (1997): 274.

5. James Madison, Veto Message (Jan. 30, 1815), in James D. Richardson, ed., *A Compilation of the Messages and Papers of the Presidents, 1789–1897*, 10 vols. (Washington, DC: Government Printing Office, 1899), 1:555.

6. See Carlton Jackson, *Presidential Vetoes* (Athens: University of Georgia Press, 1967), 11. The contrast between Madison's incremental approach and Jackson's bull-in-a-china-shop attitude is explored in chapter 4.

7. M'Culloch, 17 U.S. (4 Wheat.) at 404.

8. Ibid. at 408.

9. Ibid. at 411–23.

10. Ibid. at 415.

11. Ibid.

12. This pattern was repeated in the modern era by *Roe v. Wade*, which represented the peak of modern liberalism yet also served as an instrument of its downfall by driving social conservatives into the constitutional generation led by Ronald Reagan.

13. The relative ineffectiveness of Jeffersonian Democracy is a complex issue, but there are at least three factors that helped Marshall resist the tide of reform. First, Jeffersonians were unlucky in their attempt to pick people to challenge the chief justice. There were no vacancies on the Court from 1811 to 1823, which made it hard to use judicial appointments to change the law. Furthermore, Madison saw one of his nominees rejected in 1811 and ended up choosing Joseph Story, who became Marshall's right-hand man! Next, the War of 1812, like all wars, tended to exert a pull in the direction of a stronger national government. Seeing the White House and the Capitol burned to the ground by British troops was a traumatic event that shifted attitudes away from states' rights. Third, Jefferson's commitment to limited national government was more rhetorical than real. After all, he was the president who undertook the Louisiana Purchase, which John Quincy Adams described "as greater in itself and more comprehensive in its consequences than all the assumptions of implied powers in the years of the Washington and Adams administrations." Skowronek, *Politics*, 79. A few years later, Jefferson surpassed himself with the Embargo Act, a statute banning all exports to France and Britain, which was later cited as the broadest exercise of federal power in the antebellum era. See United States v. Marigold, 50 U.S. (9 How.) 560, 566-67 (1850).

14. A sample of Taylor's views on the great issues of the day can be found in John Taylor, *An Inquiry into the Principles and Policy of the Government of the United States* (Indianapolis: Bobbs-Merrill, 1969). On the question of federalism, Jacksonian Democracy was more like a revival of the Jeffersonian ideal than an innovation, as Jackson himself indicated in the Maysville Turnpike Veto discussed in chapter 2. The clash in the 1830s was between this vision and the views of Chief Justice Marshall, which represented the consensus of Jeffersonian Democracy as it evolved after the War of 1812.

15. See David McCullough, *1776* (New York: Simon and Schuster, 2005), 281; and Newmyer, *John Marshall*, 22. See also Sean Wilentz, *The Rise of American Democracy* (New York: W. W. Norton, 2005), 202 (noting that Monroe represented "the tag end of the Revolutionary generation").

16. See, e.g., Robert V. Remini, *Andrew Jackson: The Course of American Freedom, 1822–1832* (Baltimore: Johns Hopkins University Press, 1981), 15 (calling this the "Era of Corruption").

17. See, e.g., Ralph C. Catterall, *The Second Bank of the United States* (Chicago: University of Chicago Press, 1902), 31, 51-52; see also Carl B. Swisher, ed., "Roger B. Taney's 'Bank War Manuscript,'" *Maryland Historical Magazine* 53 (1958): 115 (explaining that the Bank's "most dangerous and formidable power when it entered the political arena, was the corrupt and corrupting influence it had acquired over the press").

18. See Newmyer, *John Marshall*, 294; Remini, *Jackson: The Course of American Freedom*, 27.

19. For a stimulating essay on how people behave in these speculative times, see Charles Mackay, *Extraordinary Popular Delusions and the Madness of Crowds* (London: Richard Bentley, 1841), reprinted with preface by Bernard M. Baruch (New York: L. C. Page, 1932), 1-97.

20. See Remini, *Jackson: The Course of American Freedom*, 27; cf. Newmyer, *John Marshall*, 333 (observing that for states' rights activists the "Bank of the United States under the mismanagement of William Jones was a gift from on high").

21. See Theodore W. Ruger, "'A Question Which Convulses a Nation': The Early Republic's Greatest Debate about the Judicial Review Power," *Harvard Law Review* 117 (2004): 826-97.

22. See Donald B. Cole, *A Jackson Man: Amos Kendall and the Rise of American Democracy* (Baton Rouge: Louisiana State University Press, 2004), 165-71.

23. Ibid., 69.

24. This "Era of Corruption" is well documented in Remini, *Jackson: The Course of American Freedom*, 11–25.

25. Perhaps a better metaphor is a lighted taper, since the chief justice explained that it would be a waste of time to explain why Maryland's view of the Necessary and Proper Clause was wrong, akin to holding "a lighted taper to the sun." See *M'Culloch*, 17 U.S. (4 Wheat.) at 419.

26. See Cole, *Amos Kendall*, 70 (describing a Kentucky law imposing a $60,000 tax on the Bank's local offices); and Newmyer, *John Marshall*, 299 (recounting a similar Ohio law that levied a $50,000 tax); see also Bank of the United States v. Planters' Bank of Georgia, 22 U.S. (9 Wheat.) 904 (1824) (rejecting Georgia's effort to tax the Bank in a case consolidated with *Osborn v. Bank of the United States*).

27. See Newmyer, *John Marshall*, 300.

28. See Osborn v. Bank of the United States, 22 U.S. (9 Wheat.) 735, 860 (1824).

29. A recent Jackson biography that explores his military career is H. W. Brands, *Andrew Jackson* (New York: Doubleday, 2005).

30. John Spencer Bassett, ed., *The Correspondence of Andrew Jackson*, 7 vols. (Washington DC: Carnegie Institute, 1926–35), 3:164 (quoting a letter from Jackson to Calhoun on June 28, 1822).

31. Needless to say, the "spoils system" of rotation in office only created a different corruption problem of unqualified people getting jobs as a reward for partisan service.

32. See Schlesinger, *Age of Jackson*, 330–33.

33. See Steven P. Croly, "The Majoritarian Difficulty: Elective Judiciaries and the Rule of Law," *University of Chicago Law Review* 62 (1995): 716–17.

34. Jacob E. Cooke, ed., *The Federalist* (Hanover, NH: Wesleyan University Press, 1961), 64. To be fair, Madison's Federalist #10 did not get much attention in the nineteenth century, thus it is a little anachronistic to emphasize the distinction between Jackson's attitude and Madison's. See Akhil Reed Amar, *America's Constitution: A Biography* (New York: Random House, 2005), 43.

35. Schlesinger, *Age of Jackson*, 29; see Remini, *Jackson: The Course of American Freedom*, 33.

36. Joel H. Silbey, ed., *The American Party Battle: Election Campaign Pamphlets, 1828–1876*, 2 vols. (Cambridge: Harvard University Press, 1999), 1:16 (italics in original).

37. Thomas Hart Benton, *Thirty Years' View*, 2 vols. (New York: D. Appleton, 1859), 1:225.

38. The chaotic backdrop to the Framers' deliberations is set out in Gordon S. Wood, *The Creation of the American Republic, 1776–1787* (Chapel Hill: University of North Carolina Press, 1969), 393–425.

39. Federalism is not the only legal principle that follows this pattern. See, e.g., Akhil Reed Amar, *The Bill of Rights* (New Haven: Yale University Press, 1998) (explaining how the Founding and Reconstruction generations gave different readings to the Bill of Rights based on their unique experiences). Constitutional theory itself is usually nothing more than a reaction to recent events. See John Hart Ely, *Democracy and Distrust* (Cambridge: Harvard University Press, 1980), 73 (using the Warren Court's cases as the basis for a general theory); and Herbert Wechsler, "Toward Neutral Principles of Constitutional Law," *Harvard Law Review* 73 (1959): 31–35 (articulating a general approach in response to *Brown v. Board of Education*); see generally Charles Austin Beard, *An Economic Interpretation of the Constitution of the United States* (New York: Macmillan, 1913) (redirecting the author's frustration with *Lochner v. New York* by claiming that the Framers were principally concerned with protecting property).

40. See, e.g., Eric Foner, *The Story of American Freedom* (New York: W. W. Norton, 1998), 71.

41. Robert V. Remini, Jackson's most distinguished modern biographer, argues that it was Jefferson who transformed Native American policy and set the stage for the Trail of Tears. See Robert V. Remini, *Andrew Jackson and His Indian Wars* (New York: Viking, 2001), 115–16. It is

true that Jefferson suggested the removal of the Tribes to the West, and some small-scale and voluntary removals were negotiated after that. Nevertheless, this was much different from Jackson's large, involuntary, and brutal removal of the Cherokees. See Joseph C. Burke, "The Cherokee Cases: A Study in Law, Politics, and Morality," *Stanford Law Review* 21 (1969): 504: "A vital difference remained between [prior presidents'] policy and that of Jackson. While Monroe and Adams had urged removal by every kind of inducement, officially, they continued to treat the tribes as more or less sovereign nations and to respect their right to remain on the treaty lands."

42. See U.S. Const., art. I, § 8, cl. 3.

43. See, e.g., William G. McLoughlin, *Cherokees and Missionaries, 1789–1839* (Norman: University of Oklahoma Press, 1984), 33–34.

44. See Rogers M. Smith, *Civic Ideals: Conflicting Visions of Citizenship in U.S. History* (New Haven: Yale University Press, 1997), 145; Anthony F. C. Wallace, *Jefferson and the Indians: The Tragic Fate of the First Americans* (Cambridge: Harvard University Press, 1999), 169–70.

45. See Wallace, *Tragic Fate*, 170.

46. Tim Alan Garrison, *The Legal Ideology of Removal* (Athens: University of Georgia Press, 2002), 17 (quoting a letter from Knox to George Washington). The point is that Native Americans retained sovereign rights only as a group. Once a tribe dissolved or an individual left a tribe, those people were subject to state law—often, as we shall see, with a status lower than whites.

47. Wallace, *Tragic Fate*, 168.

48. Ibid.

49. See McLoughlin, *Cherokees*, 106.

50. See Francis Paul Prucha, *The Great Father: The United States Government and the American Indians*, 2 vols. (Lincoln: University of Nebraska Press, 1984), 1:151–52. Most federal aid for the missionaries did not come until after the War of 1812, although Knox recognized the need for this support from the beginning. See McLoughlin, *Cherokees*, 33–34.

51. See Remini, *Jackson: The Course of American Freedom*, 265.

52. McLoughlin, *Cherokees*, 3.

53. Garrison, *Legal Ideology*, 22.

54. See Remini, *Jackson: The Course of American Freedom*, 83.

55. Merrill D. Peterson, *The Great Triumvirate: Webster, Clay, and Calhoun* (New York: Oxford University Press, 1987), 130.

56. See Skowronek, *Politics*, 89. Skowronek's work is an elegant description of the cyclical nature of political change that should be read by any serious student of American government.

57. One of the major contributions of Jacksonian Democracy to constitutional politics was the permanent establishment of a two-party system. This development is covered in several fine books, particularly Hofstadter, *Party System*.

58. The most notable example is the Censure Resolution discussed in chapter 5, but other instances of "creative" thinking will pop up throughout this book.

59. This is a theme that cuts across constitutional time, though I can only provide a taste of how this played out in other eras. In the 1790s, the Federalists feared that the Jeffersonians would launch a purge akin to the French Revolution. See Ron Chernow, *Alexander Hamilton* (New York: Penguin, 2004), 609–10; and David McCullough, *John Adams* (New York: Simon and Schuster, 2001), 543. In the 1890s, even progressives such as Theodore Roosevelt said the Populists would usher in "a red government of lawlessness and dishonesty as phantastic [sic] and vicious as the Paris Commune itself." Sundquist, *Dynamics*, 156. (Apparently, France was always the bogeyman for conservatives.) And chapter 8 details the panic that gripped Democrats when they confronted the Republican Party.

60. This dynamic is best captured by the concept of mutual transformation in war. See Carl von Clausewitz, *On War* (Princeton: Princeton University Press, 1984), 75–77; see also

Garry Wills, *Certain Trumpets: The Call of Leaders* (New York: Simon and Schuster, 1994), 86 (calling mutual transformation the idea that "each side is increasingly enraged by the other's efforts to meet violence with greater violence"). Others have drawn comparisons between war and constitutional politics. See Richard A. Posner, *An Affair of State* (Cambridge: Harvard University Press, 1999), 249–58 (using Clausewitz to explain the Clinton impeachment saga).

61. Remini, *Jackson: The Course of American Freedom*, 91.

62. Ibid., 129 (quoting a letter from Jackson to John Branch dated June 24, 1828).

63. See Donald B. Cole, *The Presidency of Andrew Jackson* (Lawrence: University Press of Kansas, 1993), 18. The text passes over the details of the 1828 campaign because the constitutional issues were more clearly framed in the 1830s.

64. Remini, *Jackson: The Course of American Freedom*, 147.

65. Carl B. Swisher, *The Taney Period, 1836–64*, vol. 5 of *History of the Supreme Court of the United States* (New York: Macmillan, 1974), 4.

Chapter 2: Presidential Reconstruction

1. This is one of the insights from Bruce Ackerman's theory of "dualist democracy." See Ackerman, *We the People: Foundations*.

2. See Martin Van Buren, *The Autobiography of Martin Van Buren*, ed. John Clement Fitzpatrick (New York: Da Capo Press, 1973), 289 (explaining that many Democrats in Congress were not "well instructed or very deeply imbued in the principles of the party they had joined"). When the new ideological movement takes over an existing party rather than forming a new one, this problem shows up as a split between people hewing to the old beliefs and the revolutionaries. Lincoln had to persuade former Whigs, FDR had to handle Southern Democrats, and Reagan had to bring along Rockefeller Republicans.

3. See Charles Warren, *The Supreme Court in United States History*, 2 vols. (Boston: Little, Brown, 1928), 1:738. In fact, Justice McLean, the president's first appointment, was a holdover from the Adams administration and evolved into a critic of Jacksonian principles. See Dred Scott v. Sandford, 60 U.S. (19 How.) 393, 542 (1857) (McLean, J., dissenting).

4. The Cherokee Nation was not the only Tribe removed from its homeland by the Jackson administration, but its plight was the one that captured national attention. For a description of the brutality inflicted on the Chickasaws, Choctaws, Creeks, and Seminoles, see Garrison, *Legal Ideology*, 2–3.

5. See Burke, "Cherokee Cases," 503; see also Worcester v. Georgia, 31 U.S. (6 Pet.) 515, 583 (1832) (McLean, J., concurring) (quoting the 1802 compact as stating "that the United States should, at their own expense, extinguish, for the use of Georgia, as early as the same can be peaceably obtained, on reasonable terms, the Indian title to lands within the state of Georgia").

6. See Prucha, *Great Father*, 1:145.

7. See McLoughlin, *Cherokees*, 102; and Mary Hershberger, "Mobilizing Women, Anticipating Abolition: The Struggle against Indian Removal in the 1830s," *Journal of American History* 86 (1999): 18.

8. McLoughlin, *Cherokees*, 143. Note that there was no recognition—even among officials friendly to the Tribes—that they should be allowed to keep their traditional culture and stay where they were. The distinction between the Knox and the Jackson approaches is probably best described as "benign" versus "malign" imperialism.

9. Ibid.

10. Ibid., 252.

11. See ibid., 240.

12. See Burke, "Cherokee Cases," 503.

13. *Worcester*, 31 U.S. (6 Pet.) at 525.

14. See ibid. at 521–22.

15. See ibid. at 524.

16. See McLoughlin, *Cherokees*, 246–47; and Letter of S. C. Stambaugh and Amos Kendall to the Secretary of War (Dec. 26, 1845), reprinted in S. Rep. 29-298, at 48–49 (1846) (laying out the background to the 1846 treaty between rival factions of the Cherokee Nation and the United States).

17. *Worcester*, 31 U.S. (6 Pet.) at 528.

18. See Letter of S. C. Stambaugh and Amos Kendall to the Secretary of War (Dec. 26, 1845), reprinted in S. Rep. 29-298, at 49–50 (1846).

19. *Worcester*, 31 U.S. (6 Pet.) at 522–23, 526–27.

20. Ibid. at 523. The oath went as follows: "I do solemnly swear [or affirm, as the case may be] that I will support and defend the constitution and laws of the state of Georgia, and uprightly demean myself as a citizen thereof, so help me God."

21. McLoughlin, *Cherokees*, 248–49.

22. In fact, the Georgia legislature waited until Jackson's election was assured before passing the first part of the Cherokee Codes. See Prucha, *Great Father*, 1:192.

23. See Remini, *Andrew Jackson and His Indian Wars*, 232; see also U.S. Const., art. IV, § 3: "No new State shall be formed . . . within the Jurisdiction of any other State." Jackson also discussed the issue in his Inaugural Address, which was the first time a president talked about Native American policy in that forum. See Van Buren, *Autobiography*, 285.

24. Andrew Jackson, Annual Message (Dec. 8, 1829), in Richardson, *Compilation*, 2:457.

25. Ibid., 2:458.

26. There is no doubt that at least some Jacksonians saw their plan as a humanitarian exercise to save the Tribes from destruction. See Wilentz, *Rise of American Democracy*, 324–27 (taking a somewhat more sympathetic view of Jackson's motivations). Putting aside the problem of what would happen when whites went further west, one flaw in this view was that the Cherokees did not want to move and could be evicted only by force. This cruel reality would be critical in convincing the next generation that repatriating slaves to Africa was also a bad idea.

27. See Smith, *Civic Ideals*, 235–36.

28. Andrew Jackson, Annual Message (Dec. 8, 1829), in Richardson, *Compilation*, 2:458-59.

29. That sad story is told in chapter 5, as the Jacksonians expelled the Tribe by ramming the fraudulent "Treaty" of New Echota through the Senate.

30. U.S. Const., art. II, § 3, cl. 1.

31. Ibid. at § 2, cl. 2.

32. Cf. Bruce Ackerman and David Golove, *Is NAFTA Constitutional?* (Cambridge: Harvard University Press, 1995) (describing the evolution of the treaty ratification process into its modern form), with Laurence H. Tribe, "Taking Text and Structure Seriously: Reflections on Free-Form Method in Constitutional Interpretation," *Harvard Law Review* 108 (1995): 1221–1303 (criticizing this development as an unjustified departure from the constitutional text).

33. For more on the significance of the repeal of the Judiciary Act, see Bruce Ackerman, *The Failure of the Founding Fathers: Jefferson, Marshall, and the Rise of Presidential Democracy* (Cambridge: Harvard University Press, 2005), 149–62.

34. Van Buren, *Autobiography*, 288.

35. See McLoughlin, *Cherokees*, 251; and Hershberger, "Anticipating Abolition," 24–25 (noting that more than 500,000 people read Evarts's pamphlet by late 1829).

36. 6 Reg. Deb. 1129 (1830) (statement of Rep. Wayne).

37. Hershberger, "Anticipating Abolition," 21 (quoting the *Journal of Commerce*).

38. "Critical State of the Cherokees," *Missionary Herald* 25 (1829): 375.

39. "Lo, the Poor Indian!," *Hamilton* (Ohio) *Intelligencer*, June 30, 1829, 2.

40. McLoughlin, *Cherokees*, 252 (quoting Rep. Lumpkin from Georgia).

41. Ibid., 253 (quoting Secretary of War John Eaton); see Ronald N. Satz, *American Indian Policy in the Jacksonian Era* (Lincoln: University of Nebraska Press, 1975), 252.

42. For a fine recent treatment of the Framers' views on the Establishment Clause, see Noah Feldman, *Divided by God* (New York: Farrar, Straus and Giroux, 2005), 19–56. To be fair, it appears that federal funding of tribal missionaries was unusual, for the Framers were otherwise rigorous in keeping public funds from religious organizations. See Douglas Laycock, "The Underlying Unity of Separation and Neutrality," *Emory Law Journal* 46 (1997): 52: "Citing this practice as evidence may prove too much. It is likely that those who voted for these funds thought it proper for government to Christianize the Indians, a purpose impossible to reconcile with any principled interpretation of the Establishment Clause."

43. This issue emerged in a different form in the heat of the 1832 election campaign, when Clay tried to push a resolution through Congress declaring a national day of prayer following a cholera epidemic. Jackson viewed this as a violation of the Establishment Clause, but the question never reached his desk because the House of Representatives tabled the measure. See Remini, *Jackson: The Course of American Freedom*, 361.

44. A similar irony runs through the Establishment Clause in the nineteenth and early twentieth centuries. For example, the phrase "separation of church and state" gained acclaim as part of anti-Catholic bigotry and was especially popular with the Ku Klux Klan. See Phillip Hamburger, *Separation of Church and State* (Cambridge: Harvard University Press, 2002), 191–251, 407–13.

45. See Cole, *Presidency of Andrew Jackson*, 72; and Remini, *Jackson: The Course of American Freedom*, 233.

46. 6 Reg. Deb. 311 (1830) (statement of Sen. Frelinghuysen).

47. See Remini, *Andrew Jackson and His Indian Wars*, 235.

48. 6 Reg. Deb. 314 (1830) (statement of Sen. Frelinghuysen).

49. This reading drew from Article One, Section 2, of the Constitution, which stated that representation was based on a state's population "excluding Indians not taxed." One implication of this exclusion was that Indians who were taxed could, under some circumstances, be part of a state and subject to its law. Whether all of the Native Americans in the North governed by state law met these conditions, however, was unclear.

50. 6 Reg. Deb. 314 (1830) (statement of Sen. Frelinghuysen).

51. Ibid. at 315.

52. Ibid. at 349 (statement of Sen. Sprague).

53. Ibid. at 315 (statement of Sen. Frelinghuysen).

54. Ibid.

55. Ibid. at 325 (statement of Sen. Forsyth).

56. Remini, *Jackson: The Course of American Freedom*, 260.

57. 6 Reg. Deb. 326 (1830) (statement of Sen. Forsyth); see Phillip P. Frickey, "Marshalling Past and Present: Colonialism, Constitutionalism, and Interpretation in Federal Indian Law," *Harvard Law Review* 107 (1993): 399–400.

58. 6 Reg. Deb. 330 (1830) (statement of Sen. Forsyth). This sounds like an argument that the United States waived its right to regulate the Cherokees.

59. Remini, *Jackson: The Course of American Freedom*, 260 (quoting Senator Adams).

60. 6 Reg. Deb. 336 (1830) (statement of Sen. Forsyth). A similar argument was made by the Alabama Supreme Court in a case involving that state's extension of jurisdiction over the Creeks. See Caldwell v. Alabama, 1 Stew. & P 327 (1832); and Garrison, *Legal Ideology*, 158 (reviewing Judge Taylor's opinion that asked how anyone who traded "millions of acres of fertile land" for "a few strings of beads, a hogshead or two of tobacco, [and] a bale or two of coarse cloth" could have the capacity to make a treaty).

61. 6 Reg. Deb. 1103 (1830) (statement of Rep. Lumpkin).

62. Ibid. at 336 (statement of Sen. Forsyth).

63. Ibid. at 1124 (statement of Rep. Wayne).

64. Remini, *Andrew Jackson and His Indian Wars*, 236.

65. See Van Buren, *Autobiography*, 288 (reproducing an amendment by Senator Freling-huysen that "until the said tribes or nations shall choose to remove, as by this act is contemplated, they shall be protected in their present possessions, and in the enjoyment of all their rights of territory and government, as heretofore exercised and enjoyed, from all interruptions and encroachments").

66. See Cole, *Presidency of Andrew Jackson*, 73; and Remini, *Andrew Jackson and His Indian Wars*, 236.

67. See Jackson, *Presidential Vetoes*, 16; and Skowronek, *Politics*, 139.

68. The Maysville Turnpike Act was even backed by Thomas Hart Benton, who was otherwise a dyed-in-the-wool Jacksonian. See Remini, *Jackson: The Course of American Freedom*, 252.

69. See U.S. Const., art. I, § 7, cl. 2.

70. See Hershberger, "Anticipating Abolition," 30; see also Andrew Jackson, Veto Message (May 27, 1830), in Richardson, *Compilation*, at 2:483.

71. There were party leaders and influential members, but the point is that they could not exercise close control of the proceedings. To take one example, the practice of moving business through the Senate by unanimous consent, which is crucial to keeping a regular schedule there, was only developed in the 1950s by Lyndon Johnson. Prior to that time, the Senate was largely ungovernable. See Robert Caro, *Master of the Senate* (New York: Knopf, 2002), 572–77.

72. See Cole, *Presidency of Andrew Jackson*, 73; and Remini, *Andrew Jackson and His Indian Wars*, 236.

73. See, e.g., Stuart v. Laird, 5 U.S. (1 Cranch) 299, 309 (1803) (upholding the practice of circuit riding and stating that "it is sufficient to observe, that practice, and acquiescence under it, for a period of several years, commencing with the organization of the judicial system, affords an irresistible answer, and has indeed fixed the construction"). This point would receive more attention in the aftermath of Jackson's Bank Veto.

74. See James Madison, Veto Message (Jan. 30, 1815), in Richardson, *Compilation*, 1:555.

75. See Letter from James Madison to Charles Ingersoll (June 25, 1831), in *Letters and Other Writings of James Madison*, 4:164–65.

76. See *Dred Scott*, 60 U.S. (19 U.S.) at 616 (Curtis, J., dissenting) (citing Madison's veto as support for the Missouri Compromise); Cong. Globe, 27th Cong., 1st Sess., app. at xv (1841) (statement of Rep. Gamble) (referring to this veto to support the Bank's constitutionality); and William Henry Harrison, Inaugural Address (Mar. 4, 1841), in Richardson, *Compilation*, 4:11 (claiming that Madison's veto stated a proper limit on presidential power).

77. Of course, the positions of the prior generation were also articulated by the Court in cases like *M'Culloch*, but Jacksonians had to address the immediate problem of convincing Congress to join their constitutional bandwagon.

78. Jackson issued twelve formal vetoes and several pocket vetoes, while his six predecessors only issued eight formal vetoes (Washington, 2; Adams, 0; Jefferson, 0; Madison, 5; Monroe, 1; John Quincy Adams, 0). All of the vetoes from this era can be found in the first three volumes of Richardson, *Compilation*.

79. See Skowronek, *Politics*, 20.

80. Andrew Jackson, Veto Message (May 27, 1830), in Richardson, *Compilation*, at 2:489.

81. See James Monroe, Veto Message (May 4, 1822), in Richardson, *Compilation*, 2:142; and James Madison, Veto Message (Mar. 3, 1817), in ibid., 1:584.

82. In fact, Jackson signed more internal improvements into law than any prior president, but they were mostly in the federal territories where no legal objection was present. See Peterson, *Great Triumvirate*, 196.

83. See Andrew Jackson, Veto Message (May 27, 1830), in Richardson, *Compilation*, at 2:487.

84. See David P. Currie, *The Constitution in Congress: Democrats and Whigs, 1829–1861* (Chicago: University of Chicago Press, 2005), 12: "Plainly the new President meant to make a sharp break with the past."

85. Andrew Jackson, Veto Message (May 27, 1830), in Richardson, *Compilation*, at 2:485.

86. Ibid. at 2:487.

87. Ibid.

88. Ibid.

89. See Peterson, *Great Triumvirate*, 195.

90. Ibid. at 195–96.

91. 6 Reg. Deb. 1141 (1830) (statement of Rep. Stanbery).

92. Burke, "Cherokee Cases," 507.

93. Hershberger, "Anticipating Abolition," 37 (quoting a poem written by Garrison in his prison cell).

Chapter 3: Judicial Resistance

1. See Benton, *Thirty Years' View*, 1:164–65; and Burke, "Cherokee Cases," 508.

2. Letter from John Marshall to Dabney Carr (June 21, 1830), in John Pendleton Kennedy, *Memoirs of the Life of William Wirt, Attorney General of the United States*, 2 vols. (Philadelphia: Lea and Blanchard, 1849), 2:253–58.

3. See Garrison, *Legal Ideology*, 100.

4. Ibid.

5. Ibid., 101. In *Johnson v. McIntosh*, 21 U.S. (8 Wheat.) 543 (1823), the Court held that lands taken from the Tribes were free and clear because the doctrine of discovery allowed the European powers and their American successor the right to acquire land as the fruits of military conflict. From a practical standpoint, this decision was unavoidable because most of the country was composed of land seized in this fashion. That decision did not say that the United States could keep annexing tribal land without cause. In fact, Marshall stated in dicta that the Tribes had a possessory interest in their land. See *Johnson*, 21 U.S. (8 Wheat.) at 574.

6. Burke, "Cherokee Cases," 508n53.

7. Garrison, *Legal Ideology*, 108 (quoting Elias Boudinot) (emphasis in original).

8. Charles Grove Haines, *The Role of the Supreme Court in American Government and Politics, 1789–1835* (Berkeley: University of California Press, 1944), 598.

9. See Garrison, *Legal Ideology*, 122; and Burke, "Cherokee Cases," 512.

10. Haines, *Supreme Court*, 598.

11. Garrison, *Legal Ideology*, 122.

12. Van Buren, *Autobiography*, 291.

13. See G. Edward White, *The Marshall Court and Cultural Change, 1815–35* (New York: Macmillan, 1988), 955–56.

14. Ibid., 956.

15. See Ex Parte McCardle, 74 U.S. (7 Wall.) 506 (1869) (upholding the jurisdiction-stripping statute); and Bruce Ackerman, *We the People: Transformations* (Cambridge: Harvard University Press, 1998), 337–40 (describing some of these New Deal amendments). The only major effort to restrict judicial review that does not correspond with a generational transition was the 1957 jurisdiction-stripping bill that came within one vote of passing the Senate. See Caro, *Master of the Senate*, 1030–31.

16. 30 U.S. (5 Pet.) 1 (1831); see Burke, "Cherokee Cases," 513.

17. See Van Buren, *Autobiography*, 291.

18. See Garrison, *Legal Ideology*, 109.

19. Ibid., 133.

20. Ibid., 130.

21. *Cherokee Nation*, 30 U.S. (5 Pet.) at 15.

22. See ibid. at 18: "At the time the constitution was framed, the idea of appealing to an American court of justice for an assertion of right or a redress of wrong, had perhaps never entered the mind of an Indian or of his tribe. . . . This was well understood by the statesmen who framed the constitution."

23. Ibid.

24. Ibid.

25. Ibid. at 19–20.

26. Ibid. at 20. The problem with Wirt's strategy was that even a Court sympathetic to his case would be skeptical of adopting a position where every tribe would be allowed to sue a state without going through the lower courts. Courts never like to open the floodgates for litigation, but that is particularly true when the cases would all involve sensitive political questions that would be decided by the justices in the first instance.

27. Van Buren, *Autobiography*, 291; see *Cherokee Nation*, 30 U.S. (5 Pet.) at 17.

28. *Cherokee Nation*, 30 U.S. (5 Pet.) at 20.

29. *Marbury* held that the Court had no jurisdiction to hear a claim that a federal justice of the peace was wrongfully deprived of his office. In the process, the chief justice also delivered a lecture on Jefferson's abuse of power in failing to obey the law and took the opportunity to articulate the idea of judicial review. See Marbury v. Madison, 5 U.S. (1 Cranch) 137 (1803). For a more thorough discussion of these dynamics, see Ackerman, *The Failure of the Founding Fathers*, 163–98.

30. See *Cherokee Nation*, 30 U.S. (5 Pet.) at 20 (Johnson, J., concurring); ibid. at 31 (Baldwin, J., concurring); and Burke, "Cherokee Cases," 516.

31. See *Cherokee Nation*, 30 U.S. (5 Pet.) at 50 (Thompson, J., concurring).

32. Burke, "Cherokee Cases," 516.

33. McLoughlin, *Cherokees*, 258.

34. Ibid.; see Garrison, *Legal Ideology*, 171 (quoting Worcester's view that "the establishment of the jurisdiction of Georgia and other states over the Cherokee people, against their will, would be an immense and irreparable injury").

35. See McLoughlin, *Cherokees*, 259; and Burke, "Cherokee Cases," 519.

36. See Burke, "Cherokee Cases," 519–20.

37. McLoughlin, *Cherokees*, 260; see *Daily National Intelligencer*, Mar. 13, 1832, 2 (reprinting a report by a special committee of a Georgia legislature stating that "removal of the whites was not so much desired, as the destruction of that influence which was at war with the interests of Georgia").

38. Ibid.

39. See Burke, "Cherokee Cases," 520; see also Althea Bass, *Cherokee Messenger* (Norman: University of Oklahoma Press, 1936), 131 (quoting a letter from Governor Gilmer to Worcester stating that "you may be under no mistake as to this matter, you are also informed that the government of the United States does not recognize as its agents the missionaries acting under the direction of the American Board of Foreign Missions").

40. Bass, *Messenger*, 130–31.

41. Ibid., 132 (quoting Worcester's letter to Gilmer of June 10, 1831).

42. Ibid., 134.

43. See ibid., 138; and McLoughlin, *Cherokees*, 262.

44. See Bass, *Messenger*, 143; and Burke, *Cherokee Cases*, 520.

45. Hershberger, "Anticipating Abolition," 32; see Haines, *Supreme Court*, 600n76 (quoting Justice Story's view that "the subject touches the moral sense of all New England. It comes home to the religious feelings of the people; it moves their sensibilities, and strikes to the very bottom of their sense of justice").

46. Worcester v. Georgia, 31 U.S. (6 Pet.) 515, 529 (1832).

47. "Georgia's Attack on the Missionaries," *Journal of Cherokee Studies* 4 (1979): 86; cf. 8 Reg. Deb. 3105 (1832) (statement of Rep. Pendleton): "Is this a question of religious enthusiasm, or of personal rights? I hesitate not to affirm that civil liberty owes as much to ecclesiastics as she owes to lawyers."

48. McLoughlin, *Cherokees*, 239; see *Liberator*, Apr. 23, 1831, 167: "Missionaries confined in a Georgia Penitentiary with felons!—for the crime of quietly teaching the poor Indians to read and write, and cultivate the soil, and imparting to them the hopes and motives of the Christian religion!"

49. Bass, *Messenger*, 141.

50. Ibid.

51. *Daily National Intelligencer*, Mar. 13, 1832, 2.

52. Ibid.

53. Ibid.

54. Ibid.

55. Ibid.

56. See Employment Div. v. Smith, 494 U.S. 872 (1990).

57. Ibid. at 885. The significance of this episode for the ongoing debate on *Smith* is discussed in chapter 9.

58. See Burke, "Cherokee Cases," 521. To a modern observer, Georgia's refusal to acknowledge the Court's authority seems impossible to defend. Yet the State offered a plausible counternarrative. In *Chisholm v. Georgia*, the State refused to appear due to a belief that sovereign immunity rendered the suit at issue unconstitutional. See Chisholm v. Georgia, 2 U.S. (2 Dall.) 419 (1793); and Padelford, Fay & Co. v. Mayor of Savannah, 14 Ga. 438, 478 (Ga. 1854) (Benning, J., concurring). Shortly thereafter, Georgia's position was vindicated by the passage of the Eleventh Amendment overruling *Chisholm*. From the State's perspective, this precedent established that a state had a duty to impede illegal actions by the Court. Indeed, judges in Georgia cited *Chisholm* and *Worcester* as examples of civil disobedience that were sustained by the American people. See *Padelford*, 14 Ga. at 478 (Benning, J., concurring).

59. *Worcester*, 31 U.S. (6 Pet.) at 559.

60. Williams v. Lee, 358 U.S. 217, 219 (1959).

61. See Bush v. Gore, 531 U.S. 98, 158 (2000) (Breyer, J., dissenting).

62. Frickey, "Marshalling Past and Present," 439.

63. In the transition between the Federalists and Jeffersonian Democracy, judicial resistance was concentrated in the lower courts, as the Supreme Court was not yet a major institution. The most interesting of these cases was *United States v. Callender*, which was also argued by Wirt, in which the Federalist justice Samuel Chase issued an opinion defending the Alien and Sedition Act right before the 1800 election. See United States v. Callender, 25 F. Cas. 239 (C.C.D. Va. 1800) (No. 14, 709) (Chase, J.); and Gerard N. Magliocca, "The Philosopher's Stone: Dualist Democracy and the Jury," *University of Colorado Law Review* 69 (1998): 204–7.

64. Burke, "Cherokee Cases," 523; see *Worcester*, 31 U.S. (6 Pet.) at 542–61.

65. *Worcester*, 31 U.S. (6 Pet.) at 561–62.

66. Ibid. at 560–61.

67. Ibid. at 541.

68. Specifically, appellate practice required that the record be authenticated by the signature of the lower court judge. Worcester and Butler only obtained the signature of the lower court clerk. Marshall ruled that this was sufficient over the dissent of Justice Baldwin. See ibid. at 536–37; and ibid. at 596 (Baldwin, J., dissenting) (stating the court reporter's summary of his view that "the record was not properly returned upon the writ of error, and ought to have been returned by the state court, and not by the clerk of that court"). The

Court's decision to overlook this technical problem was reasonable, but nothing mandated the generosity.

69. See ibid. at 576 (McLean, J., concurring).

70. Furthermore, the arrest of the missionaries was probably invalid, because there is no evidence that the State militia obtained a federal license before entering the tribal area to conduct its operation.

71. Ibid. at 574.

72. Ibid. at 552.

73. Ibid. at 561: "The whole intercourse between the United States and [the Cherokee] nation is, by our constitution and laws, vested in the government of the United States."

74. See United States v. Bailey, 24 F. Cas. 937, 940 (C.C.D. Tenn. 1834) (No. 14,495) (holding that Congress had no power to punish a murder involving a Cherokee on tribal land unless the crime had a commercial aspect); and 6 Reg. Deb. 1114-15 (1830) (statement of Rep. Lamar): "If, then, the United States cannot, in the regulations of commerce among the several States, divest the States of their jurisdiction over other subjects, how do the same words, in relation to Indian tribes, increase the powers of the Federal Government, or diminish or impair the rights of the States?"

Just to be clear, I am not saying that the Commerce Clause must be given the same reading with respect to interstate matters and tribal intercourse. There are sound arguments for thinking that Congress's power in relation to the Tribes is greater. See Amar, *America's Constitution*, 107-8. It is quite another thought, though, to say that Congress's power over the Tribes was exclusive.

75. See County of Yakima v. Confederated Tribes & Bands of the Yakima Indian Nation, 502 U.S. 251, 257 (1992).

76. See *Worcester*, 31 U.S. (6 Pet.) at 559 (using the word "nation" to attribute the independence of the "other nations of the earth" to the Cherokees). The only exceptions *Worcester* recognized were the ones that Knox had insisted upon: (1) the Tribes could not make treaties with other foreign nations; and (2) they could not sell their land to anyone other than the United States. See Smith, *Civic Ideals*, 238.

77. *Worcester*, 31 U.S. (6 Pet.) at 544-45.

78. See *Cherokee Nation*, 30 U.S. (5 Pet.) 1, 22 (1831) (Johnson, J., concurring); and Frickey, "Marshalling Past and Present," 396-97.

79. *Worcester*, 31 U.S. (6 Pet.) at 547.

80. *Cherokee Nation*, 30 U.S. (5 Pet.) at 23 (Johnson, J., concurring).

81. Ibid. at 23; Frickey, "Marshalling Past and Present," 399-400.

82. *Cherokee Nation*, 30 U.S. (5 Pet.) at 24 (Johnson, J., concurring); see ibid. at 38 (Baldwin, J., concurring).

83. See ibid. at 24-25 (Johnson, J., concurring).

84. See *Worcester*, 31 U.S. (6 Pet.) at 553 ("with respect to the words 'hunting grounds'"): "Hunting was at that time the principal occupation of the Indians, and their land was more used for that purpose than for any other. It could not, however, be supposed that any intention existed of restricting the full use of the lands they reserved." And ibid. at 555 (stating that the Treaty of Holston referred to the "boundary" between the Tribe and the United States and that "we hear no more of 'allotments' or of 'hunting grounds'"); and ibid. at 556 (noting that in that latter treaty "no claim is made to the management of all [the Tribe's] affairs").

85. Frickey, "Marshalling Past and Present," 402.

86. Ibid., 551, 553.

87. Ibid., 554.

88. Ibid., 559; see ibid., 550 (noting that the treaty "regulates the trade between the contracting parties, in a manner entirely equal").

89. See ibid., 551 (noting that the Treaty of Hopewell provided for an equal exchange of intruders); ibid., 555 (explaining the reciprocal rules for punishment of intruders); and ibid., 556 (stating that the Treaty of Holston provided for a "perfectly equal" exchange of prisoners).

90. Ibid., 553; see ibid., 556: "The remaining articles [of the Treaty of Holston] are equal, and contain stipulations which could be made only with a nation admitted to be capable of governing itself."

91. Although Marshall implied that the Removal Act was invalid, he did not specifically address the issue. Justice McLean, who concurred in *Worcester*, did conclude that the Removal Act was illegal. See ibid., 596 (McLean, J., concurring).

92. See Hershberger, "Anticipating Abolition," 32 (citing the reactions of Arthur Tappen and Lyman Beecher to *Worcester*); and *Liberator*, Mar. 10, 1832, 39 (stating that when news of *Worcester* reached an abolitionist meeting it "was received with the most enthusiastic applause," and nothing since the Revolution had "created a livelier sensation of joy in Boston and its vicinity, than this decision of the Supreme Court"). It should be said, however, that Marshall certainly did not anticipate the evolution of equal protection as we understand that concept.

93. For example, Wirt correctly concluded that the Cherokee Codes violated the Contracts Clause. Likewise, the provision barring Cherokees from testifying in litigation involving whites could have been the basis for a personal rights' opinion on discrimination. For a modern analysis of group rights, see Owen M. Fiss, "Groups and the Equal Protection Clause," *Journal of Philosophy of Public Affairs* 5 (1976): 107–77.

Chapter 4: The Bank Veto and the Election of 1832

1. See, e.g., *Daily National Intelligencer*, Mar. 10, 1832, 1; and ibid., Mar. 12, 1832, 1.

2. See 8 Reg. Deb. 2010–12 (1832) (explaining that the missionaries were imprisoned "for no other offense than a refusal to take an oath of allegiance to the State"); *National Intelligencer*, Mar. 6, 1832, 1; and ibid., Mar. 8, 1832, 1.

3. See 8 Reg. Deb. 2015–16 (1832).

4. See ibid. at 2013 (statement of Rep. Clayton).

5. See Burke, "The Cherokee Cases," 526. After the *Worcester* crisis passed, the Force Act of 1833 was enacted to fix the problem. See ibid., 531.

6. Remini, *Jackson: The Course of American Freedom*, 276.

7. Ibid., 277.

8. *The Missionaries and the State of Georgia–Address of the Democratic Committee of Correspondence for the City of Philadelphia*, Oct. 29, 1832, 3; see ibid., 2: "The Supreme Court has issued no process to the Marshal of Georgia or any other officer, to execute their decree or mandate—there has been no opposition to any law of the United States, to any process of the Supreme Court or the execution thereof."

9. Remini, *Jackson: The Course of American Freedom*, 276; see Burke, "Cherokee Cases," 527.

10. See U.S. Const., art. III, § 2 (stating that the judicial power may only be exercised in "cases" or "controversies"); and Muskrat v. United States, 219 U.S. 346 (1911) (reviewing the long-standing practice barring advisory opinions).

11. Unlike the typical advisory opinion, *Worcester* did have parties with real interests at stake. The problem was that Marshall seemed uninterested in providing a remedy, and one might wonder whether a court can properly rule on a case while taking no interest in enforcing its ruling. That could be characterized as a commentary on the law that judges may not engage in under the federal system. Modern declaratory judgments do serve this purpose in a way, but that was not an option then.

12. 8 Reg. Deb. 3105 (1832) (statement of Rep. Pendleton).

13. Ibid. at 3118 (statement of Rep. Pendleton).

14. Ibid. at 3419 (statement of Rep. Foster).

15. Andrew Jackson, Veto Message (July 10, 1832), in Richardson, *Compilation*, 2:581.

16. See Cole, *Amos Kendall*, 161; and Remini, *Jackson: The Course of American Freedom*, 343.

17. Peterson, *Great Triumvirate*.

18. See Michael F. Holt, *The Rise and Fall of the American Whig Party* (New York: Oxford University Press, 1999), 11; and Remini, *Jackson: The Course of American Freedom*, 348–49.

19. Remini, *Jackson: The Course of American Freedom*, 369; see Cole, *Amos Kendall*, 170.

20. Van Buren, *Autobiography*, 625; see Andrew Jackson, Removal of the Public Deposits, in Richardson, *Compilation*, 3:6: "There are strong reasons for believing that the motive of the bank in asking for a recharter at that session of Congress was to make it a leading question in the election of a President of the United States the ensuing November."

21. See Cole, *Amos Kendall*, 164–65.

22. Henry Cabot Lodge, ed., *The Works of Alexander Hamilton*, 12 vols. (New York: G. P. Putnam's, 1904), 3:338 (quoting a letter from Hamilton to Robert Morris).

23. See Andrew Jackson, Veto Message (July 10, 1832), in Richardson, *Compilation*, 2:576–77. In essence, Jackson's criticism was that the recharter would increase the value of the Bank's shares, but that no new shares would be issued. Accordingly, the benefits of the bill were concentrated among a tiny elite.

24. Ibid., 577.

25. Ibid., 580–81; see ibid., 581: "Is there no danger to our liberty and independence in a bank that in its nature has so little to bind it to our country?"

26. Ibid., 578.

27. Ibid., 580.

28. Ibid., 581.

29. Ibid., 589–90; see also Andrew Jackson, Removal of the Public Deposits (Sept. 18, 1833), in Richardson, *Compilation*, 3:6 (documenting the expansion of loans from the Bank prior to the 1832 election and stating that "the leading object of this immense extension of its loans was to bring as large a portion of the people as possible under its power and influence. . . . some of the largest sums were granted on very unusual terms to the conductors of the public press").

30. Andrew Jackson, Veto Message (July 10, 1832), in Richardson, *Compilation*, 2:591.

31. Ibid., 2:590.

32. Ibid.

33. Ibid., 2:582.

34. The president also argued, rather implausibly, that the prior recognitions by Congress were ambiguous because the First National Bank was allowed to lapse in 1811 and a new charter was not passed until 1816. See ibid.

35. Ibid.

36. To be sure, Jackson did say that precedent was controlling "where the acquiescence of the people and the States can be considered as well settled." Ibid., 581–82. His application of that standard, though, was sharply different from Madison's and drained it of any real significance.

37. See 8 Reg. Deb. 1221–40 (1832) (statement of Sen. Webster).

38. Ibid. at 1231.

39. Ibid.

40. Ibid.

41. Andrew Jackson, Veto Message (July 10, 1832), in Richardson, *Compilation*, 2:581–82.

42. For the modern commentary, see, e.g., Wilfred E. Binkley, *President and Congress* (New York: Alfred A. Knopf, 1947), 70–74; Jackson, *Presidential Vetoes*, 33; and Skowronek, *Politics*, 142. By contrast, Webster's address to the Senate on the veto spent about three pages on

M'Culloch (see 8 Reg. Deb. 1231, 1239–40 [1832] [statement of Sen. Webster]) and seventeen pages on the legislative precedents and policy objections in the Veto Message (see ibid. at 1221–30, 1232–38).

43. See Kramer, *The People Themselves* (emphasizing this point and arguing against judicial supremacy). Though I disagree with some of Kramer's conclusions, his survey of constitutional attitudes during the early Republic is well worth reading.

44. See Andrew Jackson, Veto Message (July 10, 1832), in Richardson, *Compilation*, 2:583; see also ibid., 2:582: "The authority of the Supreme Court must not, therefore, be permitted to control the Congress or the Executive when acting in their legislative capacities, but to have only such influence as the force of their reasoning may deserve."

45. See Burke, "Cherokee Cases," 528–29.

46. This is the most powerful theme to emerge from Stephen Skowronek's scholarship in political science. See Skowronek, *Politics*; see also Bruce Ackerman's work on the law side, *We the People: Foundations*.

47. These comparisons are scattered throughout the book, but for another example see 10 Reg. Deb. 801 (1834) (statement of Sen. Hill). In an institutional sense, one can say that Jacksonians took Jefferson's tentative innovations (political parties and robust executive power) and made them permanent.

48. See Thomas Jefferson, Annual Message (Dec. 8, 1801), in Richardson, *Compilation*, 1:331–32: "Nothing shall be wanting on my part to inform as far as in my power the legislative judgment, nor to carry that judgment into faithful execution." See also Binkley, *President and Congress*, 58–59: "Republican doctrine made Congress the fundamental organ, the mainspring of government and peculiarly the agent of the people."

49. 10 Reg. Deb. 1688 (1834) (statement of Sen. Webster) (responding to Jackson's Protest Message making this claim); see ibid. at 1646 (statement of Sen. Calhoun): "What effrontery! What boldness of assertion! The immediate representative! Why, he never received a vote from the American People. He was elected by electors, elected either by the people of the States or by their Legislatures."

50. See Abraham Lincoln, Inaugural Address (Mar. 4, 1861), in Richardson, *Compilation*, 6:9: "If the policy of the government upon vital questions affecting the whole people is to be irrevocably fixed by decisions of the Supreme Court . . . the people will have ceased to be their own rulers, having to that extent practically resigned their Government into the hands of that eminent tribunal"; and 12 Stat. 432 (1862) (abolishing slavery in the territories).

51. See Robert H. Jackson, *That Man: An Insider's Portrait of Franklin D. Roosevelt*, ed. John Q. Barrett (New York: Oxford University Press, 2003), 65–66 (describing the president's search for a way to avoid complying with such a decision); and William Leuchtenberg, *The Supreme Court Reborn* (New York: Oxford University Press, 1995), 86–88 (quoting FDR's draft speech citing Lincoln's First Inaugural and saying he would not "permit the decision of the Supreme Court to be carried through to its logical inescapable conclusion"); see also Norman v. Baltimore & Ohio R.R. Co. (Gold Clause Cases), 294 U.S. 240 (1935) (upholding the abandonment of the gold standard 5 to 4).

52. Andrew Jackson, Veto Message (July 10, 1832), in Richardson, *Compilation*, 2:584; see U.S. Const., art. I, § 8, cl. 8 (describing the patent and copyright powers).

53. Andrew Jackson, Veto Message (July 10, 1832), in Richardson, *Compilation*, 2:584.

54. This comment was made in the context of a broader argument that the Bank was unlawful because its twenty-year charter restricted the discretion of a future Congress. Jackson said that he was defending the legislature's ability to select appropriate means by vetoing an attempt by one Congress to bind another. Though this argument has force, his view would have made it almost impossible to charter a bank. If each Congress was required to renew the charter (every two years), the uncertainty created would cripple a Bank's ability to attract investors or assure borrowers that their credit line would not disappear. Thus, Jackson's

purported attempt to protect congressional flexibility had the effect of barring any Congress from choosing a Bank.

55. Andrew Jackson, Veto Message (July 10, 1832), in Richardson, *Compilation*, 2:585; see U.S. Const., art. I., § 8, cl. 18; and Benton, *Thirty Years' View*, 1:252.

56. Andrew Jackson, Veto Message (July 10, 1832), in Richardson, *Compilation*, 2:586.

57. This argument would appear in another major implied power debate sparked by the resistance to the New Deal generation's rise to power. See A.L.A. Schechter Poultry Corp. v. United States, 295 U.S. 495, 529–42 (1935) (concluding that the National Industrial Recovery Act's delegation of regulatory authority to private cartels was invalid). It should be said, though, that Jackson was not the first person to raise a nondelegation argument against the Bank. The lawyers for Maryland made this same point in M'Culloch. *See* Harold J. Plous and Gordon E. Baker, "McCulloch v. Maryland, Right Principle, Wrong Case," *Stanford Law Review* 9 (1957): 721. The chief justice, though, ignored the issue.

58. Andrew Jackson, Veto Message (July 10, 1832), in Richardson, *Compilation*, 2:590–91.

59. 8 Reg. Deb. 1240 (1832) (statement of Sen. Webster).

60. See Cole, *Amos Kendall*, 174–75.

61. 8 Reg. Deb. 1274 (1832) (statement of Sen. Clay).

62. Burke, "Cherokee Cases," 528.

63. Ibid., 520–21 (quoting James Barbour, Address to the National Republican Convention [Dec. 24, 1831]).

64. Ibid., 520; see Van Buren, *Autobiography*, 293–94.

65. *Pittsburgh Gazette*, Oct. 26, 1832, 2; see Satz, *American Indian Policy in the Jacksonian Era*, 51 (noting that opposition papers called Jackson "the persecutor of the missionaries").

66. *The Missionaries and the State of Georgia–Address of the Democratic Committee of Correspondence for the City of Philadelphia*, Oct. 29, 1832, 1.

67. Ibid.

68. See Holt, *Whig Party*, 17; and Remini, *Jackson: The Course of American Freedom*, 390.

69. See Skowronek, *Politics*, 470n9.

70. Letter from John Marshall to Joseph Story (Sept. 22, 1832), in *Proceedings of the Massachusetts Historical Society* 14: (1901) 351–52.

71. See Holt, *Whig Party*, 26.

72. See Cole, *Presidency of Andrew Jackson*, 158.

73. See Proclamation, Andrew Jackson (Dec. 10, 1832), in Richardson, *Compilation*, 2:643: "I consider, then, the power to annul a law of the United States, assumed by one State, incompatible with the existence of the Union, contradicted expressly by the letter of the Constitution, unauthorized by its spirit, inconsistent with every principle on which it was founded, and destructive of the great object for which it was formed."

74. See Cole, *Presidency of Andrew Jackson*, 115; and Michael J. Klarman, "How Great Were the 'Great' Marshall Court Decisions?" *Virginia Law Review* 87 (2001): 1177–78.

Chapter 5: Triumph and Tears

1. Schlesinger, *Age of Jackson*, 65; see Skowronek, *Politics*, 149. At that time, there was a significant debate about whether a president had the power to fire cabinet members, even though that authority was first established in Washington's administration. See Stephen G. Calabresi and Christopher S. Yoo, "The Unitary Executive during the First Half-Century," *Case Western Reserve Law Review* 47 (1997): 1538–58; see also Gerhard Casper, "An Essay in Separation of Powers: Some Early Versions and Practices," *William and Mary Law Review* 30 (1987): 234–41 (describing the debate over the removal power during Washington's presidency).

2. Andrew Jackson, Removal of the Public Deposits (Sept. 18, 1833), in Richardson, *Compilation*, 3:7.

3. See 10 Reg. Deb. 58–59 (1834) (statement of Sen. Clay). The resolution read as follows: "That, by dismissing the late Secretary of the Treasury because he would not, contrary to his sense of his own duty, remove the money of the United States in deposite with the Bank of the United States and its branches, in conformity with the President's opinion; and by appointing his successor to effect such removal, which has been done, the President has assumed the exercise of a power over the treasury of the United States, not granted to him by the constitution and laws, and dangerous to the liberties of the people."

4. Ibid. at 434 (statement of Sen. Clay).

5. Benton, *Thirty Years' View*, 1:423.

6. 10 Reg. Deb. 1318 (1834) (protest of President Jackson). The principal argument against the Censure Resolution was that the Senate could not condemn conduct that might be the subject of an article of impeachment from the House. As Jackson said, the Senate "converted themselves into accusers, witnesses, counsel, and judges, and prejudged the whole case—thus presenting the appalling spectacle, in a free state, of judges going through a labored preparation for an impartial hearing and decision, by a previous ex parte investigation and sentence against the supposed offender." Ibid. at 1322. When the Senate expunged the Censure Resolution in 1837, an act discussed later in this chapter, this was the basis for its decision. See 13 Reg. Deb. 504 (1837) (the Expunging Resolution).

7. It is interesting to note that censure was never classified as a "bill of attainder," even though one could say that a resolution targeting one person is problematic. See U.S. Const., art. I, § 9, cl. 3. On the other hand, Jackson argued that censure was a kind of legislative punishment, which might be the same point dressed up in different language. Cf. 10 Reg. Deb. 1321 (1834) (protest of President Jackson) (calling censure "the very essence of . . . punishment"), with ibid. at 1569 (statement of Sen. Clay) (disputing this assertion).

8. 10 Reg. Deb. 1653 (1834) (statement of Sen. Forsyth); see ibid. at 1158 (statement of Sen. Wright); ibid. at 1319 (protest of President Jackson); and ibid. at 1697 (statement of Sen. Benton).

9. Ibid. at 1569 (statement of Sen. Clay).

10. Ibid. at 84–85 (statement of Sen. Clay).

11. Ibid. at 344 (statement of Sen. Forsyth).

12. One example is the argument by Democrats against the Civil Rights Act of 1866, which led to the enactment of the Fourteenth Amendment. Likewise, Republicans and some Democrats argued during the New Deal that only a textual amendment would do, which FDR denounced as a desperate tactic designed to "fool the American people." See Samuel Rosenman, ed., *The Public Papers and Addresses of Franklin D. Roosevelt* (New York: Russell and Russell, 1938), 132.

13. Benton, *Thirty Years' View*, 1:409.

14. 10 Reg. Deb. 774 (1834) (statement of Sen. Hill).

15. See Ackerman, *We the People: Transformations*, 49–53 (describing the proposal of the original Constitution in a manner contrary to the Articles of Confederation).

16. 10 Reg. Deb. 1335 (1834) (protest of President Jackson).

17. Ibid. at 1570 (statement of Sen. Clay).

18. Ibid. at 1376 (statement of Sen. Leigh).

19. Ibid. at 1349 (statement of Sen. Benton).

20. Ibid. at 1689 (statement of Sen. Webster).

21. See Robert V. Remini, *Andrew Jackson: The Course of American Democracy, 1833–1845* (Baltimore: Johns Hopkins University Press, 1981), 315; and Skowronek, *Politics*, 153, 470n9.

22. See United States v. Darby, 312 U.S. 100 (1941) (overruling *Hammer v. Dagenhart* and holding that Congress can reach any form of intrastate activity as an appropriate means of regulating interstate commerce); Erie R.R. v. Tompkins, 304 U.S. 64, 79 (1938) (overruling *Swift v. Tyson* and abolishing federal common law in diversity cases); West Coast Hotel Co. v. Parrish, 300 U.S. 379 (1937) (overruling *Adkins v. Children's Hospital* and upholding state

minimum wage laws); and Jackson, *Struggle for Judicial Supremacy* (giving a contemporary account of these changes).

23. See an act supplemental to the act entitled "An Act to Amend the Judicial System of the United States," 5 Stat. 176–77 (1837).

24. See Cole, *Presidency of Andrew Jackson*, 253; and Swisher, *The Taney Period*, 54.

25. See Swisher, *The Taney Period*, 23–24.

26. Warren, *Supreme Court*, 2:16.

27. See Stanley I. Kutler, ed., *The Dred Scott Decision: Law and Politics* (Boston: Houghton Mifflin, 1967), xviii.

28. See 11 Reg. Deb. 586 (1835) (statement of Sen. Frelinghuysen).

29. In the antebellum era, the Supreme Court did not have appellate jurisdiction over most criminal and some civil cases. See ibid. at 589–90 (statement of Sen. Bibb).

30. Ibid. at 288 (statement of Sen. Frelinghuysen); see Warren, *Supreme Court*, 2:39.

31. See Letter from Daniel Webster to Warren Dutton (Jan. 30, 1835), in Charles M. Wiltse and Harold D. Moser, eds., *The Papers of Daniel Webster*, 15 vols. (Hanover, NH: University Press of New England, 1980), 4:24.

32. Ibid., 4:26.

33. See Ackerman, *The Failure of the Founding Fathers*, 150–51.

34. 11 Reg. Deb. 586 (1835) (statement of Sen. Benton).

35. Ibid. at 585.

36. Ibid. at 1498 (statement of Rep. Carmichel).

37. See Swisher, *The Taney Period*, 27–28.

38. See ibid., 28; and Warren, *Supreme Court*, 2:14–15.

39. The Duvall seat was filled by Representative Phillip B. Barbour, who was a strong foe of the Bank and of internal improvements. See Swisher, *The Taney Period*, 56–57. As for the seats created by the court-packing law, the first was given to John Catron, who ruled that *Worcester* was not controlling authority in a case before the Tennessee Supreme Court. See State v. Foreman, 16 Tenn. 256; and Swisher, *The Taney Period*, 62–63. Catron, like Justices Wayne and Taney, would compose part of the majority in *Dred Scott*. The other open seat went to John McKinley, who was a rather undistinguished supporter of the Jacksonian movement. See Swisher, *The Taney Period*, 66–67.

40. See Swisher, *The Taney Period*, 78.

41. See Cole, *Presidency of Andrew Jackson*, 116.

42. See ibid.

43. See Remini, *Jackson: The Course of American Democracy*, 266, 299.

44. Benton, *Thirty Years' View*, 1:625.

45. See ibid. When the House of Representatives was asked for additional funds to facilitate the Removal, a few votes were raised in protest. One member said "he did not regard this as a treaty at all, and would not vote this appropriation under any consideration. Should it be said that the Government, because it had the power, should force this fraud upon the Cherokee nation?" See 12 Reg. Deb. 4565 (1836) (statement of Rep. Calhoun).

46. See Garrison, *Legal Ideology*, 209.

47. Ibid. This decision was not appealed for reasons that remain murky. See ibid., 229–30. Nevertheless, one issue raised by the attorney general's argument is how preemptive opinions or other cases decided under generational pressures should be viewed once the immediate storm passes. In part, that turns on how the transition plays out (i.e., who wins and how). Beyond that, one could argue, as in *Foreman*, that these cases deserve less deference because of their partisan origins. Or one could take the opposite view and say that if a decision survives in spite of its tainted birth, then it takes on extra authority.

48. *Foreman*, 1835 WL 945 at *40. Catron advanced an analysis of *Worcester* similar to the one provided in chapter 3, which was that the holding was correct but the analysis of tribal

independence was erroneous dicta. See ibid. at *42 (stating that "sooner or later [that analysis] must be abandoned").

49. Ibid.

50. Ibid. at *41.

51. See Swisher, *The Taney Period*, 53.

52. Jackson issued a Farewell Address that reiterated these twin themes of his presidency. In recounting the Bank War, he drew the lesson that "the powers enumerated in that instrument do not confer on Congress the right to establish such a corporation as the Bank of the United States, and the evil consequences which followed may warn us of the danger of departing from the true rule of construction and of permitting temporary circumstances or the hope of better promoting the public welfare to influence in any degree our decisions upon the extent of the authority of the General Government." See Andrew Jackson, Farewell Address, in Richardson, *Compilation*, 3:304.

53. See 13 Reg. Deb. 504 (1837) (the Expunging Resolution).

54. Ibid. at 387 (statement of Sen. Benton) (emphasis added).

55. Ibid. at 469 (statement of Sen. Bayard).

56. "Military Orders and Correspondence on the Cherokee Removal," *Journal of Cherokee Studies* 3 (1978): 145.

57. Garrison, *Legal Ideology*, 1; see Remini, *Jackson: The Course of American Democracy*, 302.

58. Garrison, *Legal Ideology*, 1. For a chilling account of the brutality of the United States Army during the removal, see Stanley W. Hoig, *The Cherokees and Their Chiefs* (Fayetteville: University of Arkansas Press, 1998), 167–69.

59. See Remini, *Jackson: The Course of American Democracy*, 302.

60. Satz, *American Indian Policy in the Jacksonian Era*, 101. Jackson used somewhat more moderate language, stating that "the States which had so long been retarded in their improvement by the Indian tribes residing in the midst of them are at length relieved from the evil, and this unhappy race . . . has been at length placed beyond the reach of injury or oppression, and that the paternal care of the General Government will hereafter watch over them and protect them." See Andrew Jackson, Farewell Address, in Richardson, *Compilation*, 3:294.

61. Van Buren, *Autobiography*, 275–76.

Chapter 6: Chance and the Whig False Positive

1. See James Fitzjames Stephen, *Liberty, Equality, Fraternity* (New York: Hoyt and Williams, 1873), 70 (stating that a "minority gives way not because it is convinced that it is wrong, but because it is convinced that it is a minority").

2. See generally Joseph Alsop and Turner Catledge, *The 168 Days* (Garden City, NY: Doubleday, Doran, 1938) (describing the "switch-in-time" and the defeat of FDR's Court-packing plan).

3. See Ackerman, *We the People: Transformations*, 227–29 (describing President Andrew Johnson's choice to halt his resistance to the Fourteenth Amendment following his impeachment).

4. See Holt, *Whig Party*, 112–31; and Norma Lois Peterson, *The Presidencies of William Henry Harrison and John Tyler* (Lawrence: University Press of Kansas, 1989), 29–30. To be fair, the 1840 presidential campaign was not issue oriented, as the Whigs refused to issue a platform for fear of blowing their big chance to ride popular discontent back into power. Nevertheless, the views of Whig leaders like Clay and Webster were well known before the election and the party's plans were clearly stated after the vote.

5. See William Henry Harrison, Inaugural Address (Mar. 4, 1841), in Richardson, *Compilation*, 4:5–21.

6. See Peterson, *Great Triumvirate*, 301–2; and Peterson, *Presidencies of Harrison and Tyler*, 19.

7. See Holt, *Whig Party*, 61–62; and Peterson, *Presidencies of Harrison and Tyler*, 21–23.

8. Harrison, Inaugural Address (Mar. 4, 1841), in Richardson, *Compilation*, 4:5.

9. Ibid., 10; see ibid. (distinguishing Jackson's veto practice from that of the first six presidents).

10. Ibid., 11. Whig senators and representatives repeatedly asserted the superiority of practice and legislative precedent. See Cong. Globe, 27th Cong., 1st Sess., app. at viii (1841) (statement of Rep. Jones); ibid., app. at 364 (statement of Sen. Clay); and ibid., app. at 371–72 (statement of Sen. Morehead).

11. With the Whigs declaring their intention to reverse the recent constitutional transformation, the death of Justice Phillip B. Barbour in February 1841 took on special significance. See Swisher, *The Taney Period*, 39; and Warren, *Supreme Court*, 2:80n1; see also Holt, *Whig Party*, 126 (stating that in the lame-duck session the Whigs "mercilessly and obnoxiously taunt[ed] the Democrats about the impending overthrow of their measures"). Justice Barbour was appointed to the bench by Jackson, and hence Harrison would get a chance to add a conservative to the Court right away. Democrats who controlled the lame-duck session of Congress decided to play some hardball. President Van Buren moved the nomination of Peter Daniel through the Senate a week before Harrison's inauguration. See Warren, *Supreme Court*, 2:79. The Whigs boycotted this vote and denounced Daniel as an illegitimate "Midnight Judge" no different from the ones that the lame-duck Federalist Congress confirmed before Jefferson took over in 1801. See ibid., 2:80–81: "The public cannot fail to contrast the conduct of the party, fortunately now no longer dominant, when Mr. Adams was going out of power, with what it is when Mr. Buren is retiring." See Swisher, *The Taney Period*, 69. This desperate action fits in within a broader pattern found on the boundaries between constitutional generations, where traditionalists often try to rush through changes at the last minute before reformers gain a foothold in Congress. See Edward McPherson, *The Political History of the United States of America during the Great Rebellion* (Washington, DC: Philp and Solomons, 1864), 59–60 (describing the attempt in the 1860 lame-duck session to pass a constitutional amendment making slavery permanent); cf. Comprehensive Environmental Response, Compensation and Liability Act (CERCLA), 42 U.S.C. § 9601 et seq. (2000) (remaking environmental law in the lame-duck session on the eve of the Reagan Revolution).

12. See Holt, *Whig Party*, 126–27; and Peterson, *Presidencies of Harrison and Tyler*, 37–39; see also U.S. Const., art. II, § 3 (stating that the president "may, on extraordinary Occasions, convene both Houses").

13. 40 U.S. (15 Pet.) 449 (1841).

14. See ibid. at 497.

15. Thus, the case presented a straightforward Dormant Commerce Clause issue. Unfortunately, the Dormant Commerce Clause did not exist yet. In fact, Chief Justice Taney's concurring opinion in *Groves* stated that such an issue was "little more than an abstract question, which the court may never be called upon to decide." Ibid. at 510 (Taney, C.J., concurring). This was not a good prediction.

16. See ibid. at 483, 490–91; and Swisher, *The Taney Period*, 365.

17. See *Groves*, 40 U.S. (15 Pet.) at 486, 489.

18. Ibid. at 485.

19. See Remini, *Jackson: The Course of American Democracy*.

20. This outcome was not likely, but an antebellum court could have held that an elected state judiciary violated the Guarantee Clause of Article Four. See U.S. Const., art. IV, § 4: "The United States shall guarantee to every State in this Union a Republican Form of Government." And with an adverse precedent in *Groves*, a postbellum court might have held that a litigant facing an elected judge was deprived of due process in violation of the Fourteenth Amendment. Even without such a finding, elected state judiciaries have always coexisted uneasily with other constitutional principles. See, e.g., Republican Party of Minnesota v. White,

536 U.S. 765 (2002) (holding that a canon of ethics restricting campaign statements in judicial elections violated the First Amendment); and ibid. at 788–92 (O'Connor, J., concurring) (criticizing the practice of electing judges).

21. *Groves,* 40 U.S. (15 Pet.) at 495.

22. Indeed, Webster was attacked on the Senate floor for this aspect of his argument in *Groves.* See Peterson, *Great Triumvirate,* 299.

23. In fairness, some of the hostility directed at *M'Culloch* in the 1820s can be attributed to the slavery crisis that led to the Missouri Compromise. Some southerners objected to Marshall's reasoning because they feared it could justify a federal law abolishing slavery in the states. See Newmyer, *John Marshall,* 334. Nevertheless, a review of the sources from that time shows that this was a relatively minor concern.

24. See New York v. Miln, 36 U.S. (11 Pet.) 102, 143 (1837). Justice Story said that Marshall shared his view that the New York statute was invalid on Commerce Clause grounds, but this claim is hard to verify given that the chief justice was dead. See ibid. at 161 (Story, J., dissenting).

25. Ibid. at 139.

26. See Charles River Bridge v. Warren Bridge, 36 U.S. (11 Pet.) 420 (1837); and Swisher, *The Taney Period,* 87–90. Though some historians put a lot of emphasis on these 1837 decisions, the Jacksonians themselves ignored them. Consequently, this analysis follows their attitude.

27. *Charles River Bridge,* 36 U.S. (11 Pet.) at 545–46.

28. See *Groves,* 40 U.S. (15 Pet.) at 499–503. Two justices dissented on this point, and two did not participate in the case at all. See ibid. at 517.

29. Ibid. at 608 (Taney, C.J., concurring).

30. See Dred Scott v. Sandford, 60 U.S. (19 How.) 393, 432–42 (1857); see also U.S. Const., art. IV, § 3: "The Congress shall have power to dispose of and make all needful Rules and Regulations respecting the Territory or other Property belonging to the United States."

31. *Groves,* 40 U.S. (15 Pet.) at 515 (Baldwin, J., concurring). One caution in reading any opinion by Justice Baldwin is that he went insane early in his tenure and was—to put it mildly—erratic afterward. See David J. Garrow, "Mental Decrepitude on the U.S. Supreme Court: The Historical Case for a 28th Amendment," *University of Chicago Law Review* 67 (2000): 1002–3 (describing Justice Story's comment that Baldwin was "partially deranged at all times" and other lawyers who called Baldwin "crazy").

32. *Groves,* 40 U.S. (15 Pet.) at 515 (Baldwin, J., concurring).

33. See *Dred Scott,* 60 U.S. (19 Pet.) at 397.

34. Another example of this two-step process came during the intersection of the Reconstruction and Populist generations. At that time, the Court began its resistance in a case that expressly avoided the issue of whether the Sherman Antitrust Act was valid under the Commerce Clause. See United States v. E. C. Knight, 156 U.S. 1, 16 (1895). That tentative start was followed by a preemptive opinion striking down the federal income tax statute. See Pollock v. Farmers' Home Loan & Trust, 157 U.S. 429, 570 (1895); and Magliocca, "Constitutional False Positives," 868–72.

35. Letter from Henry Clay to N. Beverley Tucker (Apr. 15, 1841), in Lyon G. Tyler, *The Letters and Times of the Tylers,* 3 vols. (Richmond, VA: Whittet and Shepperson, 1885), 2:30.

36. See Peterson, *Presidencies of Harrison and Tyler,* 19; see also 10 Reg. Deb. 677–78 (1834) (statement of Sen. Tyler) (attacking the removal of the deposits from the Bank).

37. 10 Cong. Deb. 677 (1834) (statement of Sen. Tyler).

38. John Tyler, Veto Message (Sept. 9, 1841), in Richardson, *Compilation,* 4:63–64.

39. See ibid., 4:66–68. Moreover, the proposed charter allowed states to reject a branch only if the legislature did so expressly and immediately. See ibid., 4:66.

40. Ibid., 4:68.

41. Binkley, *President and Congress*, 94–95. See Cong. Globe, 27th Cong., 1st Sess., app. at 391 (1841) (statement of Rep. Mason); and ibid., app. at 472 (statement of Rep. Thompson).

42. See Binkley, *President and Congress*, 95; and Peterson, *Presidencies of Harrison and Tyler*, 85–87.

43. Peterson, *Presidencies of Harrison and Tyler*, 90; see Holt, *Whig Party*, 137.

44. Jackson, *Presidential Vetoes*, 66 (quoting the *Jonesborough Whig*, July 13, 1842).

45. Some other leading examples of chance influencing constitutional law include (1) Lincoln's death, which forced Republicans to draft the Fourteenth Amendment (a topic discussed in chapter 9); and (2) the assassination of Huey Long in 1935, which probably saved the New Deal. The last point is interesting because there is evidence that the Second New Deal (i.e., the redistributive and regulatory laws enacted in 1935) was a response to Long's presidential ambitions. See Alan Brinkley, *Voices of Protest: Huey Long, Father Coughlin, and the Great Depression* (New York: Alfred A. Knopf, 1982), 80.

46. Clausewitz, *On War*, 85.

47. In recent years, this tendency has diminished as the national parties have become more unified. Although there are significant personality differences between Bill Clinton and Al Gore, or George W. Bush and Dick Cheney, it would be hard to say that they represent different constituencies or outlooks the way Lincoln and Andrew Johnson did.

48. See Ackerman, *We the People: Transformations*, 276–77 (describing this as the vice presidential exception).

49. Not every presidential death has led to a major constitutional shake-up, but the ones near a generational transition (Harrison/Tyler, Lincoln/Johnson, and McKinley/Roosevelt) all had a significant impact.

50. There is a significant parallel here with the generational confrontation during Reconstruction, where congressional Republicans were forced in 1866 to seek a supermajority to overcome President Johnson's resistance. The difference between 1842 and 1866 is that in the first case the congressional party failed while in the second they succeeded.

51. See Cong. Globe, 27th Cong., 2d Sess., 164 (1842); see also ibid., app. at 136 (statement of Sen. Buchanan) (stating that "the fallacy of [Clay's] argument, from beginning to end, consists in the assumption that Congress, in every situation and under every circumstance, truly represent the deliberate will of the people").

52. Cong. Globe, 27th Cong., 1st Sess., app. 344 (1841) (statement of Sen. Clay).

53. This opportunity for mischief arose because the compromise tariff that ended the Nullification Crisis expired in 1842. See Act of March 2, 1833, ch. 55, 4 Stat. 629; and Remini, *Jackson: The Course of American Democracy*, 38–39. Unless another tariff was passed, rates would plummet and starve the government of revenue. See Jackson, *Vetoes*, 64; and Peterson, *Presidencies of Harrison and Tyler*, 98–101; see also Cong. Globe, 27th Cong., 2d Sess., 706 (1842) (statement of Sen. Crittenden) (describing the crunch facing the Treasury).

54. See John Tyler, Veto Message (Aug. 9, 1842), in Richardson, *Compilation*, 4:183–89 (vetoing the second tariff bill); (John Tyler, Veto Message (June 29, 1842), in Richardson, *Compilation*, 4:180–83 (vetoing the first tariff bill).

55. See Cong. Globe, 27th Cong., 2d Sess., 875 (1842).

56. Ibid., 871 (statement of Rep. Adams). It is safe to say that Adams was still bitter over his defeat in 1828. See ibid., 906 (statement of Rep. Adams): "The vetoes of President Jackson were all, in [my] opinion, among the most pernicious acts that could have been committed for the people of the United States and their highest interests."

57. Ibid., 896 (report of the Select Committee).

58. Ibid. Needless to say, the Democrats on the committee dissented from this conclusion, and they argued that the voters would vindicate the president. See ibid., 901 (minority report of the committee): "Let the battlements of this Capitol continue to rock with salutary agitation. Our reliance is in the majestic strength and serenity of a sovereign people."

59. John Tyler, Protest (Aug. 30, 1842), in Richardson, *Compilation*, 4:191–92.

60. Ibid., 4:193.

61. Holt, *Whig Party*, 151; see Peterson, *Presidencies of Harrison and Tyler*, 167. In case there is any confusion, the reason there were fewer total seats up for grabs in 1842 was because of the recent census. One lesson of this result, which Republicans learned again in 1995, is that people react badly to a government shutdown. Indeed, Thomas Gilmer, the only Whig member on the Select Committee who dissented from its report, foresaw this problem when he asked: "Will the country tolerate a suspension of the entire Government until a political dispute is settled?" See Cong. Globe, 27th Cong., 2d Sess., 896 (1842) (report of Rep. Gilmer).

62. See Holt, *Whig Party*, 194; and Peterson, *Presidencies of Harrison and Tyler*, 243. To the extent that the Whigs did execute a "switch-in-time," one could say this happened in 1848 when Zachary Taylor was elected president. Taylor was a general who believed "that traditional Whig policies must be shelved and that he [should] run a non-partisan, rather than an exclusively Whig, administration." Holt, *Whig Party*, 413. Taylor, like Harrison, died shortly after taking office.

63. Though the Bank issue was the focus of intense discussion during this time, the other major issue of the 1830s—Indian Removal—did not come up. Thus, even the most rabid conservatives accepted that this part of the Jacksonian agenda could not be reversed.

64. See Skowronek, *Politics*, 43–46 (describing the category of preemptive presidents).

65. Cong. Globe, 27th Cong., 1st Sess., 299 (1841) (statement of Rep. Wise).

66. For example, Chief Justice Taney helped draft Jackson's Bank veto and was instrumental in carrying out the president's constitutional death sentence by removing the deposits. Justice Daniel, the "Midnight Justice" appointed by Van Buren, opposed virtually every exercise of implied power as unconstitutional and said that supporting the legality of the Bank "is an objection which with me would overrule any and every recommendation which could be urged" for a candidate. John P. Frank, *Justice Daniel Dissenting: A Biography of Peter V. Daniel, 1784–1860* (Cambridge: Harvard University Press, 1964), 77. In a slightly different vein, Justice Catron was willing to disregard (and effectively overrule) *Worcester*, and there is every reason to think he would do the same for *M'Culloch*. Likewise, Justice Wayne was a rabid supporter of Jackson's stand on the Bank and on removal. See Alexander A. Lawrence, *James Moore Wayne: Southern Unionist* (Chapel Hill: University of North Carolina Press, 1943), 72. I thank Mark Graber for his work on the views of these justices.

67. See Peterson, *Great Triumvirate*, 306 (stating that Webster warned his colleagues that that the Bank bill would be struck down by the justices).

68. See Mark A. Graber, "Naked Land Transfers and American Constitutional Development," *Vanderbilt Law Review* 53 (2000): 76 (stating that the Taney Court lacked the opportunity, not the will, to strike down federal statutes).

69. John Tyler, Veto Message (June 11, 1844), in Richardson, *Compilation*, 4:330 (vetoing an internal improvements bill).

70. James K. Polk, Veto Message (Aug. 3, 1846), in Richardson, *Compilation*, 4:461 (vetoing an appropriation for harbor and river improvements).

71. James Buchanan, Veto Message (Feb. 1, 1860), in Richardson, *Compilation*, 5:603 (vetoing an internal improvements bill). By Buchanan's time, Congress began overriding some vetoes of internal improvements, which preceded the total rejection of Jacksonian understandings of federal power in Reconstruction.

72. This may explain why many scholars think that the Taney Court did not represent a major change from the Marshall Court. See Swisher, *The Taney Period*, 97–98 (stating that "the Court was careful to adhere to traditional patterns"); and Warren, *Supreme Court*, 2:33 (stating that the Jacksonian hopes of overturning Marshall's precedents were unfulfilled). The problem is that their focus is too narrow. Once the practices of all three branches are taken into account, the scope of the change becomes more obvious.

Chapter 7: The Rise of Abolitionism

1. This shift was foreshadowed by the separate opinions in *Groves* described in chapter 6.

2. That point struck me quite forcefully during a recent stay in China. In talking to scholars and government officials pursuing legal reform, a central premise of their thinking was that they should do the opposite of what was done during the Cultural Revolution. That view stems from the fact that the current generation of leaders in China lived through that chaos and has that terrible experience burned into its collective memory.

3. See, e.g., Michael Kent Curtis, *No State Shall Abridge: The Fourteenth Amendment and the Bill of Rights* (Durham, NC: Duke University Press, 1986), 6; Don E. Fehrenbacher, *The Dred Scott Case: Its Significance in American Law and Politics* (New York: Oxford University Press, 1978), 117–20; and Smith, *Civic Ideals*, 231, 246–47.

4. See Hershberger, "Anticipating Abolition," 35.

5. Ronald G. Walters, *The Antislavery Appeal: American Abolitionism after 1830* (Baltimore: Johns Hopkins University Press, 1976), ix.

6. See, e.g., Sundquist, *Dynamics*, 54.

7. See Eric Foner, *Free Soil, Free Labor, Free Men: The Ideology of the Republican Party before the Civil War* (New York: Oxford University Press, 1970), 100–101; see also Primus, *American Language of Rights*, 139 (quoting a member who said that the rule barring slavery petitions from being debated "made more abolitionists in one year, by identifying the right of petition with the question of slavery, than the abolitionists would have made for themselves in twenty-five years").

8. A major exception is Mary Hershberger, whose essay on the connection between these developments broke new ground. See Hershberger, "Anticipating Abolition," 15–40; see also *Liberator*, July 21, 1832, 114 (decrying "Andrew Jackson, and all his subordinate land-stealing, negro-thieving, missionary-persecuting, and Cherokee-murdering gang").

9. See ibid., 35–40; and Linda Kerber, "The Abolitionist Perception of the Indian," *Journal of American History* 62 (1975): 272–73.

10. See Hershberger, "Anticipating Abolition," 35.

11. Henry Mayer, *All on Fire: William Lloyd Garrison and the Abolition of Slavery* (New York: St. Martin's, 1998), 138.

12. Ibid.

13. See Robert Winston Mardock, *The Reformers and the American Indian* (Columbia: University of Missouri Press, 1971), 8; Hershberger, "Anticipating Abolition," 37; and *Liberator*, Apr. 23, 1831, 67: "We present our patrons to-day, a new head for the Liberator. . . . Down in the dust, our Indian Treaties are seen."

14. See "Brutality of the Administration toward the Cherokees," *Liberator*, Mar. 23, 1838, 48: "We have hitherto devoted a large portion of our columns to the defence of this injured people."

15. See Hershberger, "Anticipating Abolition," 38; see also Howard Jay Graham, "Our 'Declaratory' Fourteenth Amendment," *Stanford Law Review* 7 (1954): 6–7 (describing Birney's influence on the structure of Section One of the Amendment).

16. See Hershberger, "Anticipating Abolition," 38.

17. Letter from James Gillespie Birney, Late Vice President, Kentucky Colonization Society, to Reverend Thornton J. Mills, Corresponding Secretary, Kentucky Colonization Society, in *New York Office of the Anti-Slavery Reporter* (1834), 25, 30; see also *Liberator*, Jan. 26, 1833, 15: "So said the government of Georgia, in regard to the removal of the Indians—we don't compel them to go. No, Sir, they *did not* compel the Indians *to go*; but then, they rendered them so uncomfortable, by their oppression and injustice, that the poor Indians *can't stay*. And just so it is, Sir, with the Blacks."

18. See Beriah Green, *Sketches of the Life and Writings of James Gillespie Birney* (Utica, NY: Jackson and Chaplin, 1844), 17.

19. Ibid., 10.

20. Cf. Hershberger, "Anticipating Abolition," 39 (listing Green, Tappan, Garrison, Wright, and Vaux as founding members of the American Anti-Slavery Society), with ibid., 35 (listing the same people as supporters of colonization in the 1820s).

21. See Kerber, "Abolitionist Perception," 277–78.

22. Ibid., 278 (quoting the *Sixth Annual Report of the Board of Managers of the Massachusetts Anti-Slavery Society* (1838), 2–4).

23. Aida Donald and David Donald, eds., *Diary of Charles Francis Adams*, 8 vols. (Cambridge: Harvard University Press, 1964), 8:50.

24. Although this section dwells on the rising generation's connection between the tribal and slavery questions, it is worth recalling that Judge Catron also made this comparison in *Foreman*. So would Chief Justice Taney in *Dred Scott*.

25. Kerber, "Abolitionist Perception," 290.

26. Mardock, *Reformers*, 12; see L. Maria Child, *Letters from New York, Second Series* (New York, C. S. Francis, 1849), 160–61: "When either of the races come in contact with us, they must either consent to be our beasts of burden, or be driven to the wall, and perish!"; Letter from William Lloyd Garrison to Louis Kossuth (Feb. 1852), in Louis Ruchames, ed., *The Letters of William Lloyd Garrison: 1850–1860*, 6 vols. (Cambridge: Harvard University Press, 1975), 4:97, 100 (condemning "the stain on our national escutcheon. . . . this is the blood of the almost exterminated Indian tribes, and of millions of the descendants of Africa").

27. See Kerber, "Abolitionist Perception," 273–74; and John Greenleaf Whittier, "Letter from the Editor," *Pennsylvania Freeman*, May 10, 1838, 2.

28. See Mardock, *Reformers*, 9; and Kerber, "Abolitionist Perception," 273–74.

29. Letter from James Birney to Joshua Levitt (Jan. 10, 1842), in Dwight L. Dumond, ed., *Letters of James Gillespie Birney, 1831–1857* (New York: D. Appleton, 1938), 652; see ibid., 645, 650 (emphasizing that the Removal was "instigated by the slaveholding States"). On the origins of the Liberty Party, see Holt, *Whig Party*, 155–57.

30. See, e.g., Foner, *American Freedom*, 85.

31. See Cong. Globe, 26th Cong., 1st Sess., 185 (1840); and Kerber, "Abolitionist Perception," 278.

32. See Kerber, "Abolitionist Perception," 278. For more on Giddings's role as the leader of the abolitionist cause, see Richard L. Aynes, "The Antislavery and Abolitionist Background of John A. Bingham," *Catholic University Law Review* 37 (1988): 927–29.

33. See George W. Julian, *The Life of Joshua R. Giddings* (Chicago: A. C. McClurg, 1892), 398–99; and Aynes, "John A. Bingham," 929. Bingham's role in linking that episode with the constitutional amendment he took the lead in drafting is a significant theme in chapters 8 and 9.

34. Cong. Globe, 28th Cong., 1st Sess., 64 (1843); see U.S. Const., art. I, § 2, cl. 3.

35. Diary entry of Salmon P. Chase (July 2, 1843), in John Niven et al., eds., *The Salmon P. Chase Papers: Correspondence, 1823–1857* (Kent, OH: Kent State University Press, 1993), 169.

36. Ableman v. Booth, 11 Wis. 498, 529 (1859). This pamphlet was attached as an appendix to the second decision of the Wisconsin Supreme Court in the *Booth* case. In its initial ruling, the court held that a state writ of habeas corpus could issue against a person tried by federal commissioners under the Fugitive Slave Act. *In re* Booth, 3 Wis. 13, 54 (1854). The U.S. Supreme Court reversed, holding that state habeas corpus did not lie against a judgment by a federal adjudicatory body. Ableman v. Booth, 62 U.S. (21 How.) 506, 526 (1859). On remand, the state supreme court wrote a lengthy opinion responding to this order. 11 Wis. at 529.

37. See, e.g., Cong. Globe, 42d Cong, 1st Sess., app. at 84 (1871) (statement of Rep. Bingham); and Cong. Globe, 34th Cong., 3d Sess., app. at 139 (1857) (statement of Rep. Bingham).

38. The text refers to the best Supreme Court opinion because there was a circuit opinion by Justice Bushrod Washington on the rights of citizens that was even more widely cited by abolitionists. See Corfield v. Coryell, 6 F. Cas. 546 (C.C.E.D. Pa. 1823) (No. 3,230).

39. See Alschuler, *Law without Values*, 181; see also Buck v. Bell, 274 U.S. 200 (1927) (upholding a state law permitting the sterilization of the mentally retarded). Most of Holmes's dissents took a deferential stance toward progressive legislation not because he thought these measures were wise, but because he believed that majorities should almost always have their way.

40. Van Buren, *Autobiography*, 275–76.

41. See Graham, "Fourteenth Amendment," 5–6; see also Jacobus tenBroek, *Equal under Law* (New York: Collier Books, 1965), 243–80 (reproducing Weld's 1836 pamphlet on Congress's power to bar slavery in the District of Columbia).

42. See Graham, "Fourteenth Amendment," 6.

43. Ibid., 6–7, 7nn21,22. Other adherents of the Birney-Weld school included Justin Morrill, who served on the Joint Committee on Reconstruction; Salmon P. Chase, who was recruited to the abolitionist cause by Birney; the aforementioned Joshua R. Giddings, who was converted by Weld; and Benjamin Wade, who was Giddings's law partner. Ibid., 6–7, 6nn18,19, 7n20.

44. See Howard Jay Graham, "The Early Antislavery Backgrounds of the Fourteenth Amendment," *Wisconsin Law Review* (1950): 623–24. Bingham did not become a committed abolitionist until some years later. Nevertheless, his draft of the Fourteenth Amendment drew heavily on Birney-Weld ideas.

45. See Letter from Horace Greeley to Salmon P. Chase (Apr. 16, 1852), in Niven, *Salmon P. Chase Papers*, 346–47 (using the Cherokee Removal as an example).

46. Each generation grapples with the problem of whether liberty is best secured through structural reform (e.g., separation of powers, more democracy) or through remedies in the courts (e.g., the Bill of Rights, civil rights laws).

47. See Harold Holzer, *Lincoln at Cooper Union* (New York: Simon and Schuster, 2004), 284 (quoting Lincoln's speech to the Cooper Union).

48. See Foner, *American Freedom*, 87; and Primus, *American Language of Rights*, 144–46.

49. See Amar, *The Bill of Rights*, 237–38; Curtis, *No State Shall Abridge*, 36–40; and Primus, *American Language of Rights*, 136–44.

50. For a classic (and still hard to beat) analysis of this aspect of antebellum thought, see tenBroek, *Equal under Law*, 122–31.

51. See, e.g., Adamson v. California, 332 U.S. 46, 112 (1947) (Black, J., dissenting): "It is true that they were designed to meet ancient evils. But they are the same kind of human evils that have emerged from century to century wherever excessive power is sought by the few at the expense of the many."

52. See tenBroek, *Equal under Law*, 296–319 (reproducing one of Birney's pamphlets on the question).

53. Cong. Globe, 39th Cong., 1st Sess., 1118 (1866) (statement of Rep. Wilson); see ibid. at 1836 (statement of Rep. Lawrence) (discussing the case in reference to the Civil Rights Act of 1866); and ibid. at 768 (statement of Sen. Sumner) (same); see also Stephen A. Engel, "The McCulloch Theory of the Fourteenth Amendment: *City of Boerne v. Flores* and the Original Understanding of Section 5," *Yale Law Journal* 109 (1999): 141–45 (surveying the legislative debate and noting the frequency with which *M'Culloch* was invoked).

54. 45 U.S. (4 How.) 567 (1846).

55. See ibid. at 571.

56. See ibid.

57. Ibid. at 573.

58. Ibid.

59. Ibid. at 572. One could read this as an endorsement of tribal autonomy, but the states were still free to prosecute intratribal crimes if they wished.

60. Ibid. at 573.

61. Ibid.

62. See Sundquist, *Dynamics*, 73–82.

63. One theme of Stephen Skowronek's work is that our political institutions are thickening (i.e., becoming more entrenched) over time and making it more difficult to achieve radical change. See Skowronek, *Politics*, 31. Though this thesis is too broad in my view—Jefferson faced the weakest institutions of all and achieved less than other presidents—it does seem to apply here.

64. See Holt, *Whig Party*, 804–5; and Sundquist, *Dynamics*, 74–79.

65. See, e.g., David Herbert Donald, *Lincoln* (New York: Simon and Schuster, 1995), 167–68. For a sensitive analysis of the dynamic behind the Democrats' thinking on the Kansas-Nebraska Act, see Skowronek, *Politics*, 193–95.

66. See Donald, *Lincoln*, 206. One can see the start of the tit-for-tat escalation pattern here, for the trump card of the Kansas-Nebraska Act (at least from the point of view of slaveholders) boomeranged by intensifying abolitionist feeling and making the end of slavery more likely. *Dred Scott*, which is the focus of chapter 8, was the next step in this retaliatory process.

67. See Richard Hofstadter, *The Paranoid Style in American Politics* (New York: Knopf, 1965).

68. See, e.g., Ackerman, *The Failure of the Founding Fathers*, 25 (describing Jefferson's monocrat charge); and David M. Kennedy, *Freedom from Fear: The American People in Depression and War, 1929–1945* (New York: Oxford University Press, 2005), 280 (explaining FDR's venom against economic royalists).

69. Of course, there was an Anti-Masonic Party that arose at about the same time as the abolitionists. Indeed, Thaddeus Stevens started his career as an Anti-Mason. See Hans L. Trefousse, *Thaddeus Stevens* (Chapel Hill: University of North Carolina Press, 1997), 30–34. As for Skull and Bones, a conspiracy theorist might note that both presidential candidates in 2004 hailed from that secret group.

70. The point is that there is nothing inevitable about the success of any political movement, just as there is no guarantee about exactly how a generational confrontation will play out. For example, while the Republicans were getting together, another new party—the Know-Nothings—emerged as an alternative for the new generation. See Holt, *Whig Party*, 844–50. This nativist organization just never got the spark it needed to become the main challenger to the Democrats.

71. See Sundquist, *Dynamics*, 98; see also Wilentz, *Rise of American Democracy*, 675: "For all practical political purposes, the national Whig Party died on May 22, 1854."

72. See Holt, *Whig Party*, 763.

73. See Fehrenbacher, *Dred Scott*, 202.

74. See ibid., 291; and Holt, *Whig Party*, 978.

75. Franklin Pierce, Annual Message (Dec. 31, 1855), in Richardson, *Compilation*, 5:349–50.

76. Silbey, *American Party Battle*, 1:36.

Chapter 8: Judicial Resistance: *Dred Scott v. Sandford*

1. Dred Scott v. Sandford, 60 U.S. (19 How.) at 407 (1857). The best recent work on *Dred Scott* is by Mark Graber, who provides a thoughtful analysis instead of taking the easy route of labeling the case an obvious mistake. See Mark A. Graber, *Dred Scott and the Problem of Constitutional Evil* (New York: Cambridge University Press, 2006).

2. See *Dred Scott*, 60 U.S. (19 How.) at 450–51. There is a long-standing controversy about whether this aspect of the Court's opinion was dicta or holding. The analysis in this chapter

passes over this point because it is irrelevant to the constitutional dynamics that are the focus of this book.

3. See, e.g., Cong. Globe, 41st Cong., 2d Sess., 1513 (1870) (statement of Rep. Nye) (stating that the justices "were throwing a breastwork around a corrupt and tottering party; it was a legal breastwork thrown around Buchanan and his administration").

4. See Cass R. Sunstein, "Foreword: Leaving Things Undecided," *Harvard Law Review* 110 (1996): 49: "One of the notable features of [*Dred Scott*] was that far from deciding only those issues that were necessary for disposition, the Court decided every issue that it was possible to decide. If the Court had wanted to do so, it could have avoided the controversial issues entirely."

5. Of course, the idea of using the Due Process Clause to protect slavery was first suggested by Justice Baldwin in *Groves*, which was a decision issued under political conditions that some thought required a preemptive opinion.

6. Benton, *Examination*, 123. Benton opposed the decision on the Missouri Compromise issue because he was a moderate on slavery issues and felt that Congress ought to have broad discretion on the question.

7. For a fine discussion of this issue, see Richard Primus, "Canon, Anti-Canon, and Judicial Dissent," *Duke Law Journal* 48 (1998): 243–303.

8. Lincoln saw this basic truth when he said: "The *Dred Scott* decision . . . never would have been made in its present form if the party that made it had not been sustained previously by the elections." Mark A. Graber, "Desperately Ducking Slavery: *Dred Scott* and Contemporary Constitutional Theory," *Constitutional Commentary* 14 (1997): 285 (quoting the Fifth Lincoln-Douglas Debate). To take another example, even most supporters of *Roe v. Wade* are unwilling to describe the Court's opinion as brilliant reasoning. See generally J. M. Balkin, ed., *What Roe v. Wade Should Have Said* (New York: New York University Press, 2005) (offering a host of better alternatives). *Roe* is a landmark because of what it does, not because of what it says. If a future constitutional generation convinces voters that *Roe*'s premise of reproductive autonomy is wrong, it would be easy for some future scholar to attack *Roe* for its "obvious" errors in the same way that people attack *Dred Scott* now. That is the principal flaw of the otherwise excellent study by Don E. Fehrenbacher, *Dred Scott*.

9. See *Dred Scott*, 60 U.S. (19 How.) at 400.

10. See Fehrenbacher, *Dred Scott*, 253–57.

11. Scott v. Emerson, 15 Mo. 576, 586 (1852).

12. Strader v. Graham, 51 U.S. (10 How.) 82 (1852).

13. Ibid. This was dicta because prior cases held that the Ordinance had no legal force once a state was created. See ibid.

14. See *Dred Scott*, 60 U.S. (19 How.) at 601–2. Unfortunately, the structure of the case is confusing because it fused the normally distinct issues of jurisdiction and merits. Scott's suit sought a ruling that he was free. The jurisdictional issue, though, also turned on whether Scott was free. That was because a slave was not a citizen of a state and could not invoke the diversity jurisdiction of the federal courts. Thus, all of the determinations about his legal status could be reasonably characterized as rulings on jurisdiction or on the merits.

15. This point is worth remembering because even though Justice Curtis's dissent in *Dred Scott* is justly praised for its powerful denunciation of Taney's legal vision, in the most basic sense—who should win the case—it was wrong. One particularly troubling aspect of his opinion was his refusal to accept the Missouri Supreme Court's reading of state law on the issue of whether Scott was a citizen of the state. See ibid. at 604 (Curtis, J., dissenting): "I do not feel at liberty to surrender my own convictions of what the law requires, to the authority of the decision in 15 Missouri Reports."

16. Benton, *Examination*, 11.

17. See *Dred Scott*, 60 U.S. (19 How.) at 602–14 (Curtis, J., dissenting) (naming several alternative grounds for decision).

18. See ibid. at 458 (Nelson, J., concurring); ibid. at 518 (Catron, J., concurring); and ibid. at 530 (McLean, J., dissenting).

19. See ibid. at 401–3.

20. See Smith, *Civic Ideals*, 264.

21. See *Dred Scott*, 60 U.S. (19 How.) at 492–93 (Daniel, J., concurring). This was contrary to the argument made by the justices who asserted waiver, since they were saying that the Court could not independently examine the jurisdictional issue.

22. Diversity jurisdiction allows citizens of one state to sue citizens of another state even if no federal issue is present. See U.S. Const., art. III, § 2, cl. 1. At this point, Scott's master lived outside of Missouri.

23. See *Dred Scott*, 60 U.S. (19 How.): "Can a negro, whose ancestors were imported into this country, and sold as slaves, become a member of the political community formed and brought into existence by the Constitution of the United States, and as such become entitled to all the rights, and privileges, and immunities, guarantied [sic] by that instrument to the citizen?"

24. See ibid. at 403–5; ibid. at 580–81 (Curtis, J., dissenting); Fehrenbacher, *Dred Scott*, 344–46; and Smith, *Civic Ideals*, 270–71. Perhaps a more charitable reading of Justice Curtis's position is that he assumed for the sake of argument that national citizenship was required for a diversity suit.

25. The decision of some justices to write President-elect Buchanan and tell him about their internal deliberations on *Dred Scott* makes the political thrust of the case rather obvious. See Swisher, *The Taney Period*, 615–18. With advance knowledge of the result, Buchanan blandly informed the public in his Inaugural Address that "to their decision, in common with all good citizens, I shall cheerfully submit, whatever this may be." James Buchanan, Inaugural Address (Mar. 4, 1857), in Richardson, *Compilation*, 5:431.

26. See Smith, *Civic Ideals*, 245 (calling *Dred Scott* "the masterwork of Jacksonian racist constitutionalism").

27. See *Dred Scott*, 60 U.S. (19 How.) at 403–4; and Fehrenbacher, *Dred Scott*, 342 (stating that there was "no logical reason" for drawing this comparison).

28. *Dred* Scott, 60 U.S. (19 How.) 403–4.

29. See ibid. at 407.

30. Taney also repeated Marshall's false assertion that no power had ever claimed dominion over the Tribes. See ibid. at 403: "Neither the English nor colonial Governments claimed or exercised any dominion over the tribe or nation by whom it was occupied, nor claimed the right to the possession of the territory, until the tribe or nation consented to it."

31. This legal legerdemain would be repeated when the Reconstruction Court revived *M'Culloch*. See Hepburn v. Griswold, 75 U.S. (8 Wall.) 603, 615 (1870) (as chapter 9 explains).

32. See, e.g., United States v. Ritchie, 58 U.S. (17 How.) 525 (1854). This makes sense given that Jackson saw Native Americans as aliens. Aliens, of course, can become citizens. On the other hand, some of the treaties that naturalized Native Americans also granted citizenship rights to African Americans, which was a fact Taney ignored. See *Dred Scott*, 60 U.S. (19 How.) at 587 (Curtis, J., dissenting).

33. See *Dred Scott*, 60 U.S. (19 How.) at 572–73, 582 (Curtis, J., dissenting).

34. Ibid. at 411.

35. Of course, the chief justice was not the first representative of the Jacksonian generation to make this comparison. See 7. Op. Att'y Gen. 746, 751 (1856); see also State v. Foreman, 16 Tenn. 256 (1835) (drawing this link).

36. Ibid. at 410. Lincoln was quite fond of using the Declaration in support of his arguments against slavery, but Taney was not replying directly to Lincoln. See Pauline Maier, *American Scripture: Making the Declaration of Independence* (New York: Vintage Books, 1997), 201–6.

37. See *Dred Scott*, 60 U.S. (19 How.) at 412–17, 419–21. One problem with the Court's analysis was that women were citizens, even though plenty of legislation discriminated against them. See ibid. at 583 (Curtis, J., dissenting).

38. Ibid. at 582 (Curtis, J., dissenting).

39. See ibid. at 572–76, 586–88 (Curtis, J., dissenting).

40. See ibid. at 426; see also Christopher L. Eisgruber, "Dred Again: Originalism's Forgotten Past," *Constitutional Commentary* 10 (1993): 46 (calling *Dred Scott* "a riot of originalism"). The most effective argument against Taney's false originalism was Lincoln's Cooper-Union Speech, where he produced evidence that the Framers did not intend to limit Congress's power over slavery in the territories. See Holzer, *Lincoln at Cooper Union*, 252–84.

41. See *Dred Scott*, 60 U.S. (19 How.) at 442.

42. Moreover, Benton claimed that in legislating for the territories Congress ignored constitutional rights when they were deemed inappropriate and never considered itself bound by the document. See Benton, *Examination*, 12n, 14–15n, 26–27, 31–32. Yet all nine justices accepted the principle that the Constitution applied to the territories. Taney stated for the Court that "citizens of the United States who migrate to a Territory belonging to the people of the United States, cannot be ruled as mere colonists, dependent upon the will of the General Government, and to be governed by any laws it may think proper to impose." *Dred Scott*, 60 U.S. (How.) at 447.

43. See 26 U.S. (1 Pet.) 511, 542 (1828).

44. Ibid. at 546.

45. *Dred Scott*, 60 U.S. (19 How.) at 444.

46. Ibid.

47. U.S. Const., art. IV, § 3, cl. 2; see *Dred Scott*, 60 U.S. (19 How.) at 444.

48. See *Dred Scott*, 60 U.S. (19 How.) at 444.

49. See Cross v. Harrison, 57 U.S. (16 How.) 164, 194 (1853); *Canter* 26 U.S. (1 Pet.) at 541; and Sere v. Pitot, 10 U.S. (6 Cranch) 332, 336–37 (1810).

50. See Stuart A. Streichler, "Justice Curtis's Dissent in the Dred Scott Case: An Interpretative Study," *Hastings Constitutional Law Quarterly* 24 (1997): 540n233 (citing Scott's brief in the Supreme Court).

51. M'Culloch v. Maryland, 17 U.S. (4 Wheat.) 316, 422 (1819).

52. Moreover, the chief justice stated that the power of Congress to create territorial governments lent support to the idea that it could establish other corporate bodies like the Bank. See ibid. at 422: "All admit the constitutionality of a territorial government, which is a corporate body." Thus, the link between *M'Culloch* and the Missouri Compromise was strong even if the question was framed in terms of implied power rather than the specific application of the Territory Clause.

53. See *Dred Scott*, 60 U.S. (19 How.) at 542 (McLean, J., dissenting).

54. Ibid. at 614–15 (Curtis, J., dissenting).

55. See ibid. at 442: "We put aside, therefore, any argument, drawn from precedents, showing the extent of the power which the General Government exercised over slavery in this Territory, as altogether inapplicable to the case before us."

56. Although due process was the headline novelty in *Dred Scott*, other justices offered their own creative ideas on how to strike down the ban on territorial slavery. For instance, Justice Daniel wrote that the Missouri Compromise "establish[ed] inequalities amongst those citizens by creating privileges in one class of those citizens." Ibid. at 489 (Daniel, J., concurring). Meanwhile, Justice Catron, the old Jacksonian warhorse, argued that a slave owner gained the right to enter a territory with his property "through the equality of his State, by virtue of that great fundamental condition of the Union—the equality of the States." Ibid. at 527 (Catron, J., concurring).

57. Ibid. at 451. This analysis also invalidated the Kansas-Nebraska Act, since Congress presumably also did not have the implied power to authorize settlers in the territories to bar slavery. See ibid. at 451. The technique of reading implied power in conjunction with express textual prohibitions was used in subsequent cases; see, e.g., Hepburn v. Griswold, 75 U.S. (8 Wall.) 603, 622–25 (1870). What makes *Dred Scott* unique is its view that this interpretive stance was appropriate in the absence of state authority.

58. See Allgeyer v. Louisiana, 165 U.S. 278 (1897); and Magliocca, "Constitutional False Positives," 884–87; see also Lochner v. New York, 198 U.S. 45 (1905) (expanding this doctrine).

59. *Dred Scott*, 60 U.S. (19 How.) at 621 (Curtis, J., dissenting).

60. The original formulation of this issue was by Alexander M. Bickel, *The Least Dangerous Branch*, rev. ed. (1962; repr., New Haven: Yale University Press, 1986), 16.

61. In addition to the examples discussed thus far, see, e.g., Pollock v. Farmers' Home Loan & Trust Co., 157 U.S. 429, 570 (1895) (declaring the income tax statute unconstitutional as applied to certain revenue streams), modified on reh'g, 158 U.S. 601 (striking down the entire income tax act); ibid. at 157 U.S. 652 (White, J., dissenting): "Let it be felt that on great constitutional questions this court is to depart from the settled conclusions of its predecessors, and to determine them all according to the mere opinion of those who temporarily fill its bench, and our constitution will . . . be bereft of value"; United States v. Callender, 25 F. Cas. 239 (C.C.D. Va. 1800) (No. 14, 709) (Chase, J.); and Kramer, *The People Themselves*, 135 (noting that Justice Chase's conduct of the *Callender* trial was the basis of an article of impeachment). The New Deal is also replete with examples of massive judicial resistance. See A.L.A. Schechter Poultry Corp. v. United States, 295 U.S. 495 (1935) (invalidating the National Recovery Act on delegation and Commerce Clause grounds), though my research on that era is not as well developed.

62. Fehrenbacher, *Dred Scott*, 419 (quoting the *Philadelphia Pennsylvanian*).

63. Considering Bingham's formidable achievements, his career does not receive as much attention as it deserves. See Adamson v. California, 332 U.S. 46, 74 (1947) (Black, J., dissenting) (calling him the "Madison of the first section of the Fourteenth Amendment"). No biography has succeeded in conveying his importance to the work of Reconstruction. For an interesting take on Bingham's early activities, see C. Russell Riggs, "The Ante-Bellum Career of John A. Bingham: A Case Study in the Coming of the Civil War" (Ph.D. diss., New York University, 1958).

64. See Cong. Globe, 34th Cong., 3d Sess., app. at 135–40 (1857) (statement of Rep. Bingham).

65. See Riggs, "Ante-Bellum Career," 203. During his speech, Bingham observed that the territorial issue was sub judice and suggested that antislavery advocates expected a bad outcome. Cong. Globe, 34th Cong., 3d Sess., app. at 137 (1857) (statement of Rep. Bingham).

66. Cong. Globe, 34th Cong., 3d Sess., app. at 139 (1857) (statement of Rep. Bingham). Just to be clear, the capitalization of the word "equality" is not my handiwork. That is how it is written in the original source.

67. See Fehrenbacher, *Dred Scott*, 452. It is worth noting that the attack against the decision was aimed almost entirely at the Missouri Compromise issue. Few Republicans said anything about the citizenship ruling, probably because at that time there was considerable public support for the idea that African Americans should not be citizens. See Donald, *Lincoln*, 200; and Fehrenbacher, *Dred Scott*, 439.

68. Fehrenbacher, *Dred Scott*, 442.

69. See Garrison, *Legal Ideology*, 209.

70. Warren, *Supreme Court*, 2:357. In fact, in the aftermath of *Dred Scott* it was the Democrats who benefited politically. Results from state elections in 1857 went against the Repub-

licans, and there is good reason to think that this was caused by initial public approval for Chief Justice Taney's opinion. See Graber, *Dred Scott*, 40.

71. Cong. Globe, 35th Cong., 1st Sess., 943 (1858) (statement of Sen. Seward).

Chapter 9: The Fourteenth Amendment in Jackson's Shadow

1. One could say that the tit-for-tat pattern of retaliation evident during a generational transition is, to use a term from ancient astronomy, an epicycle (i.e., a cycle within a cycle).

2. See Abraham Lincoln, Inaugural Address (Mar. 4, 1861), in Richardson, *Compilation*, 6:5.

3. Indeed, congressional Republicans passed a law over President Johnson's veto that reduced the number of justices so that the president would get no appointments. See Warren, *Supreme Court*, 2:501.

4. See, e.g., Slaughter-House Cases, 83 U.S. (16 Wall.) 36, 71 (1873) (stating that the "pervading purpose" of the Reconstruction Amendments was "the freedom of the slave race").

5. See Eric L. McKitrick, *Andrew Johnson and Reconstruction* (Chicago: University of Chicago Press, 1960), 90n10; see also Kenneth M. Stampp, *The Era of Reconstruction, 1865–77* (New York: Knopf, 1965), 50 (calling Johnson the "Last Jacksonian"); ibid. at 54–55 (describing Johnson's background in Tennessee).

6. See, e.g., W. R. Brock, *An American Crisis: Congress and Reconstruction, 1865–1877* (New York: St. Martin's, 1963), 30.

7. See Andrew Johnson, Veto Message (Jan. 5, 1867), in Richardson, *Compilation*, 6:472–83 (vetoing a bill extending the vote to African Americans in the District of Columbia); and Andrew Johnson, Veto Message (Mar. 27, 1866), in ibid., 6:405–13 (vetoing the Civil Rights Act of 1866); see also Andrew Johnson, Veto Message (Mar. 2, 1867), in ibid., 6:492–98 (vetoing the Tenure of Office Act).

8. Benjamin Perley Poore, ed., *Trial of Andrew Johnson, President of the United States, before the Senate of the United States, on Impeachment by the House of Representatives for High Crimes and Misdemeanors*, 3 vols. (Washington, DC: Government Printing Office, 1868), 2:123; see Brock, *American Crisis*, 35 (stating that southerners saw Johnson "as a new Andrew Jackson"); and Poore, *Trial*, at 1:332 (quoting a spectator during a Johnson speech who remarked, "Here's a second Jackson").

9. James G. Blaine, *Twenty Years of Congress*, 2 vols. (Norwich, CT: Henry Bill, 1884), 2:241; see ibid. at 2:308: "In many features of [Johnson's] career [he] has been suspected of an attempted imitation of Jackson."

10. Cong. Globe, 39th Cong., 2d Sess., 1524 (1867) (statement of Rep. Schenck).

11. Specifically, Johnson dismissed Edwin M. Stanton for supporting congressional efforts to coerce the southern states to ratify the Fourteenth Amendment. See Ackerman, *We the People: Transformations*, 222–23.

12. See, e.g., Poole, *Trial*, 2:36–37 (discussing the Deposit Crisis); and ibid. at 2:314 (describing "the great party exacerbations between the democracy, under the lead of General Jackson, and the whigs").

13. The issue is even more complicated than it looks because the generational ebb and flow often shifts attitudes toward past precedents and presidents. Though unpopular during his tenure, Johnson's reputation rose over the next several decades as the egalitarian ideals of the Reconstruction era fell into disfavor. By the 1940s, he received the ultimate encomium—a Hollywood biography. Starring Van Heflin as Johnson and Lionel Barrymore as Thaddeus Stevens, this film made Johnson the hero who fought against evil Republican schemes to brutalize the South. See *Tennessee Johnson* (Metro-Goldwyn-Mayer, 1942). It was only after the civil rights revolution of the 1960s that Johnson's reputation took another nosedive.

14. This point is stressed by Stephen Skowronek, who argues that the temporal relationship of a president to his political generation is far more important to his reputation than leadership skills. The worst presidents, he notes, tend to cluster at the end of a given regime (the two Adams, James Buchanan, Herbert Hoover, Jimmy Carter), while the best usually come at the beginning (Jefferson, Jackson, Lincoln, FDR, Reagan). See Skowronek, *Politics*, 8.

15. Andrew Johnson, Veto Message (Mar. 27, 1866), in Richardson, *Compilation*, 6:413.

16. Ibid.

17. Ibid., 6:406.

18. See Amar, *America's Constitution*, 547n21.

19. See Andrew Johnson, Veto Message (Mar. 27, 1866), in Richardson, *Compilation*, 6:406: "When eleven of the thirty-six States are unrepresented in Congress at the present time, is it sound policy to make our entire colored population and all other excepted classes citizens of the United States?" Whether Congress possessed the power to exclude the South, and if so on what grounds, is an oft-debated question that this analysis will pass over. For a more detailed discussion, see Ackerman, *We the People: Transformations*, 99–119; and Amar, *America's Constitution*, 368–80.

20. See Cong. Globe, 39th Cong., 1st Sess., 3349 (1866) (protest of President Johnson).

21. Ibid.

22. This theme continued with the amendment's ratification in the southern states, as Congress took the lead role in organizing their elections (with the help of federal troops) and required them to ratify the amendment as a condition to being readmitted into the Union. See Ackerman, *We the People: Transformations*, 201–6.

23. It would be a stretch to take the further step and say that Lincoln's death put Reconstruction on a firmer footing. Our history suggests that constitutional text is no better than Supreme Court opinions or customs in achieving concrete results. Granted, there are certain structural changes that can only be achieved with an amendment, but many textual provisions are not enforced at all. For instance, the Fifteenth Amendment guaranteeing African Americans the right to vote was ignored in the decades between the unsuccessful Populist generation and the civil rights movement of the 1960s. See C. Vann Woodward, *The Strange Career of Jim Crow* (New York: Oxford University Press, 2002), 77–90. By contrast, there are many Court opinions and informal practices that proved more durable.

24. U.S. Const., amend. XIV, § 1; see, e.g., tenBroek, *Equal under Law*, 145–47 (describing Bingham's drafting role).

25. The relationship between Section One and the Civil Rights Act is not disputed, but the claim that the Fourteenth Amendment incorporated the Bill of Rights against the states is. At first, academic opinion was very critical of Justice Black's view that the Reconstruction generation incorporated the Bill of Rights; cf. Adamson v. California, 332 U.S. 46, 71 (1947) (Black, J., dissenting); and Charles Fairman, "Does the Fourteenth Amendment Incorporate the Bill of Rights?" *Stanford Law Review* 2 (1949): 139. Recent scholarship confirms that Justice Black was largely correct; see, e.g., Amar, *The Bill of Rights*, 163–214; and Curtis, *No State Shall Abridge*, 26–170. Although the Court has never accepted his version of "total incorporation," a series of cases have held most of these provisions applicable to the states under the standard articulated in *Palko v. Connecticut*, 302 U.S. 319, 325 (1937) (stating that a provision of the Bill of Rights applies to the states if it is in the "very essence of a scheme of ordered liberty"). The evolution of this case law is complex, but the upheaval created by the next generational transition in the 1890s was an important factor. See Magliocca, "Constitutional False Positives," 823n9.

26. U.S. Const., amend. XIV, § 5.

27. See, e.g., Katzenbach v. Morgan, 384 U.S. 641, 651 (1966): "The McCulloch v. Maryland standard is the measure of what constitutes 'appropriate legislation' under § 5 of the Fourteenth Amendment." Engel, "*McCulloch* Theory of the Fourteenth Amendment," 141–45.

28. United States v. Rhodes, 27 F. Cas. 785, 791 (C.C.D. Ky. 1866) (No. 16,151). As one might expect, President Johnson disagreed with this interpretation. In his veto of the Civil Rights Act, Johnson replied, in tones reminiscent of the Bank Veto, that "it can not . . . be justly claimed that, with a view to the enforcement of this article of the Constitution, there is at present any necessity for the exercise of all the powers which this bill confers." Andrew Johnson, Veto Message (Mar. 27, 1866), in Richardson, *Compilation*, 6:411. Some Republicans, notably John Bingham, were also uneasy about the Civil Rights Act, which was a factor in the decision to write the Fourteenth Amendment.

29. It is worth noting that Republicans did not criticize Jackson himself. Instead, they praised the president for his steadfast opposition to secession during the Nullification Crisis.

30. Indeed, there are commonalities in the language used in the Fourteenth Amendment and in the Cherokee experience. See, e.g., *Liberator*, Apr. 4, 1838, 56: "It is a mistaken impression with regard to the Cherokees, that they object to becoming citizens of the United States. . . . they have required *the protection and the privileges* of our laws, to accompany that conformity on their part. *They have asked this repeatedly, and repeatedly has it been denied*" (italics in original). Another notable example is the 1846 treaty between the Cherokee Nation and the United States, which required that within the Tribe, "laws shall be passed for equal protection, and for sanctity of life, liberty, and property." Treaty with the Cherokees, Aug. 6, 1846, art. 2, 9 Stat. 871.

31. See S. Rep. No. 38-25, at 1 (1864).

32. See ibid. at 3 (quoting the Virginia law stating that "a negro or Indian" could not be a witness when whites were parties); ibid. at 4 (describing the Kentucky law providing that "a slave, negro, or Indian" could not testify against whites); ibid. (discussing statutes of North Carolina and Tennessee); ibid. at 4–5 (stating that South Carolina's exclusions included "free Indians and slaves"); and ibid. at 4–6 (describing the practice in Georgia, Alabama, and Texas).

33. Ibid. at 24 (quoting Letter from Hon. John Appleton, Chief Justice of Maine, to Hon. Charles Sumner [Jan. 24, 1864]).

34. Ibid. at 26.

35. Although Sumner could not get his bill through the 38th Congress, the essence of his proposal was codified in the Civil Rights Act. See Curtis, *No State Shall Abridge*, 71.

36. *National Anti-Slavery Standard*, Apr. 10, 1869, 2; see Mardock, *Reformers*, 15 (citing Lydia Maria Child's post–Civil War efforts on behalf of Native Americans because "their wrongs' . . . have been almost equal to those of the black race"); and ibid. at 48 (quoting the abolitionist Wendell Phillips, who said that the "great poison of the age is race hatred. . . . We must see the man, not the negro, the man and not the Indian, the man and not the Chinaman").

37. See Cong. Globe, 40th Cong., 3d Sess., 801 (1869) (statement of Rep. Mullins): "Why, when all are treated alike, should the Indians not be included?"; ibid. at 21 (statement of Rep. Garfield) (alluding to *Dred Scott* by attacking the idea that the tribes "shall be confined to reservations and not have any rights which white men are bound to respect"); and Cong. Globe, 40th Cong., 2d Sess., 1956 (1868) (statement of Rep. Broomall) (refuting the doctrine "that black men and red men have no rights whatever except by the grace and favor of the white men").

38. Cong. Globe, 39th Cong., 1st Sess., 154 (1866) (statement of Rep. Morrill).

39. Cong. Globe, 38th Cong., 2d Sess., 260 (1865) (statement of Rep. Rollins). Another piece of evidence reinforcing the link between African American and Native American rights involved the Thirteenth Amendment. When the core of that provision was applied for the first time, Congress focused on the Tribes. In 1867, the Senate began investigating the peonage system in New Mexico in order "to prevent the enslavement of Indians." Cong. Globe, 39th Cong., 2d Sess., 239–41 (1867) (statement of Sen. Sumner). The Senate later passed a bill that attempted to abolish peonage. See ibid. at 1571–72.

40. Alexander Keyssar, *The Right to Vote: The Contested History of Democracy in the United States* (New York: Basic Books, 2000), 165.

41. See Majority Report of the Joint Committee on Reconstruction, reprinted in Edward McPherson, ed., *The Political History of the United States of America during the Period of Reconstruction* (Washington, DC: Solomons and Chapman, 1880), 86–88; and S. Rep. No. 39-156 (1867) (stating the findings and recommendations of the Joint Committee on the Tribes).

42. 16 Stat. 566 (1871). The president and the Tribes still negotiated agreements, but after 1871 they needed the approval of a majority of both houses of Congress rather than a supermajority of the Senate. See Mardock, *Reformers*, 105. Existing treaties with the Tribes remained in force. See Cong. Globe, 41st Cong., 3d Sess., 1811 (1871) (statement of Rep. Sargent). This change in the form of tribal relations was not a comment on their sovereignty but the product of a long campaign by the House of Representatives to wrest from the Senate its exclusive power over Native American affairs. See, e.g., Cong. Globe, 41st Cong., 2d Sess., 1517 (1870) (statement of Sen. Sumner); and Smith, *Civic Ideals*, 319.

43. See Smith, *Civic Ideals*, 318–19.

44. Ibid., 318.

45. See S. Rep. No. 41-268, at 10 (1870) (Senate Judiciary Committee Report): "Those who framed the fourteenth amendment . . . understood that the Indian tribes were not made citizens, but were excluded by the restricting phrase, 'and subject to the jurisdiction.'"; and Cong. Globe, 39th Cong., 1st Sess., 2890 (1866) (statement of Sen. Howard): "Indians born within the limits of the United States, and who maintain their tribal relations, are not, in the sense of this amendment, born subject to the jurisdiction of the United States." Some complained that this language was inexact because many federal laws regulated aspects of tribal life and did subject their members to national jurisdiction. See ibid. at 2895–96 (1866) (statement of Sen. Doolittle); ibid. at 2893–94 (statement of Sen. Johnson); and ibid. at 2894–95 (statement of Sen. Hendricks).

46. Ibid. at 527 (statement of Sen. Trumbull). Put another way, there was no analogous group of African Americans who refused to recognize federal authority, and therefore some distinction had to be made between the Tribes and the freedmen.

47. Cong. Globe, 39th Cong., 1st Sess., 574 (1866). Given the strong objections to tribal citizenship, the remarkable thing is that so many Republicans fought for the idea and upheld the abolitionist position that tribal rights were inextricably linked to African American freedom. See Cong. Globe, 41st Cong., 2d Sess., 1670 (1870) (statement of Rep. Paine); ibid. at 125–26 (1869) (statement of Rep. Niblack); Cong. Globe, 41st Cong., 1st Sess., 560 (1869) (statement of Rep. Butler); and Cong. Globe, 39th Cong., 1st Sess., 571 (1866) (statement of Sen. Henderson).

48. Elk v. Wilkins, 112 U.S. 94, 112 (1884) (Harlan, J., dissenting).

49. *Cincinnati Daily Commercial*, Aug. 9, 1866, 9. Citizenship was extended to all Native Americans by Congress in 1924.

50. The Senate Judiciary Committee Report on the relationship between the Tribes and the Fourteenth Amendment made this point: "To maintain that the United States intended, by a change of its fundamental law, which was not ratified by these tribes . . . to annul treaties then existing between the United States as one party, and the Indian tribes as the other parties respectively, would be to charge upon the United States repudiation of national obligations" (S. Rep. No. 41-268, at 11 [1870]). Some members also had a hard time understanding how the United States could make treaties with people who were also citizens. See, e.g., Cong. Globe, 39th Cong., 1st Sess., 2893 (1866) (statement of Sen. Trumbull): "We cannot make a treaty with ourselves; it would be absurd."

51. S. Rep. No. 41-268 (1870) at 9 (Senate Judiciary Committee Report). Of course, the modern solution to this issue allows the Tribes to exercise sovereignty in addition to their

rights as U.S. citizens, but the Reconstruction Framers should not be blamed for failing to see this option.

52. This exposes a flaw in the argument that the language of the Fourteenth Amendment barring the Tribes from citizenship can be interpreted to exclude children born here to illegal alien parents. See Peter H. Schuck and Rogers H. Smith, *Citizenship without Consent* (New Haven: Yale University Press, 1985), 76–83. These scholars assume that the drafters were expressing a theory of citizenship that sought to limit the rights granted by the state, when in reality the clause was written as part of a concrete response to precedent that made every effort to expand rights.

53. Cong. Globe, 40th Cong., 3d Sess., app. at 142 (1869) (statement of Rep. Burleigh); see Cong. Globe, 41st Cong., 2d Sess., 4137 (1870) (statement of Rep. Davis) (summarizing the history of Removal).

54. Cong. Globe, 41st Cong., 2d Sess., 1671 (1870) (statement of Rep. Maynard).

55. Cong. Globe, 39th Cong., 1st Sess., 1684 (1866) (statement of Rep. Stevens).

56. The case was raised by Reverdy Johnson, a leading Democrat who represented the slaveholder in *Dred Scott*, and led to a dialogue with Senators Trumbull and Sumner about the status of Native Americans under the bill. See ibid. at 505–6.

57. See ibid. at 1756 (statement of Sen. Trumbull). Even Andrew Johnson saw the importance of *Worcester* for his generational foes. During the impeachment trial, his counsel sought to reassure the Senate that the president was now on board with their constitutional program by comparing the Cherokee Removal with Reconstruction: "I knew a case where the State of Georgia undertook to make it penal for a Christian missionary to preach the gospel to the Indians. . . . And I knew the great leader of the moral and religious sentiment of the United States [Theodore Frelinghuysen], who, representing in this body . . . the State of New Jersey, tried hard to save his country from the degradation of the oppression of the Indians at the [insistence] of the haughty planters of Georgia. The Supreme Court of the United States held the law unconstitutional and issued its mandate, and the State of Georgia laughed at it and kept the missionary in prison. . . . But the war came, and as from the clouds from Lookout Mountain swooping down upon Missionary Ridge came the thunders of the violated Constitution of the United States, and the lightnings of its power over the still home of the missionary Worcester, taught the State of Georgia what comes of violating the Constitution" (Poole, *Trial*, 2:35–58). This tribute to *Worcester* was directed at Senator Frederick Frelinghuysen, the nephew of the "great leader" who fought so hard against Removal.

58. Cong. Globe, 42d Cong., 1st Sess., 335 (1871) (statement of Rep. Hoar) (discussing the Ku Klux Klan Act); see Curtis, *No State Shall Abridge*, 161–64 (noting that this was a major contemporary interpretation of the Fourteenth Amendment by Congress).

59. Cong. Globe, 42d Cong., 1st Sess., 335 (1871) (statement of Rep. Hoar).

60. See Cong. Globe, 42d Cong., 1st Sess., app. at 84 (1871) (statement of Rep. Bingham) (quoting the first eight amendments and stating that "these eight articles I have shown never were limitations upon the power of the States, until made so by the fourteenth amendment").

61. Ibid.

62. *Cincinnati Daily Commercial*, Aug. 10, 1866, 1; see ibid., Aug. 27, 1866, 9 (making the same point in an article entitled "The Constitutional Amendment—Discussed by Its Author").

63. See Employment Div. v. Smith, 494 U.S. 872 (1990).

64. There is one wrinkle to this discussion. *Smith* did qualify its holding by saying that "the First Amendment bars application of a neutral, generally applicable law to religiously motivated action . . . involv[ing] not the Free Exercise Clause alone, but the Free Exercise Clause in conjunction with other constitutional protections." Ibid. at 881. In other words, an action that burdens religious expression and another right is invalid. The missionaries'

imprisonment clearly fit under this rule, since the oath law burdened their free exercise and free speech rights. Thus, Bingham's use of this episode to define the incorporated First Amendment does not necessarily undermine *Smith*.

The problem with this saving interpretation is that virtually nobody, in the 1830s or during Reconstruction, saw the jailing of the missionaries as a free speech issue. For instance, the Georgia legislature's Special Committee Report, which gave the most detailed analysis of those events, did not cast the objections in terms of free speech. Likewise, the criticisms of the religious organizations in the 1830s focused entirely on free exercise concerns. Nor do Bingham's comments in the text say anything about free speech. To my mind, this suggests that a broader interpretation of Reconstruction repudiating *Smith*'s holding makes more sense.

That was the position that I took in a prior article, subject to the discovery of additional evidence. In researching this book, I came across another statement of Bingham's (as reported in a newspaper article) in which he did describe the issue as a free speech problem. See *Cincinnati Daily Commercial*, Aug. 27, 1866, 9: "Hereafter the American people can not have peace, if, as in the past, States are permitted to take away freedom of speech, and to condemn men, as felons, to the penitentiary for teaching their fellow men that there is a hereafter, and a reward for those who learn to do well." Granted, this quote does not mention Georgia or Indians, but it sounds like his other references to *Worcester*. This clouds the picture somewhat, but I think that my original conclusion stands for two reasons. First, since the reference is a secondhand quote of a speech he gave, I cannot be sure that his language on freedom of speech is accurate. Second, even if the statement is correct, the evidence is still tilted in the direction of a pure free exercise interpretation.

65. One scholar has focused on *Smith* in relation to the abolitionist generation's views, though *Worcester* is not discussed. See Kurt T. Lash, "The Second Adoption of the Free Exercise Clause: Religious Exemptions under the Fourteenth Amendment," *Northwestern University Law Review* 88 (1994): 1133–37.

66. Of course, even if my historical interpretation is accepted, that does not mean that *Smith* is wrong. History has a powerful claim on the law, but it is not the be-all and end-all of resolving constitutional issues.

67. That oversight is particularly unfortunate since both *Smith* and the oath law affected the religious freedom of Native Americans, in one case to practice their religion and in the other to receive religious instruction.

68. See, e.g., Jeffrey Tulis, *The Rhetorical Presidency* (Princeton: Princeton University Press, 1987), 87–93 (discussing Johnson's ill-fated "swing around the circle" campaign).

69. See Ackerman, *We the People: Transformations*, 212–23.

70. See Hans L. Trefousse, *Andrew Johnson* (New York: W. W. Norton, 1989), 323–24.

71. S. Rep. No. 41-268, at 6 (1870) (Senate Judiciary Committee Report).

72. Ibid. at 7. Unfortunately, this victory for tribal rights proved short-lived, as Native Americans (along with African Americans) suffered serious setbacks in the years following Reconstruction. That story is important, but this book cannot provide an adequate treatment.

73. Ibid.

74. What this shows is that courts will usually bend over backwards to present their work as consistent with past practice. Judges are reluctant to admit that they are adjusting precedent because the illusion of continuity is critical to legal authority. See, e.g., Wills, *Certain Trumpets*, 132–33 (explaining that courts fit Max Weber's model of traditional authority).

75. See Hepburn v. Griswold, 75 U.S. (8 Wall.) 603 (1870). Paper money means notes that are not backed by gold or silver but must be accepted as payment.

76. Ibid. at 614 (footnote omitted).

77. Ibid. at 615.

78. This performance is similar to the famous one given by Chase a year earlier in *Ex Parte McCardle*, 74 U.S. (7 Wall.) 506 (1869). In that case, the chief justice held that a jurisdiction-stripping statute was valid by glossing over the fact that Congress intended to prevent the Court from hearing any challenge to military Reconstruction, not just the challenge brought under the specific habeas corpus statute that was repealed.

79. *Hepburn*, 75 U.S. (8 Wall.) at 615.

80. Of course, this did not resolve the question of how *M'Culloch* should be interpreted. After embracing Marshall's test, Chief Justice Chase proceeded to hold that paper money exceeded Congress's powers. See ibid. at 625. One year later, though, the Court reversed itself and advanced a broader reading of *M'Culloch*. See Knox v. Lee, 79 U.S. (12 Wall.) 457, 541 (1871).

81. William M. Safire, *Lend Me Your Ears: Great Speeches in History* (New York: W. W. Norton, 1992), 772 (quoting Bryan's speech to the 1896 Democratic Convention).

Conclusion: In Search of the Missing Constitution

1. Frickey, "Marshalling Past and Present," 383.

2. See Korematsu v. United States, 323 U.S. 214 (1944).

3. See Kenji Yoshino, *Covering: The Hidden Assault on Our Civil Rights* (New York: Random House, 2006).

4. In this respect, there is a deep symmetry between the criticism leveled at the *Smith* rule and the Cherokee resistance to Removal. A doctrine holding that minority religions must always conform to majority policy preferences is clearly about assimilation and not about respecting diverse beliefs.

5. There is evidence that the abolitionist generation saw tribal identity in cultural terms. The Senate that gave us the Fourteenth Amendment also ratified a treaty holding that any white person who married into or joined the Choctaw or Chickasaw Tribes was under their legal authority, which contradicted the Taney Court's holding in *Rogers* that a white could never become a tribal member. See Treaty with the Choctaw and Chickasaw, Apr. 28, 1866, art. 38, 14 Stat. 769, 779. Shortly after, following Reconstruction, the Supreme Court held that the Pueblos were not a Tribe for purposes of a federal law because they practiced settled agriculture and lived in villages. See United States v. Joseph, 94 U.S. 614 (1876). Though the Court conceded that the Pueblos had some unusual cultural practices, it concluded that "they only resemble in this regard the Shakers and other communistic societies in this country and cannot for that reason be classed with the Indian Tribes." Ibid. at 617–18.

6. One example of this is the way in which the "liberty of contract" is sometimes falsely attributed to the Framers of the Fourteenth Amendment, when it was, in fact, caused by intergenerational friction of the 1890s. See Magliocca, "Constitutional False Positives," 884–87. Similarly, the decisions holding that Congress may not abrogate state sovereign immunity are grounded in the text of the Eleventh Amendment, which has nothing to say about that issue, when that rule really emanates from the federalism of the Reagan Revolution. See, e.g., Seminole Tribe of Florida v. Florida, 517 U.S. 1133 (1996).

7. Chambers v. Florida, 309 U.S. 227, 241 (1940).

8. For an interesting discussion on the mutually reinforcing relationship between the Court's decisions and popular opinion, see Michael Abramowicz, "Constitutional Circularity," *UCLA Law Review* 49 (2001): 1–90.

9. This reasoning could offer a new justification for the Court's decision to overrule *Plessy v. Ferguson* in *Brown v. Board of Education*. *Plessy* was one of many cases decided by the Court during its resistance to the Populist generation. See Magliocca, "Constitutional False Positives," 823n9 and 855–73. By the 1950s, however, *Plessy* was the only one of those cases that

remained good law. Even though the other preemptive opinions of the 1890s were about unrelated topics such as the income tax, the justices in *Brown* could have noted that the invalidity of these temporally related cases undermined *Plessy*'s holding by indicating that the values reflected by that opinion no longer enjoyed the support of the nation.

10. Abraham Lincoln, Inaugural Address (Mar. 4, 1861), in Richardson, *Compilation*, 6:11.

Bibliography

Frequently Cited Works

Congressional Globe (citation format: Cong. Globe, Congress, Session, Page, Year, Member)
Daily National Intelligencer (citation format: Date and Page)
Liberator (citation format: Title, Date, Page)
Register of Debates (citation format: Reg. Deb., Volume, Page, Year, Member)

Books, Articles, and Miscellaneous Sources

Abramowicz, Michael. "Constitutional Circularity." *UCLA Law Review* 49 (2001): 1–90.
Ackerman, Bruce. *We the People: Foundations.* Cambridge: Harvard University Press, 1991.
———. *We the People: Transformations.* Cambridge: Harvard University Press, 1998.
———. *The Failure of the Founding Fathers: Jefferson, Marshall, and the Rise of Presidential Democracy.* Cambridge: Harvard University Press, 2005.
Ackerman, Bruce, and David Golove. *Is NAFTA Constitutional?* Cambridge: Harvard University Press, 1995.
Adkins, Nelson F., ed. *Common Sense and Other Political Writings.* New York: Bobbs-Merrill, 1953.
Alexander, Larry, and Lawrence B. Solum. "Popular? Constitutionalism?" *Harvard Law Review* 118 (2005): 1594–1640.
Alschuler, Albert W. *Law without Values.* Chicago: University of Chicago Press, 2000.
Alsop, Joseph, and Turner Catledge. *The 168 Days.* Garden City, NY: Doubleday, Doran, 1938.
Amar, Akhil Reed. *America's Constitution: A Biography.* New York: Random House, 2005.
———. *The Bill of Rights.* New Haven: Yale University Press, 1998.
Arnold, Richard S. "How James Madison Interpreted the Constitution." *New York University Law Review* 72 (1997): 267–93.
Aynes, Richard L. "The Antislavery and Abolitionist Background of John A. Bingham." *Catholic University Law Review* 37 (1988): 881–933.
Balkin, J. M., ed. *What* Roe v. Wade *Should Have Said.* New York: New York University Press, 2005.
Bass, Althea. *Cherokee Messenger.* Norman: University of Oklahoma Press, 1936.
Bassett, John Spencer, ed. *The Correspondence of Andrew Jackson.* 7 vols. Washington DC: Carnegie Institute, 1926–35.
Beard, Charles Austin. *An Economic Interpretation of the Constitution of the United States.* New York: Macmillan, 1913.
Benton, Thomas Hart. *An Examination of the Dred Scott Case.* New York: D. Appleton, 1857.

———. *Thirty Years' View*. 2 vols. New York: D. Appleton, 1859.

Bernstein, David B., and Ilya Somin. "Judicial Power and Civil Rights Reconsidered." *Yale Law Journal* 114 (2001): 595–657.

Bickel, Alexander M. *The Least Dangerous Branch*. Rev. ed., 1962; repr., New Haven: Yale University Press, 1986.

Binkley, Wilfred E. *President and Congress*. New York: Alfred A. Knopf, 1947.

Blaine, James G. *Twenty Years of Congress*. 2 vols. Norwich, CT: Henry Bill, 1884.

Bork, Robert H. *The Tempting of America*. New York: Free Press, 1990.

Brands, H. W. *Andrew Jackson*. New York: Doubleday, 2005.

Brinkley, Alan. *Voices of Protest: Huey Long, Father Coughlin, and the Great Depression*. New York: Alfred A. Knopf, 1982.

Brock, W. R. *An American Crisis: Congress and Reconstruction, 1865–1877*. New York: St. Martin's, 1963.

Bryan, William J. *The First Battle: A Story of the Campaign of 1896*. Chicago: W. B. Conkey, 1896.

Burke, Joseph C. "The Cherokee Cases: A Study in Law, Politics, and Morality." *Stanford Law Review* 21 (1969): 500–531.

Calabresi, Stephen G., and Christopher S. Yoo. "The Unitary Executive during the First Half-Century." *Case Western Reserve Law Review* 47 (1997): 1451–1561.

Caro, Robert. *Master of the Senate*. New York: Knopf, 2002.

Casper, Gerhard. "An Essay in Separation of Powers: Some Early Versions and Practices." *William and Mary Law Review* 30 (1987): 211–61.

Catterall, Ralph C. *The Second Bank of the United States*. Chicago: University of Chicago Press, 1902.

Chernow, Ron. *Alexander Hamilton*. New York: Penguin, 2004.

Child, L. Maria. *Letters from New York, Second Series*. New York: C. S. Francis, 1849.

Clausewitz, Carl von. *On War*. Princeton: Princeton University Press, 1984.

Cole, Donald B. *A Jackson Man: Amos Kendall and the Rise of American Democracy*. Baton Rouge: Louisiana State University Press, 2004.

———. *The Presidency of Andrew Jackson*. Lawrence: University Press of Kansas, 1993.

Cooke, Jacob E., ed. *The Federalist*. Hanover, NH: Wesleyan University Press, 1961.

Croly, Steven P. "The Majoritarian Difficulty: Elective Judiciaries and the Rule of Law." *University of Chicago Law Review* 62 (1995): 689–790.

Currie, David P. *The Constitution in Congress: Democrats and Whigs, 1829–1861*. Chicago: University of Chicago Press, 2005.

Curtis, Michael Kent. *No State Shall Abridge: The Fourteenth Amendment and the Bill of Rights*. Durham, NC: Duke University Press, 1986.

Donald, Aida, and David Donald, eds. *Diary of Charles Francis Adams*. 8 vols. Cambridge: Harvard University Press, 1964.

Donald, David Herbert. *Lincoln*. New York: Simon and Schuster, 1995.

Dumond, Dwight L., ed. *Letters of James Gillespie Birney, 1831–1857*. New York: D. Appleton, 1938.

Eisgruber, Christopher L. "Dred Again: Originalism's Forgotten Past." *Constitutional Commentary* 10 (1993): 37–65.

Ely, John Hart. *Democracy and Distrust*. Cambridge: Harvard University Press, 1980.

Engel, Stephen A. "The McCulloch Theory of the Fourteenth Amendment: *City of Boerne v. Flores* and the Original Understanding of Section 5." *Yale Law Journal* 109 (1999): 115–54.

Fairman, Charles. "Does the Fourteenth Amendment Incorporate the Bill of Rights?" *Stanford Law Review* 2 (1949): 5–139.

Fehrenbacher, Don E. *The Dred Scott Case: Its Significance in American Law and Politics*. New York: Oxford University Press, 1978.

Feldman, Noah. *Divided by God.* New York: Farrar, Straus and Giroux, 2005.

Fiss, Owen M. "Groups and the Equal Protection Clause." *Journal of Philosophy of Public Affairs* 5 (1976): 107–77.

Foner, Eric. *Free Soil, Free Labor, Free Men: The Ideology of the Republican Party before the Civil War.* New York: Oxford University Press, 1970.

———. *The Story of American Freedom.* New York: W. W. Norton, 1998.

Frank, John P. *Justice Daniel Dissenting: A Biography of Peter V. Daniel, 1784–1860.* Cambridge: Harvard University Press, 1964.

Frickey, Phillip P. "Marshalling Past and Present: Colonialism, Constitutionalism, and Interpretation in Federal Indian Law." *Harvard Law Review* 107 (1993): 381–440.

Garrison, Tim Alan. *The Legal Ideology of Removal.* Athens: University of Georgia Press, 2002.

Garrow, David J. "Mental Decrepitude on the U.S. Supreme Court: The Historical Case for a 28th Amendment." *University of Chicago Law Review* 67 (2000): 995–1087.

"Georgia's Attack on the Missionaries." *Journal of Cherokee Studies* 4 (1979): 82–92.

Graber, Mark. "Desperately Ducking Slavery: *Dred Scott* and Contemporary Constitutional Theory." *Constitutional Commentary* 14 (1997): 285–318.

———. *Dred Scott and the Problem of Constitutional Evil.* New York: Cambridge University Press, 2006.

———. "Naked Land Transfers and American Constitutional Development." *Vanderbilt Law Review* 53 (2000): 76–121.

Graham, Howard Jay. "Our "Declaratory" Fourteenth Amendment." *Stanford Law Review* 7 (1954): 3–39.

———. "The Early Antislavery Backgrounds of the Fourteenth Amendment." *Wisconsin Law Review* (1950): 610–61.

Green, Beriah. *Sketches of the Life and Writings of James Gillespie Birney.* Utica, NY: Jackson and Chaplin, 1844.

Haines, Charles Grove. *The Role of the Supreme Court in American Government and Politics, 1789–1835.* Berkeley: University of California Press, 1944.

Hamburger, Phillip. *Separation of Church and State.* Cambridge: Harvard University Press, 2002.

Hershberger, Mary. "Mobilizing Women, Anticipating Abolition: The Struggle against Indian Removal in the 1830s." *Journal of American History* 86 (1999): 15–40.

Hofstadter, Richard. *The Idea of a Party System.* Berkeley: University of California Press, 1969.

———. *The Paranoid Style in American Politics.* New York: Knopf, 1965.

Hoig, Stanley W. *The Cherokees and Their Chiefs.* Fayetteville: University of Arkansas Press, 1998.

Holt, Michael F. *The Rise and Fall of the American Whig Party.* New York: Oxford University Press, 1999.

Holzer, Harold. *Lincoln at Cooper Union.* New York: Simon and Schuster, 2004.

Jackson, Carlton. *Presidential Vetoes.* Athens: University of Georgia Press, 1967.

Jackson, Robert H. *The Struggle for Judicial Supremacy.* New York: Alfred A. Knopf, 1941.

———. *That Man: An Insider's Portrait of Franklin D. Roosevelt.* Edited by John Q. Barrett. New York: Oxford University Press, 2003.

Julian, George W. *The Life of Joshua R. Giddings.* Chicago: A. C. McClurg, 1892.

Kennedy, David M. *Freedom from Fear: The American People in Depression and War, 1929–1945.* New York: Oxford University Press, 2005.

Kennedy, John Pendleton. *Memoirs of the Life of William Wirt, Attorney General of the United States.* 2 vols. Philadelphia: Lea and Blanchard, 1849.

Kerber, Linda. "The Abolitionist Perception of the Indian." *Journal of American History* 62 (1975): 271–95.

Keyssar, Alexander. *The Right to Vote: The Contested History of Democracy in the United States.* New York: Basic Books, 2000.

Klarman, Michael J. "How Great Were the 'Great' Marshall Court Decisions?" *Virginia Law Review* 87 (2001): 1111–84.

Kramer, Larry D. *The People Themselves: Popular Constitutionalism and Judicial Review.* New York: Oxford University Press, 2004.

Kuhn, Thomas S. *The Structure of Scientific Revolutions.* Chicago: University of Chicago Press, 1996.

Kutler, Stanley I., ed. *The Dred Scott Decision: Law and Politics.* Boston: Houghton Mifflin, 1967.

Lash, Kurt T. "The Second Adoption of the Free Exercise Clause: Religious Exemptions under the Fourteenth Amendment." *Northwestern University Law Review* 88 (1994): 1106–56.

Lawrence, Alexander A. *James Moore Wayne: Southern Unionist.* Chapel Hill: University of North Carolina Press, 1943.

Laycock, Douglas. "The Underlying Unity of Separation and Neutrality." *Emory Law Journal* 46 (1997): 43–73.

Letters and Other Writings of James Madison. Philadelphia: J. B. Lippincott, 1867.

Leuchtenberg, William. *The Supreme Court Reborn.* New York: Oxford University Press, 1995.

Lodge, Henry Cabot, ed. *The Works of Alexander Hamilton.* 12 vols. New York: G. P. Putnam's, 1904.

Mackay, Charles. *Extraordinary Popular Delusions and the Madness of Crowds.* London: Richard Bentley, 1841. Reprinted with preface by Bernard M. Baruch, New York: L. C. Page, 1932.

Magliocca, Gerard N. "Constitutional False Positives and the Populist Moment." *Notre Dame Law Review* 81 (2006): 821–88.

——. "The Philosopher's Stone: Dualist Democracy and the Jury." *University of Colorado Law Review* 69 (1998): 175–221.

Maier, Pauline. *American Scripture: Making the Declaration of Independence.* New York: Vintage Books, 1997.

Mardock, Robert Winston. *The Reformers and the American Indian.* Columbia: University of Missouri Press, 1971.

Mayer, Henry. *All on Fire: William Lloyd Garrison and the Abolition of Slavery.* New York: St. Martin's, 1998.

McCullough, David. *John Adams.* New York: Simon and Schuster, 2001.

——. *1776.* New York: Simon and Schuster, 2005.

McKitrick, Eric L. *Andrew Johnson and Reconstruction.* Chicago: University of Chicago Press, 1960.

McLoughlin, William G. *Cherokees and Missionaries, 1789–1839.* Norman: University of Oklahoma Press, 1984.

McPherson, Edward, ed. *The Political History of the United States of America during the Great Rebellion.* Washington, DC: Philp and Solomons, 1864.

——. *The Political History of the United States of America during the Period of Reconstruction.* Washington, DC: Solomons and Chapman, 1880.

Menand, Louis. *The Metaphysical Club.* New York: Farrar, Straus and Giroux, 2001.

"Military Orders and Correspondence on the Cherokee Removal." *Journal of Cherokee Studies* 3 (1978): 143–52.

The Missionaries and the State of Georgia–Address of the Democratic Committee of Correspondence for the City of Philadelphia. Oct. 29, 1832.

Newmyer, R. Kent. *John Marshall and the Heroic Age of the Supreme Court.* Baton Rouge: Louisiana State University Press, 2001.

Niven, John, et al., eds. *The Salmon P. Chase Papers: Correspondence, 1823–1857.* Kent, OH: Kent State University Press, 1993.

Peterson, Merrill D. *The Great Triumvirate: Webster, Clay, and Calhoun.* New York: Oxford University Press, 1987.

Peterson, Norma Lois. *The Presidencies of William Henry Harrison and John Tyler.* Lawrence: University Press of Kansas, 1989.

Plous, Harold J., and Gordon E. Baker. "McCulloch v. Maryland, Right Principle, Wrong Case." *Stanford Law Review* 9 (1957): 710–30.

Poore, Benjamin Perley, ed. *Trial of Andrew Johnson, President of the United States, before the Senate of the United States, on Impeachment by the House of Representatives for High Crimes and Misdemeanors.* 3 vols. Washington, DC: Government Printing Office, 1868.

Posner, Richard A. *An Affair of State.* Cambridge: Harvard University Press, 1999.

Primus, Richard. *The American Language of Rights.* United Kingdom: Cambridge University Press, 1999.

——. "Canon, Anti-Canon, and Judicial Dissent." *Duke Law Journal* 48 (1998): 243–303.

Proceedings of the Massachusetts Historical Society 14: (1901).

Prucha, Francis Paul. *The Great Father: The United States Government and the American Indians.* 2 vols. Lincoln: University of Nebraska Press, 1984.

Remini, Robert V. *Andrew Jackson: The Course of American Freedom, 1822–1832.* Baltimore: Johns Hopkins University Press, 1981.

——. *Andrew Jackson: The Course of American Democracy, 1833–1845.* Baltimore: Johns Hopkins University Press, 1981.

——. *Andrew Jackson and His Indian Wars.* New York: Viking, 2001.

Richardson, James D., ed. *A Compilation of the Messages and Papers of the Presidents, 1789–1897.* 10 vols. Washington, DC: Government Printing Office, 1899.

Riggs, Russell C. "The Ante-Bellum Career of John A. Bingham: A Case Study in the Coming of the Civil War." Ph.D. diss., New York University, 1958.

Rosenman, Samuel, ed. *The Public Papers and Addresses of Franklin D. Roosevelt.* New York: Russell and Russell, 1938–1950.

Rowe, Gary D. "Constitutionalism in the Streets." *Southern California Law Review* 78 (2005): 401–56.

Rubenfeld, Jed. *Freedom and Time.* New Haven: Yale University Press, 2001.

Ruchames, Louis, ed. *The Letters of William Lloyd Garrison, 1850–1860.* 6 vols. Cambridge: Harvard University Press, 1975.

Ruger, Theodore W. " 'A Question Which Convulses a Nation': The Early Republic's Greatest Debate about the Judicial Review Power." *Harvard Law Review* 117 (2004): 826–97.

Ryder, Norman. *The Cohort Approach: Essays in the Measurement of Temporal Variations in Demographic Behavior.* New York: Arno Press, 1980.

Safire, William M. *Lend Me Your Ears: Great Speeches in History.* New York: W. W. Norton, 1992.

Satz, Ronald N. *American Indian Policy in the Jacksonian Era.* Lincoln: University of Nebraska Press, 1975.

Schlesinger, Arthur M., Jr. *The Age of Jackson.* Boston: Little, Brown, 1945.

Schuck, Peter H., and Rogers M. Smith. *Citizenship without Consent.* New Haven: Yale University Press, 1985.

Schumpeter, Joseph. *Capitalism, Socialism, and Democracy.* New York: Harper and Row, 1976.

Silbey, Joel H., ed. *The American Party Battle: Election Campaign Pamphlets, 1828–1876.* 2 vols. Cambridge: Harvard University Press, 1999.

Simpson, Brooks D. *The Reconstruction Presidents.* Lawrence: University Press of Kansas, 1998.

Skowronek, Stephen. *The Politics Presidents Make.* Rev. ed., 1993; repr., Cambridge: Harvard University Press, 1997.

Smith, Rogers M. *Civic Ideals: Conflicting Visions of Citizenship in U.S. History.* New Haven: Yale University Press, 1997.

Stampp, Kenneth M. *The Era of Reconstruction, 1865–77.* New York: Knopf, 1965.

Stephen, James Fitzjames. *Liberty, Equality, Fraternity.* New York: Hoyt and Williams, 1873.

Streichler, Stuart A. "Justice Curtis's Dissent in the Dred Scott Case: An Interpretative Study." *Hastings Constitutional Law Quarterly* 24 (1997): 509–44.

Sundquist, James L. *Dynamics of the Party System.* Washington, DC: Brookings Institution, 1983.

Sunstein, Cass R. "Foreword: Leaving Things Undecided." *Harvard Law Review* 110 (1996): 6–101.

Swisher, Carl B. *The Taney Period, 1836–64.* Vol. 5 of *History of the Supreme Court of the United States.* New York: Macmillan, 1974.

Swisher, Carl B., ed. "Roger B. Taney's 'Bank War Manuscript.'" *Maryland Historical Magazine* 53 (1958): 103–30.

Taylor, John. *An Inquiry into the Principles and Policy of the Government of the United States.* Indianapolis: Bobbs-Merrill, 1969.

TenBroek, Jacobus. *Equal under Law.* New York: Collier Books, 1965.

Tennessee Johnson. Metro-Goldwyn Mayer, 1942.

Trefousse, Hans L. *Andrew Johnson.* New York: W. W. Norton, 1989.

———. *Thaddeus Stevens.* Chapel Hill: University of North Carolina Press, 1997.

Tribe, Laurence H. "Taking Text and Structure Seriously: Reflections on Free-Form Method in Constitutional Interpretation." *Harvard Law Review* 108 (1995): 1221–1303.

Tulis, Jeffrey. *The Rhetorical Presidency.* Princeton: Princeton University Press, 1987.

Tushnet, Mark V. *Taking the Constitution from the Courts.* Princeton: Princeton University Press, 1999.

Tyler, Lyon G. *The Letters and Times of the Tylers.* 3 vols. Richmond, VA: Whittet and Shepperson, 1885.

Van Buren, Martin. *The Autobiography of Martin Van Buren.* Edited by John Clement Fitzpatrick. New York: Da Capo Press, 1973.

Wallace, Anthony F. C. *Jefferson and the Indians: The Tragic Fate of the First Americans.* Cambridge: Harvard University Press, 1999.

Walters, Ronald G. *The Antislavery Appeal: American Abolitionism after 1830.* Baltimore: Johns Hopkins University Press, 1976.

Warren, Charles. *The Supreme Court in United States History.* 2 vols. Boston: Little, Brown, 1928.

Wechsler, Herbert. "Toward Neutral Principles of Constitutional Law." *Harvard Law Review* 73 (1959): 1–35.

White, G. Edward. *The Marshall Court and Cultural Change, 1815–35.* New York: Macmillan, 1988.

Whittier, John Greenleaf. "Letter from the Editor." *Pennsylvania Freeman,* May 10, 1838.

Wilentz, Sean. *The Rise of American Democracy.* New York: W. W. Norton, 2005.

Wills, Garry. *Certain Trumpets: The Call of Leaders.* New York: Simon and Schuster, 1994.

Wiltse, Charles M., and Harold D. Moser, eds. *The Papers of Daniel Webster.* 15 vols. Hanover, NH: University Press of New England, 1980.

Wood, Gordon S. *The Creation of the American Republic, 1776–1787.* Chapel Hill: University of North Carolina Press, 1969.

Yoshino, Kenji. *Covering: The Hidden Assault on Our Civil Rights.* New York: Random House, 2006.

Cases and Statutes

Ableman v. Booth, 11 Wis. 498 (1859).

Ableman v. Booth, 62 U.S. (21 How.) 506 (1859).

Act of March 2, 1833, ch. 55, 4 Stat. 629.

Adamson v. California, 332 U.S. 46 (1947).

A.L.A. Schechter Poultry Corp. v. United States, 295 U.S. 495 (1935).

Allgeyer v. Louisiana, 165 U.S. 578 (1897).

American Ins. Co. v. Canter, 26 U.S. (1 Pet.) 511 (1828).

Bank of the United States v. Planters' Bank of Georgia, 22 U.S. (9 Wheat.) 904 (1824).

Barron v. Baltimore, 32 U.S. (7 Pet.) 243 (1833).

Buck v. Bell, 274 U.S 200 (1927).

Bush v. Gore, 531 U.S. 98 (2000).

Caldwell v. Alabama, 1 Stew. & P. 327 (1832).

Chambers v. Florida, 309 U.S. 227 (1940).

Charles River Bridge v. Warren Bridge, 36 U.S. (11 Pet.) 420 (1837).

Cherokee Nation v. Georgia, 30 U.S. (5 Pet.) 1 (1831).

Chisholm v. Georgia, 2 U.S. (2 Dall.) 419 (1793).

Comprehensive Environmental Response, Compensation and Liability Act (CERCLA), 42 U.S.C. § 9601 et seq. (2000).

Corfield v. Coryell, 6 F. Cas. 546 (C.C.E.D. Pa. 1823) (No. 3,230).

County of Yakima v. Confederated Tribes & Bands of the Yakima Indian Nation, 502 U.S. 251 (1992).

Cross v. Harrison, 57 U.S. (16 How.) 164 (1853).

Dartmouth College v. Woodward, 17 U.S. (4 Wheat.) 518 (1819).

Dred Scott v. Sandford, 60 U.S. (19 How.) 393 (1857).

Elk v. Wilkins, 112 U.S. 94 (1884).

Employment Div. v. Smith, 494 U.S. 872 (1990).

Erie R.R. v. Tompkins, 304 U.S. 64, 79 (1938).

Ex Parte McCardle, 74 U.S. (7 Wall.) 506 (1869).

Groves v. Slaughter, 40 U.S. (15 Pet.) 449 (1841).

Hepburn v. Griswold, 75 U.S. (8 Wall.) 603 (1870).

In re Booth, 3 Wis. 13 (1854).

In re Debs, 158 U.S. 564 (1895).

Johnson v. M'Intosh, 21 U.S. (8 Wheat.) 543 (1823).

Katzenbach v. Morgan, 384 U.S. 641 (1966).

Knox v. Lee, 79 U.S. (12 Wall.) 457 (1871).

Korematsu v. United States, 323 U.S. 214 (1944).

Lochner v. New York, 198 U.S. 45 (1905).

Marbury v. Madison, 5 U.S. (1 Cranch) 137 (1803).

M'Culloch v. Maryland, 17 U.S. (4 Wheat.) 316 (1819).

Muskrat v. United States, 219 U.S. 346 (1911).

New York v. Miln, 36 U.S. (11 Pet.) 102 (1837).

Norman v. Baltimore & Ohio R.R. Co. (Gold Clause Cases), 294 U.S. 240 (1935).

Osborn v. Bank of the United States, 22 U.S. (9 Wheat.) 738 (1824).

Padelford, Fay & Co. v. Mayor of Savannah, 14 Ga. 438 (Ga. 1854).

Palko v. Connecticut, 302 U.S. 319 (1937).

Pollock v. Farmers' Home Loan & Trust Co. 157 U.S. 429 (1895), modified on reh'g, 158 U.S. 601 (1895).

Republican Party of Minnesota v. White, 536 U.S. 765 (2002).

Scott v. Emerson, 15 Mo. 576 (1852).

Seminole Tribe of Florida v. Florida, 517 U.S. 1133 (1996).

Sere v. Pitot, 10 U.S. (6 Cranch) 332 (1810).

Slaughter-House Cases, 83 U.S. (16 Wall.) 36 (1873).

State v. Foreman, 16 Tenn. 256 (1835).

Strader v. Graham, 51 U.S. (10 How.) 82 (1852).
Stuart v. Laird, 5 U.S. (1 Cranch) 299 (1803).
Sturges v. Crowinshield, 17 U.S. (4 Wheat.) 122 (1819).
United States v. Bailey, 24 F. Cas. 937, 940 (C.C.D. Tenn. 1834) (No. 14,495).
United States v. Callender, 25 F. Cas. 239 (C.C.D. Va. 1800) (No. 14,709).
United States v. Darby, 312 U.S. 100 (1941).
United States v. E. C. Knight, 156 U.S. 1 (1895).
United States v. Joseph, 94 U.S. 614 (1876).
United States v. Marigold, 50 U.S. (9 How.) 560 (1850).
United States v. Rhodes, 27 F. Cas. 785, 791 (C.C.D. Ky. 1866) (No. 16,151).
United States v. Ritchie, 58 U.S. (17 How.) 525 (1854).
United States v. Rogers, 45 U.S. (4 How.) 567 (1846).
West Coast Hotel Co. v. Parrish, 300 U.S. 379 (1937).
Williams v. Lee, 358 U.S. 217 (1959).
Worcester v. Georgia, 31 U.S. (6 Pet.) 515 (1832).

Index

CPSIA information can be obtained at www.ICGtesting.com
Printed in the USA
BVOW08s0253230716

456433BV00001B/56/P

9 780700 617869